JAMES MADISON ON THE CONSTITUTION AND THE BILL OF RIGHTS

**Recent Titles in
Contributions in Legal Studies**
Series Editor: Paul L. Murphy

JAMES MADISON
ON THE
CONSTITUTION
AND THE
BILL OF RIGHTS

Robert J. Morgan

Contributions in Legal Studies, Number 48

GREENWOOD PRESS
New York • Westport, Connecticut • London

Library of Congress Cataloging-in-Publication Data

Morgan, Robert J.
  James Madison on the Constitution and the Bill of Rights / Robert
J. Morgan.
    p.   cm. — (Contributions in legal studies, ISSN 0147-1074 ;
no. 48)
  Bibliography: p.
  Includes index.
  ISBN 0-313-26394-9 (lib. bdg. : alk. paper)
  1. United States—Constitutional history.   2. United States—
Constitutional law—Amendments—1st-10th.   3. Madison, James,
1751-1836—Views on the Constitution.   I. Title.   II. Series.
KF4541.M675   1988
342.73'029—dc19
[347.30229]   88-10243

British Library Cataloguing in Publication Data is available.

Library of Congress Catalog Card Number: 88-10243
ISBN: 0-313-26394-9
ISSN: 0147-1074

First published in 1988

Greenwood Press, Inc.
88 Post Road West, Westport, Connecticut 06881

Printed in the United States of America

The paper used in this book complies with the
Permanent Paper Standard issued by the National
Information Standards Organization (Z39.48-1984).

10 9 8 7 6 5 4 3 2 1

It is as difficult a matter to reform an old constitution as it is to construct a new one; as hard to unlearn a lesson as it was to learn it initially.

Aristotle, *Politics*, Book IV, chap. 1

Contents

Acknowledgments

During the greater part of my adult life, it has been my good fortune to be a member of a university founded, as James Madison once said, to educate "republican patriots and genuine scholars." I hope that my analysis of his immeasurable contributions to our political life does not discredit this ideal.

I owe special debts to the Center for Advanced Studies of the University of Virginia for appointments to the position of Sesquicentenniel Fellow on two occasions; to the staff of the Word Processing Center of the College of Arts and Sciences for indispensable secretarial services; and to the Center for Public Service under the direction of James A. (Dolph) Norton for producing finished copy.

Robert A. Rutland, former Editor of the Madison Papers, and his staff never failed to assist my research. Martha Derthick, Richard Marks, Clifton McCleskey, David O'Brien and Robert M. O'Neil read all or portions of this work in various stages. They are responsible only for encouraging me, however. Peter A. Lawler, Nelson B. Ong, and, especially, Jeffrey Hockett served as able research assistants. Nancy Hasler, Sharon Gingras, Pat Hudson, and Barbara Stinnett cheerfully provided secretarial services. The editorial staff of The Greenwood Press combined professional competence with personal warmth in assisting with the final preparation of the manuscript.

My wife, Naomie, has supported and encouraged me in a special way which follows from her understanding of why I needed to write this book.

Charlottesville, Virginia

June 10, 1988

Introduction

James Madison bequeathed his papers to us in order to satisfy the "laudable curiosity felt by all people to trace the origins and progress of their political institutions."[1] Few sources of this information match, and none exceed, Madison's for this purpose. More important, no one involved in these events exceeded him in analytical and creative political insight into the tasks of framing and explaining the Constitution and Bill of Rights. It is especially rewarding, therefore, to examine these events through his mind by using the whole body of his political and constitutional thought. At the same time it is important not to claim too much. Madison explicitly rejected the idea that he was "the writer" of the Constitution and the record amply supports this disclaimer.[2] Given the chance, he undoubtedly would have been equally modest in describing his role as an architect of the Bill of Rights. Even as we bear this limitation in mind we can still learn a very great deal from him about some of the most important characteristics of our constitutional system.

He became a constitutional reformer because he wanted to expand federal powers so as to preserve a republican government strong enough to fulfill America's unique destiny. He believed reforms were necessary because the Confederation created in 1781 was, like all other ancient and modern confederations, inherently vulnerable to disunion caused by either internal conflicts or foreign intervention in the affairs of the weaker members. Prompted by this chronic crisis which threatened enjoyment of the fruits of the Revolution, Madison formulated a plan of reforms in outline to transform the republic from a league of sovereign states into a national government. Among the changes he wished to make were popular ratification of the new constitution and a bicameral Congress which would include a new house having members apportioned among the states on the basis of population and chosen directly by the voters. In defending this novel addition to our political institutions, he showed that he had a clear and sensitive grasp of, as well as firm commitment to, the ideals of responsibility, accountability, responsiveness, and accessibility as essential characteristics of democratic political institutions. Also, one of his major goals was to raise the vision of federal legislators to a continental and even international level in order to improve the quality of public policy through improvements in representative institutions. This was no minor objective in an age when philosophers and politicians alike candidly admitted that self-interest is a prime mover of political elites, and parochialism is apt to be the natural offspring of social heterogeneity. He predicted that the desirable result of this reform would probably be rule by legislative majorities moderated by the diversity of opinions and interests which are natural in a society of extended scale.

He demonstrated a keen, but little known, insight into the enormous difficulties entailed in creating the office of president and maintaining it over time in a republic which had never had such an office. Constitutional provisions were needed both to support and to control the exercise of presidential power. Rarely, Madison argued, would any single person be endowed with such singular talents and superior devotion to the common good as to be chosen to exercise power without challenge by his peers. As soon as the Convention settled the question of representation in mid–July, 1787, he foresaw the need to devise a form of popular election which would make the president accountable directly to the electorate, if he were to exercise his powers without undue control by Congress. The electoral provisions which the Framers adopted could not guarantee this outcome unless the the president's election were made the focus of national politics and the electors could be made to record the voters' wishes. His Helvidius essays dealing with the separation of functions between President and Congress in the conduct of foreign relations revealed the other horn of his dilemma–the need to control the exercise of executive power because the conduct of war gives fullest scope to all of the motives which impel individuals to hold public offices. The polarity of tensions between the need to support and control the executive was part of one of the two most basic problems facing the Framers in his judgment–combining stability in the legislature with due energy in the executive.

Madison's explanation of the theory of the separation of powers was an ingenious, even original, Americanization of a constitutional dogma of ancient lineage. It served two purposes. It pointed out that a pure and rigidly dogmatic theory of separated executive and legislative functions and structures had never guided the framers of any known constitutions. The doctrine was simply an exhortation intended to guide the actions of established governments. His second aim was to assure Americans that David Hume and the Baron de Montesquieu were wrong in arguing that the avarice of legislators must be appealed to in order to subdue their ambition which drives them to encroach on the executive's powers. Starting in 1789 and until 1801 this perspective informed Madison's analyses of the problems of transforming the Constitution from a plan on paper into a functioning republic, rather than an aristocracy or a monarchy. In particular, he shared with Jefferson and such leading European thinkers as Hume, Adam Smith, Edmund Burke, and Immanuel Kant a concern for the effects of a funded war debt on the distribution of power within government and society.

It is well known that the Framers did not regulate the right to vote, and they left the original document silent on the subject of political parties. Madison's beliefs about both of these matters are relevant, however, because they shed some light from his perspective on the claim that the Framers' objective was to curb democracy, however defined. Unfortunately, it is difficult to determine exactly what limits he thought ought to be imposed on the right to vote when the Constitution was framed. It is evident, however, that he eventually embraced the universal, white, manhood suffrage. On the other hand, the evidence is quite persuasive that he always considered parties inevitable and necessary in a free government. Once the provisions of the Constitution made them necessary in effect to elect a president by popular vote, if the President were not to be subservient to Congress, Madison understood that national political associations would have to be formed to serve this end.

His commitment to freedom of speech and press as well as to the separation of religion and politics in an elective and responsible system of government is generally known, but worthy of more systematic and careful analysis than any available at present. It is especially important to be aware of his rejection of all claims that the English common law is to be incorporated by construction into the First Amendment by either Congress or the federal courts. Americans inherited the common law as a legacy to be used selectively, if at all. Unless it was explicitly adopted in the language of the Constitution, it had no validity in Madison's judgment. American governments did *not* automatically inherit from Great Britain the power to compel beliefs about religion and politics and to punish their expression simply because the common law and the First Amendment both deal with such matters in their respective political systems. The Revolution freed Americans to make their own distinctive political culture, one consistent with their unique history and republican ideals. A firm belief that American's time had come and it had been given the opportunity to regenerate the political world infused Madison's conception of the separation of religion and politics. The secular sword and religious faith ought always to be kept separate so that each realm might flourish to the benefit of humanity. Americans did not found the first new nation in order to remain Englishmen.

There are two difficulties inherent in developing a comprehensive, consistent, and unified analysis of Madison's political thought. The first is that he expounded it in more than fifty published essays, one unpublished essay, two short monographs, numerous state papers, notes on the proceedings of Congress and the Constitutional Convention between 1780 and 1787, speeches recorded with questionable accuracy, and voluminous private correspondence. Furthermore, the bulk of his published essays was composed in order to justify or explain particular characteristics of our constitutional system. All of his essays and monographs reveal him as a skilled advocate, so that one must examine the record of his private correspondence to determine just how much of public exposition was rhetoric and how much was sincere advocacy.

The second difficulty is that his published papers were written to justify and explain a Constitution framed, he declared explicitly, by sacrificing pure theory to the political situation then prevailing. Experience was regarded as a prime component of the kind of knowledge required to reform a constitution. The corrective power of our unique experience justified departures from the practices of ancient commonwealths. Those practices which had been admired by others as "beacons" to republican lawgivers provided Americans with only sufficient light "to give warning of the course to be shunned without pointing out that to be pursued," Madison declared.[3] Modern governments supplied equally deficient models for imitation. In making a revolution without precedent and reconstructing their governing institutions, Americans of this period had a decent respect for opinions held in other times and other nations, but foreign models provided no real instruction for them. The good fortune of which Americans were partly their own authors enabled them to create a new and experimental republic unsupported by either speculative political theorists or historical models.[4]

In fact, Madison was so confident that Americans were the first to understand fully and to establish the true characteristics of republican government that he sent copies of the Constitution, despite its flaws, to William Short, Jefferson's secretary in Paris, on 24 October 1787. Madison hoped to obtain European comments on it, but he did not believe that they would be useful. Although he wanted to learn the comments of the "philosophical Statesmen of Europe," he thought it unlikely that his interest would be rewarded unless "their future criticisms should evince a more thorough knowledge of our situation as well as the true genius of Republican Government, than many of their past..."[5] Many years later he conceded that the "rights of man," which served as the foundation of just government were provided by others, but the "superstructures" of governing institutions which European philosophers erected on this base "had always been sadly defective. Hume himself was among these bungling lawgivers."[6]

These observations warn us against assuming that Madison's motives and meanings can be confidently deduced by analogy from his use of words and phrases employed by European political theorists. He was obviously very familiar with their works, but he was highly selective in using them. Consequently, I have assumed that his original texts are expositions of his motives and beliefs wherever they seem to be perfectly clear. It is his perspective, rather than his predecessors' or ours, which is to be recovered. He left a voluminous record of references and allusions to the works of political philosophers, historians, and legal scholars so that only occasionally does it seem either necessary or fruitful to seek his meaning elsewhere or to point out instructive parallels of thought. This caution is of particular importance, also, because Madison was so explicit on many occasions in warning against using political terms and doctrines fashioned by European theorists favorable to monarchy in order to interpret the Constitution and Bill of Rights. Any effort to fit his thinking into a particular mold by tracing it to its alleged antecedents is likely to distort it and to mislead us. Therefore, it seems best to give the simplest interpretations consistent with the evidence from Madison's pen and to speculate to a minimum degree about sources and parallels.

Even in the face of these difficulties one can discern a clear and overriding thesis giving unity and focus to Madison's political thought. There is a natural, inescapable, and continuing tension between the democratic ideal of accountability and the tendency of all governments toward autonomy. This polarity is rooted in the sources of legitimacy and power in the American system of government in particular. In a free government, public opinion is sovereign, Madison declared. In a just government, legitimacy is derived from consent. According to the republican theory prevailing in the United States in 1787, the people are the exclusive fountain of all authority to frame and amend constitutions which create governments, endow them with legal powers to use the resources of the community for the common good, and restrict abuse of these powers. This process of *authorizing* power, Madison anticipated before the Convention, would provide the reformed government with what he and Alexander Hamilton both called constitutional energy. The *exercise* of authorized power depends, however, on the motives which impel individuals to seek public offices in order to act on a public stage. Therefore, the energy–that force naturally impelling bodies to action, according to prevailing theory–is derived from these two sources in the American political system. In the political vocabulary of the eighteenth century, constitutional authority was called artificial because it was created by humans. The second source of energy was called natural because it was given by nature to mankind as an immutable and universal condition of existence. The constitutional source of energy implies the accountability of rulers to voters. The natural source of energy drives rulers toward autonomy as they seek to exercise power without restriction in the pursuit of fame and even wealth, according to a view widely held in the late eighteenth century. It is the power to regulate relations with other nations and to wage war successfully that gives the freest scope to natural energy in search of autonomous action consistent with the love of fame. Two other conditions produce this tendency: one is an outbreak of domestic violence; the other is the absence of sufficient constitutionally authorized power, a condition which invites the creation of a government independent of society.[7]

This inherent conflict between the authorization to govern, embodied in a written constitution grounded on popular sovereignty, and the exercise of limited powers so authorized makes all textual divisions and restrictions in a written constitution fragile and of no real force unless they are supported by public opinion. It should not surprise us to find Madison explaining this phenomenon to Jefferson in a letter written in the summer of 1788 discussing the merits and limitations of a Bill of Rights. Madison believed that it is the need for both a limited authorization of power and the drive to govern which makes the proper mix of liberty and authority problematic and all solutions inevitably proximate in a constitutional democracy such as ours. This sense of the fragility of a written constitution permeates many of Madison's political essays; it explains his reliance on the constitutional text as a self–explanatory document and his insistence on formal amendment to the Constitution as the ground for expanding national powers only after the kind of debate required to mobilize public opinion on the issues.

The importance of the tendency toward autonomy was undoubtedly so evident to Madison and his contemporaries because of the military struggles of rival European imperial powers whose colonies, armies, and fleets surrounded the young American Republic on land and sea. It was this fact of eighteenth–century life which Madison recognized as a major variable to be taken into account in framing the Constitution and maintaining a republican government over time. As Bernard Bailyn and other historians of political ideas in the American revolutionary period have observed, many Americans pointed to the history of Rome in order to prove that even in a well–formed republic, the commitment to imperial conquest will ultimately result in the loss of liberty by military force turned inward.[8] This perspective defined for Madison the nature and destiny of the American republic which emerged in revolt against colonial rule in order to establish a constitutional republic secure against degeneration into a copy of the traditional political systems of Europe.

There is, also, a secondary thesis which sets this work apart from most other interpretations of Madison's motives as a Founder. It is summed up best in his own words written while he was still composing the last of his *Federalist* papers. He told Edmund Pendleton: "I have for some time been persuaded that the question on which the proposed Constitution must turn is the simple one whether the Union shall or shall not be continued. There is in my opinion no middle ground to be taken."[9] It was the need to preserve the union and republican goverment, not the desire to curb democracy that prompted Madison to become a constitutional reformer in 1787. This study will not settle the debate over all the Framers' intentions or the extent of their belief in democracy. It is not intended to do so. In Madison's judgment the Constitution was a progressive reform even though the result was more flawed than he wished. On balance, I believe that his cautious, but hopeful, explanations and assessments of the work of the Framers were justified, especially given the circumstances prevailing in a weak, divided and vulnerable confederation during an age when imperialism was ascendant and democracy was nascent. The object of constitutional reform in 1787 was to cure just these flaws which he perceived in the American Confederation so that the republic might fulfill its special destiny to become a respected and powerful nation able to maintain a middle position between the extremes of weak confederations and aggressive empires reflecting the glory that was once Rome's. To this end, Madison helped to initiate reform in 1787 and advocated limited government by constitutional majority in a socially diverse and extended society.

Academic specialists of various sorts may wish to note that this perception of the prime importance of foreign relations in determining the true characteristics of a political system is undoubtedly ignored today because it rests on a view of the relationship of society to government which is no longer in vogue. Madison's understanding of this relationship rested on a tradition of political discourse traced through Montesquieu and Hume to Machiavelli. These thinkers shared a common belief in the capacity of governments to act autonomously, although they had to take into account opinions prevailing in their respective societies. Insofar as the power to wage war accounts for this relationship, it has been missing from prevailing interpretations of Madison's political and constitutional thought, despite two calls for notice of it. In 1945 Charles A. Beard conceded that both Liberals and Marxists had created a social science which ignored the role of war by treating all political ideas and actions as the epiphenomenal resultants of domestic group conflicts. Since he attributed the latter to James Madison, whose tenth

Federalist allegedly expressed the Framers' political science, Beard's call for a restatement of the theory of motives explaining politics was of potentially great importance. The heuristic implications of Beard's new belief that economic man is dependent on political and military man were ignored, however, by critics despite Louis Hartz's call in 1955 for abandonment of the Progressives' constricting propadeutic. Hartz urged scholars to seek new fundamental categories of analysis which take into account world forces and America's relations with other nations, but he, too, was ignored.[10]

Another component of Madison's thought was a belief he shared in common with some leading European thinkers who taught a science of government that aimed at creating constitutions which control the behavior of rulers.[11] Madison's fifty–seventh *Federalist* contains a classic expression of this belief which permeates these essays. He said that every constitution, ought first of all, to obtain as rulers persons who possess the most wisdom to know and the most virtue to pursue the common good of society. Second, it ought to contain the most effectual precautions for keeping them virtuous. Elections are the characteristic means used by republican government to achieve the first goal. The means relied on in "this form ofgovernment for preventing their degeneracy are more numerous."[12]

Finally, this book may serve the additional purpose of fulfilling the hope Madison expressed to John Adams in 1823. Perhaps, Madison mused poignantly, both of them would eventually escape the "misfortune of history." He meant the gap between the knowledge which they possessed as participants in the great events of the Founding Age and posterity's search for "impartial" judgment of their handiwork.[13]

NOTES

1. James Madison, *Letters and Other Writings of James Madison*, 4 vols. (New York: Worthington, 1884),3:228; cited hereafter as *LJM*.

2. *LJM*, 4:341–42. See also, Max Farrand, ed., *The Records of the Federal Convention of 1787*, 4 vols. (New Haven, Conn.: Yale University Press, 1966; first published in 1911), 3:479; cited hereafter as Farrand, *Records*.

3. Alexander Hamilton, John Jay, and James Madison, *The Federalist*, with an introduction by Edward Mead Earle, (New York: Random House, The Modern Library,1937), 226 (No. 37); cited hereafter as *The Federalist*.

4. *The Federalist* 81, 84–85 (No. 14). For later statements that Madison mediated theory through experience see *PJM*, 13:25, 377; *LJM*, 3:52, 535; 4:388.

5. James Madison, *The Papers of James Madison*, ed. William T. Hutchinson, William M. E. Rachal, Robert A. Rutland, and others, 15 vols. to date (Chicago: University of Chicago Press; Charlottesville, Va.: University Press of Virginia, 1962 to date), 10:220–21, cited hereafter as *PJM*.

6.   *LJM*, 4:58. This statement undermines Douglas Adair's claim that Madison was the "most creative and philosophical" disciple of the Scottish philosophers at the Convention: "'That Politics May be Reduced to a Science:' David Hume, James Madison and the Tenth Federalist," *The Huntington Library Quarterly* 20 (August 1957):343–59. This thesis is found in Henry May, *The Enlightenment in America* (New York and London: Oxford University Press, 1976), 3–65; and Gary Wills, *Explaining America: The Federalist* (New York: Penguin Books, 1981); cited hereafter as *Explaining*.

7.   This thesis is taken from Robert J. Morgan, "Madison's Analysis of the Sources of Political Authority," *The American Political Science Review* 75 (September 1981): 613–25, cited hereafter as Morgan, "Madison's Analysis."

8.   Bernard Bailyn, *The Ideological Origins of the American Revolution* (Cambridge, Mass: The Belknap Press of the Harvard University Press, 1967), 55–93; cited hereafter as Bailyn, *Origins*; Gordon Wood, *The Creation of the American Republic* (New York: W. W. Norton and Co., 1972), 32–43; cited hereafter as Wood, *Creation*; Charles F. Mullett, *"Classical Influences on the American Revolution,"* Classical Journal, 35 (November, 1939): 92–104.

9.   *PJM*, 10:532; see also, 11:125–128, 135–39, 146–47, 176.

10.   See Morgan, "Madison's Analysis," 613–14, for the works cited.

11.   *LJM*, 3:238.

12.   *The Federalist*, 370 (No. 57).

13.   *LJM*, 3:308.

Part I
POWER

Chapter 1

To Improve and Perpetuate the Union

Madison provided us with an unmistakable key to understanding his thought and actions as a constitutional reformer, when he said that the rights of man are the foundation of just governments, but mankind had deduced only defective superstructures of government as of 1776. Nature had given Americans their independence and a rich land with the obligation to provide the world with a model of free government and a productive people raising the standards of material and moral well–being for the progressive betterment of the human race. Unfortunately, in their first attempt they created a government resting on "fallacious principles..." A weak government and quarreling factions threatened the success of this experiment. Therefore, the task in hand by 1787 was "to improve and perpetuate the union" by resting well–crafted institutions on sound political and constitutional principles.[1]

THE GIFT OF NATURE

When Madison became a member of the Revolutionary Congress in 1779, he had a clear understanding of the ethical, political, and constitutional issues which justified American independence. He expounded them in a notable state paper adopted by Congress in 1780 and continued to develop their full implications thereafter to strengthen the American claim to unhindered development and political incorporation of the territory ceded by Britain in 1783. The American claim to free navigation of the Mississippi River provided the occasion for his exposition, and the first ground on which he rested it is a familiar one: Americans had never explicitly consented to be ruled according to the terms of an imperial constitution as it was defined by the British government. The second basis of the American claim is not familiar and it is worthy of special note because of its great importance in Madison's conception of the destiny of the American Republic. The exercise of power is legitimate only if it is used for the benefit of those "from whom it is derived and over whom [it is] exercised." These two precepts in combination justified the American claim to all of the territory and rights pertaining to them of the former British sovereign. The rights claimed did not devolve on the United States on any of the grounds recognized by the law of nations such as priority of discovery, occupancy, or conquest. American title was secured by the "revolution" in our government effected by securing independence from Britain and becoming an equal among nations. Therefore, "equity and justice perfectly coincide with political and constitutional principles" to support the American title to this vast undeveloped area. It ought to be recognized universally because the new nation would encourage the rapid growth of population and commerce. Nations desiring to achieve these beneficial ends will agree, therefore, that no part of the American union ought ever to be subjected again to foreign rule. Forcible appropriation of its territory by another power can never be "consonant to the rights of nations or the sentiments of humanity."[2]

Europeans ought to support these doctrines because they had more to gain than to lose by eliminating governmental barriers to economic growth and international commerce. With an independent and developing United States there would be a steady increase in the production of agricultural and manufactured goods. Population of the lands virtually vacant at that time would probably double in twenty to twenty-five years with no corresponding diminution of it in the European nations from which emigration will have occurred.[3]

In private, Madison insisted that if the new republic were to achieve the level of power which would make other governments respect it, the American West must become a workshop for those whom Jefferson called the "idle poor" of Europe. In an exchange of ideas on this subject raised by Jefferson, Madison conceded that he was puzzled by the proper means of relieving the "misery of the lower classes," but he had little doubt that it will "abate wherever Government assumes a freer aspect & the laws favor a subdivision of property." It is to be suspected, however, that this difference between Europeans and Americans cannot account fully for the comparative comfort enjoyed by the latter. "Our limited population has probably as large a share in producing this effect as the political advantages which distinguish us". There is probably an inseparable relationship between poverty and density of population. Even if the land is shared among the people "ever so wisely" with a full supply of labor, there 10st be "a surplus of subsistence" because there will be "a great surplus of inhabitants". The latter will be far greater in number than those employed to supply us with every necessity and "comfort of life. What is to be done with the surplus?" Madison's answer was that all nations have a natural duty to recognize the right of individuals to emigrate from overpopulated to underpopulated nations such as the United States.[4]

He was greatly concerned, therefore, that the Count de Buffon relied on natural history to devalue nature's gift to Americans. Buffon argued that the North American continent was less favorable to the maximum growth of animals than Europe and other areas of the world. This contention was a serious challenge to the idea that nature had given Americans their independence to serve the interests of humanity in accordance with what Madison perceived to be the symmetry of nature. If the natural endowments of the American continent were as deficient as Buffon asserted, then one of the moral foundations of American independence was eroded. Consequently, Madison translated and made extensive notes on Buffon's *Natural History* and then urged Jefferson to reply to Buffon by publishing his *Notes on the State of Virginia* from the original English text because of the importance of "the subjects you have handled." Jefferson obliged by picturing an American republic in which the land would be filled with people and happiness, foreign commerce would flourish, and Americans would teach the political economists of Europe that it is false arithmetic to claim that it is in the interest of nations to go to war.[5]

The duty of nations to recognize the right of expatriation to underpopulated areas richly endowed with resources is derived, Madison believed, from natural laws of which mankind are rational observers and agents. He started a private memorandum on this subject sometime after 1784 by noting that the planetary system, the greatest part of the universe, is regulated by "fixed laws" which make the entire scene one of "order and proportion." By analogy we may infer that the entire world, including the innermost recesses of the earth, would demonstrate the same degree of rationality, if it were open to our observation. Therefore, one may conclude that "order and symmetry" are the characteristics of "nature's plan" for the universe. Our imperfect means of observation produce apparent irregularities which, if overcome, it is "extremely probable," would reveal proofs of a "general plan"of nature exhibiting "meaning & method..." Among plants and animals the "contrivance of nature strikes every observer." All living orders are related to each other in general and particular relationships, notably that of predator and prey in the food chain. They share an apparent capacity for multiplication which seems to depend on the supply of food, depredations and disease. Apparently nature has set "a certain proportion," limiting the effects of the reproductive capacity of all living things except mankind. It is not prey to the other forms of life nor is it subject to limits on its numerical increase. Humans do not depend on nature's "spontaneous" supplies of food. By exercising "reason," mankind is capable of increasing its supply of food at pleasure. This species is equally capable of destroying all forms of life which are of no utility to it and substituting fcr them others on which it feeds. Because mankind can break "the natural law of proportion" among the various forms of life, one must ask, What is to restrain the infinite growth of the human population at the cost of destroying all other forms which do not support it? The answer seems to be that nature did not intend to permit "one favorite offspring" to destroy all others. If the contrary proposition were true, then this event should have occurred by this time. Furthermore, there is no evidence that the aggregate population of the world has either increased or decreased in the whole of history. Except for some limited paleontological evidence of the disappearance of species, it is "highly probable" that limitations on the extent of human control over other forms of life for exclusive human benefit will be discovered eventually to be one of the "secret laws of nature..." Until then, the human impulse toward infinite growth, except where it is limited by the supply of food or the depredations of disease and war, will result in a continual increase simply because humans can increase the supply of food through the exercise of reason. Because the natural limits to the population of the world have not been discovered, every nation having a full population ought to permit a part of it to emigrate freely to places capable of supporting it.[6]

The fulfillment of this humane goal might call for an aggressive nationalism on the part of the new republic, however, if the fruits of the Revolution were to be enjoyed fully. The paramount need facing the infant nation was the strength to deal effectively with Europe's great imperial powers. Madison assured Jefferson that the United States was already a power which Spain ought not to "despise..." Soon the safety of her possessions "in this part of the Globe" would depend more on American "peaceableness than her power." At the moment, however, Spain did not fear the rising power of the independent United States as it had when the colonies were an extension of British imperial power. Unfortunately, Spain could hold American power in contempt because of our lack of naval force, our internal dissensions, and our existing system of government. All of these factors made it very difficult to establish and execute an aggressive foreign policy. In the long run, however, The United States might be able to prove that republics are not necessarily more peace-loving than other forms of government.[7] Imperial Spain should recognize that the security of her possessions bordering ours must depend upon "the *complexity of our federal Government and the diversity of interests* among the members of it." This combination makes offensive measures against foreign nations "improbable in Council, and difficult in execution." Indeed, Spain ought to favor American settlements between the Appalachians and the Mississippi. If the conflicting interests of thirteen states in the union could create such a hobble on foreign policy, "ought she not wish to see the number enlarged?" In fact, other European nations ought to encourage this development for the same reason.[8]

Madison shrewdly conveyed much of this message in a less bellicose tone to the Marquis de Lafayette: "Nature has given the use of the Mississippi to those who may settle on its waters, as she gave the United States their independence." Spain may try to repeat Britain's folly by attempting to retard the settlement of the western territory, but it, like Britain, will find that it cannot defeat the goal of our independence because it is in perfect accord with the natural order. Everywhere, "nature," aided by "Philosophy & Commerce," seems to be overcoming "tyranny & bigotry" which have trampled on rights for so long. It does not seem to be presumptuous, therefore, to say that those nations which ascertain nature's tendency, instead of "forcing her current into artificial channels," and anticipate its effects will both demonstrate their wisdom and acquire glory. Consequently, if the United States were to agree to Spain's closure of the Mississippi to international commerce, then Americans would be "guilty of treason against the very laws under which they obtained & hold their national existence." Spain's unwillingness to permit amicable use of this great channel of beneficial intercourse shows that its government prefers an "extensive desart [sic]" to "an extensive flourishing empire. Humanity cannot suppress the wish that some of those gifts which she abuses were placed by just means, in hands that would turn them to a wiser account."[9] If France fully understood that the effect of supporting this claim would be the full incorporation of the western territories as states standing on a constitutional par with the original members of the union, it would be rational for France to do so. With the extension of settlements, the number of states must be multiplied, and along with them the number of "Wills which are to direct the machine." As this number increases, the chances of a dangerous union of them will diminish. "We experience every day the difficulty of drawing thirteen states into the same plans. Let the number be doubled & so will the difficulty."[10]

These two letters contain the germ of theory of representation which Madison later developed to assuage the anxieties of Americans who feared either the expansion of the national domain or the dilution of the power of the original states by the addition of new ones, or both. Governing majorities created by a complex governmental structure and representing a great diversity of opinions and interests, especially those following from an increase in the number of states, are unlikely to expand, much less maximize, their power. On the contrary, such majorities tend to be incapable of doing so, especially where foreign policy is concerned.

The second ground of American independence, the consent of the governed, entailed not only the right of self-government, but an obligation as well, if it were to fulfill its promise. In one of his state papers adopted by Congress in 1783, Madison, with some passion, exhorted Americans to perform their duty to preserve republican government. They had not made a revolution to pursue "national splendor and glory" through wars of "ambition and of vain glory." If that were to happen, Americans would betray the claim of rights which justified their Revolution. It provided them with the opportunity to establish a wholly new republic which other nations might emulate. The aftermath of the Revolution provided the first real opportunity to prove to mankind the value of "unadulterated forms of Republican Government." It ought not to be the last one. If Americans were to succeed in demonstrating to the world that such governments produce those qualities which "enoble [sic] the character of a nation, and fulfill the ends of Government," then they would not fail to influence human rights favorably throughout the world. If American republicanism failed to bear its promised fruits, then the political cause which it ought to vindicate would fail.[11]

UNSOUND FOUNDATIONS

From the perspective of Europes's imperial powers the causes which Madison thought made an aggressive American foreign policy unlikely also left the members of the Confederation divided, prey to intervention in their affairs, and tempted to call on outsiders for help against each other. As such the American republic was in no position to threaten the European colonies in North America. The foundamental source of weakness in the Confederation was the provision requiring congressional decisions by a majority consisting of seven states. Madison learned very early in his congressional service that the interest of individual states and even regional groups of them might be ignored or injured by such a majority. This constitutional requirement bore no necessary relationship to a numerical majority, of course. On occasions even "the opinion of a Majority of Congress is a very different thing from a Constitutional vote." This system was so unsatisfactory, he warned in 1783, that Virginians ought to presume in making provisions for their future "security, importance & interest" that the existing Union "will but little survive the present war." Its necessity at the moment was as certain as its future dissolution was probable.[12]

A little more than a year later Madison repeated his fear that, if regional conflicts of interest unresolved by Congress were left to be inflamed by claims of "justice" unrequited, then disunion will be the fruit of the Revolution. He predicted that, unless "amicable & adequate" measures were quickly adopted for adjusting outstanding fiscal accounts and repaying the public debt, disunion is *"inevitable."* The southern states will be left rich, but weak at sea, and vulnerable, therefore, to the *"eastern* [states] *which will be powerful and rapacious."* The consequence will be that first the weaker and then the stronger of the resulting confederacies will seek foreign alliances which will then make them subservient to the *"wars and politics of Europe."*[13]

In 1785 Madison he wondered whether independence would ever secure our commercial advantages as long as we were constitutionally incapacitated from harmonizing the actions of the states in the existing Confederation. It was so constituted that this relationship could be achieved only if all states acquiesced in the opinion of a reasonable congressional majority of formally equal states. Congress was not trusted either to form or to enforce an opinion on any subject "drawn from the diversity of interests in the States..." Yet, there were so many more reasons for submitting the commercial interests of the states to "the direction and care of the Majority" than there were against doing so. The most general one must be the desire to reap the fruits of independence by creating a government to which all will give their confidence and allegiance instead of relying upon the intervention of foreign powers to relieve some parts of the country from their extreme distress. The "defects of the federal system should be amended" because they endanger "its very existence..." A minority which suffers cannot respect a government for very long, if it is too feeble to protect its interest. But when the major part suffers and despairs of "seeing a protective energy given to the General Government, from what motives is their allegiance to be any longer expected?"[14] Obviously, the suffering majority to which Madison referred consisted of the large states and Virginia in particular.

Again in 1786 Madison argued that rule by a majority Congress can result in decisions which are not "just" because they are inimical to the long-term prosperity and durability of the union. Allowing Spain to block navigation of the Mississippi River would be unjust even if the decision were made unanimously. The maxim that "the interest of the majority is the standard of right and wrong" must be qualified to avoid misapplication, he said. Taking the word interest to mean "ultimate happiness" qualified by its "necessary moral ingredient," the proposition is undoubtedly true. Taking the word *interest* in its popular sense, however, to mean the "immediate augmentation of property and wealth," the proposition is false. Applied in the latter sense, the maxim would make it the interest of the ruling majority in every political community "to despoil & enslave the minority of individuals." Applied in a "federal community," this rule would sacrifice the interests of a minority of the states composing it. The truth is that in any political community this maxim reestablishes "under another name and in a more spe[c]ious form, force as the measure of right."[15]

In December, 1786, he composed an official document adopted by Virginia's House of Delegates which declared that justice is the necessary moral ingredient supporting majority rule in most instances dividing society. Justice entails the protection of equal rights. The Confederation was created to serve as guardian of the equal rights and interests of all states. American control and beneficial use of the western territory and free navigation of the Mississippi River ought to be accepted by the whole nation as "the bountiful Gift of Nature to the United States as Proprietors...and secured by the late Revolution." Therefore, a sacrifice of the rights of only one part to the supposed or real interests of another would be a flagrant violation of the ideal of justice, a "direct contravention of the end for which the federal Government was instituted, and an alarming innovation of the System of the Union."[16]

The injustices as well as the weaknesses of the existing Confederation would be multiplied by the addition of ultramontane states. Nothing but the special circumstances prevailing during the Revolution could have produced the sacrifices of state sovereignty on which the Confederation rested. Unfortunately, the lessons learned from this experience were receding from memory so that "caprice, jealousy, and diversity of opinions" seemed likely to increase, "perhaps in greater ratio," with the addition of "ultramontane States," he complained to Washington. This change in our situation is likely to be exacerbated as foreign nations imitate a certain Macedonian Prince (Philip II) who served his purpose of weakening the Grecian confederacy through the tactic of winning over a few of the leading persons in the smaller states of the league.[17] In March, 1786, he repeated this message to Jefferson. Congress was unable to agree on fundamental issues during "the present crisis," and the prospects were for even greater impediments to "unanimity" with the admission of new states west of the Appalachians. Their interests and opinions will certainly be "*less congenial with the Atlantic states*" than the latter are with each other. This effect of extending the sphere is likely to occur "*more than proportionally*."[18] This "paroxism [*sic*] in our present affairs" was paralyzing foreign and domestic policy.[19]

Consequently, Madison decided to analyze the causes of injustice and weakness peculiar to the American confederation in light of the histories of ancient and modern confederations. This information might provide evidence of uniformities of behavior which would be of great value to anyone preparing to use constitutional science to secure some practical reforms. He concluded that all confederations had been inherently weak because they are given equal representation in the common legislature regardless of differences in their respective populations, wealth and influence. This disparity inclines them to withhold adequate legislative powers from the common legislature, especially those required by a sovereign nation. The modern Dutch Republic displayed a further anomaly which was inconsistent with the preservation of republican government. The stadtholder had accumulated a degree of power over foreign relations far greater than his nominal authority. This situation had come about by

> a strange affect of human contradictions. Men too jealous to confide their liberty to their representatives who are their equals, abandoned it to a Prince who might the more easily abuse it as the affairs of the Republic were important & had not [been] fixed [by] themselves [sic].

Hugo Grotius was correct, therefore, in saying that only his countrymen's common hatred of the Austrian monarchy had kept their constitution from being destroyed by its own vices and breaches of its fundamental principles which had resulted fro shifting power in the Dutch republic from the representatives of theoretically equal provinces to the stadtholder.[20]

Madison clearly feared that in the absence of sufficient constitutional authority in the American confederation to make the union a true sovereign government respected by other nations, this chronic crisis would be solved by imitation of the Dutch republic. Americans who were equals would place authority in the hands of a single person. Consequently, he believed that constitutional reform in 1787 might become a move to establish a monarchy of one form or another rather than to preserve republican government.

By the time Madison prepared these notes on the flaws of all confederations, he had become convinced that this form of political organization was totally unsuited for the American republic, if it were to fulfill its unique destiny as a nation. In addition to the vast disproportion between the voting power of each member and its wealth and population generally characteristic of confederations, there were other flaws specific to the American union. Madison listed twelve of them in his well-known, but little analyzed, memorandum called the "Vices of the Political System of the U. States," prepared in the months immediately before the Convention of 1787. There were three kinds of flaws. First, the state governments commonly failed to comply with Congress' requisitions of money, they encroached on the federal authority to make treaties, violated the laws of nations, trespassed on each others' rights, failed to act in unison, when the common interest required it, and lacked any federal constitutional guarantee to protect them against internal violence.

Second, the government of the Confederation could make laws in name only because its official acts could not be enforced with sanctions. "A sanction is essential to the idea of law, as coercion is to that of Government." The existing confederation lacked both of these "great vital principles of a Political Consti[tu]tion." The Articles of Confederation were no more than a treaty of friendship, alliance, and commerce among thirteen "independent and Sovereign States." This fatal flaw was caused by a misplaced confidence in the honor and sound policy of the states. Therefore, appeals to "the ordinary motives by which the laws secure the obedience of individuals" were ignored on the supposition that such a consideration was unnecessary in framing a constitution. The flaws are excusable in the authors of the Articles which were framed during the crisis of war, but it could no longer be expected that thirteen independent states will promptly andunanimously obey the acts of Congress–not even during any future war. The reasons for their refusals are clear enough: no act affects all states equally; they are all partial to their own interests and even more so when influenced by the "Courtiers of popularity" who naturally exaggerate inequality of effects when they are real and suspect them when they are fancied. Also, the distrust of voluntary compliance with congressional acts begets noncompliance, although a common trust ought to be the "latent disposition of all." Consequently, the constitutional power of Congress has been only "nominally authoritative."

Another fundamental flaw is the lack of ratification of the Articles by the people. In some states the document is incorporated in the local constitution, but in others it is recognized only by statute. Two further evils result. When a state law conflicts with an act of Congress, the question is which act has superior obligation. Since the state courts decide the issue, they tend to favor state over federal acts. This situation follows from the fact that the Articles were ratified by the state governments, not the voters of each state. In the absence of the latter form of ratification, the union was no more than a league of sovereign powers without a "political Constitution..." and joined in a compact which in theory left each member to decide for itself the extent of its obligations to the others and the occasion which might justify the dissolution of the union.

The third group of vices consisted of flaws internal to the states, although most of them had an "indirect influence on the general malady" of the Confederation. These faults were the excessive number of laws, the frequency with which they were changed, and their injustice which undermines faith in the republican theory of majority rule.[21] This last subject deserves special notice. Madison attributed the lack of such guarantees to a misapplication of the "Republican Theory," according to which power and right are synonymous because both are vested in the majority. Experience has shown, however, that three conditions vitiate this theory. First, if the minority consists of all those who "possess the skill and habits of military life, & such as possess the great pecuniary resources, one third only may conquer the remaining two thirds." The second condition leading to minority rule occurs, when one–third of the population who choose rulers becomes a majority by the "accession" of those whose poverty excludes them from the right to vote and for this reason are likely to join in "sedition" instead of supporting the established government. Where "slavery exists," republican theory is "more fallacious."[22]

He did not elaborate on this excursion into political theory, so that we are left to ponder its implications in conjunction with additional evidence which may permit a reasonable interpretation. These observations implied that a reformed constitution would authorize the federal government to guarantee the states against domestic violence, although it is by no means clear that he intended this power to extend to all three conditions mentioned in "Vices." Since Madison probably prepared this memorandum after Shays's "Rebellion" in Massachusetts had subsided, it is probable that this event stimulated these remarks. There is little, if any evidence, however, to give credence to the idea that this event was a major factor in moving Madison to become a constitutional reformer. This conclusion is dubious given the available record. After all, Madison mentioned *three* conditions under which the theory of majority rule on which republican government operates is nullified in reality: rule by a minority consisting of the military and monied interests, a minority of voters who have rallied the dispossessed to support sedition, and every political unit where slavery exists. The existing record demonstrates that he did not think that Shays' affair fitted into any of these three classes of cases in which republican governments are effectively subverted. Therefore, he did not support federal military assistance to curb those who were called rebels in Massachusetts.

Madison was serving in Congress, when he spoke for the first time about Daniel Shays's resistance to the government of that state. On 19 February 1787 he noted that Rufus King of Massachusetts "pathetically implored" Congress to continue recruiting troops. They were needed to punish the so-called rebels by disarming and disfranchising them. Madison agreed to continue recruiting troops on the pretext of needing a defense on our borders as long as any credence could be given to rumors that the British were manipulating the Shayites. On the merits, however, he did not like to intervene militarily in a state and would not do so at this time for two compelling reasons: the Articles of Confederation did not authorize it expressly; and "the principles of Republican Govts which as they rest on the sense of the majority, necessarily suppose power and right to be on the same side."[23]

Madison's reply gave little comfort to King and others who were upset by the Shays affair. By grounding his reluctance to act on the doctrine that majority rule is right, Madison was laying the ground for the position he wished to take at the Convention. He passed on to George Washington on 21 February (and Jefferson later) the report that the legislature of Massachusetts called this "mutiny" a "Rebellion." Madison was astonished by the drastic measures said to be contemplated to punish the participants because he thought that if they were carried out in the face of the popularity of Shays and his follows in parts of the state, "a new crisis may be brought on." He hoped that the affair would not deter a thorough reform of the existing Confederation so as to make the "Republican form" serve. Success in this enterprise would dissuade persons who appeared to lean toward a monarchical government. A few days later he repeated these views to Edmund Pendleton and added his concern for the growing sentiment in favor of disunion. Given the uncertainties involved, he could not predict the outcome of the Convention. He could say only that the time had come for all of the friends of the Revolution to reform the Confederation and support the republican cause.[24] What is most obvious about this limited record is that Madison regarded the Shays affair as more of a threat than an aid to the kind of reform he contemplated in the spring of 1787.

BETTER REPRESENTATIVES

Among the many deficiences of the existing Confederation which troubled Madison very greatly were three behavioral tendencies common to legislative bodies. There was the self–serving behavior of some elected representatives, the inclination to serve as advocates of particular interests at the expense of others, and the inclination to violate individual rights when acting as members of a governing majority. Therefore, one of the most important reforms which he hoped to effect was an improvement in the quality of the members of Congress. In 1783 he spoke in Congress of the need for members to act in the national interest, even if it were at the cost of a strict adherence to the wishes of the state legislatures which had chosen them to serve. In the course of debating a tax measure, Madison had to resolve the dilemma which arose when he supported it, but the legislature of Virginia withdrew its assent. This circumstance embarrassed him because he was by conviction strongly disinclined to disregard the sense of his constituents. Nevertheless, there were three circumstances which inclined him to act contrary to this theory of his duty as a representative. First, although all the members of Congress represented and were accountable to their respective states, they also "owed a fidelity to the collective interests of the whole." Second, although instructions from, or the declared sense of, a representative's constituents ought generally to be a "law" to the former, there are occasions on which a representative ought to "hazard personal consequences" out of a clear conviction that his determination of an issue is in the "true interest" of the persons served. Third, a representative is justified in acting on his own convictions if constituents would act in the same way were they in possession of the same information. On this occasion the collective interest consisted in the preservation of the union, its reputation abroad, and its internal peace.[25]

On other occasions he complained that measures in Congress were not being decided in the "spirit impartial of judges." Its members were acting as "advocates for the respective interests of their constituents."[26] There was a need, also, for more "temperate & experienced" members in Congress, if that body were to make those "catholic arrangements on which the harmony & stability of the Union must greatly depend."[27] Unfortunately, most Americans failed, or refused, to recognize the crucial relationship between external and internal circumstances which affect, and are affected by, the distribution of power within a political system. Madison was dismayed in

1785 by the failure of his fellow Virginians to grasp this truth. It did not operate with full force on minds unaccustomed to consider the interests of the state as they were intertwined with the confederacy much less as they were affected by foreign politics.[28]

Madison consolidated and elaborated many of these scattered reflections on congressional and state legislative behavior in the final sections of his memordum, "Vices." The motives which legislators have for holding office explain why some of them are self-serving to the point even of acting contrary to the known interests and views of their constituents. Such persons violate a public trust and thereby demonstrate their lack of fidelity or virtue as Madison and his contemporaries usually called this quality. There are three motives for holding public office. "1. ambition. 2. personal interest. 3. public good. Unhappily the first two are proved by experience to be the most prevalent." Those who are under these first two interests, particularly the second one, are always the most industrious and successful members in pursuing and obtaining their personal objectives. When they form majorities in legislatures, as they often do, consisting of members who are activated by "interested views," *contrary* to "the interest, and views, of their Constituents," they join in a "perfidious sacrifice" of the latter to the former. The next election is supposed to displace such offenders and replace them with others who will subsequently repair the damage. In practice, however, clever legislators mask their "base and selfish measures" with "pretexts of public good and apparent expediency." This art, industriously employed by self-serving members, too often prevails among unwary voters who misplace their confidence in such representatives. They are often enabled to form majorities, also, because they dupe other honest but unenlightened members who follow favorite leaders veiling their selfishness and varnishing their professions of devotion to the public good with "sophistical" and "popular eloquence." Self-serving behavior is manifested in the instability of laws, particularly state statutes regulating trade. This situation is an "evil in itself," but it creates an even greater one. It erodes confidence in "the fundamental principle of republican Government," according to which the majority who rule are the "safest Guardians of both public Good and of private rights."[29]

The tendency of representatives to act as mere advocates of the parochial interests of their constituents is "a still more fatal if not more frequent cause" of the loss of confidence in majority rule. The cause of partiality is found "among the people themselves." All civilized societies are divided into "interests and factions" reflecting, among other things, the many forms taken by productive property. If representatives are to be restrained in office, it must be by "public opinion" in a republic. This means in practice the opinion of the majority rules within society because it sets the standard of public conduct to be measured by elections. In a narrow constituency such as "R. Island," there is little respect among the people for opinions held by other persons living outside of it. True, individuals holding "extended views" and activated by "national pride" may elevate public opinion to this broader perspective occasionally, but the ordinary citizen and state legislator do not care in the least about the effects of their local legislation in "France or Holland; or even in Massts or Connect." It is sufficient for persons holding parochial views that their interests are served. The citizen is justified by the fact that a measure is popular in his state. The legislator is Justified in voting for it because it is popular in his district.[30]

Finally, confidence in republican government is eroded by the tendency of legislative majorities to violate the rights of minorities and individuals. In a republic, the majority, regardless of the diversity of its social composition, declares the law. If it is united by an apparent interest or common passion, then it is likely to violate the rights of minorities or individuals. Unfortunately, no mere multiplication of the numbers of persons constituting a ruling majority can in itself restrain the tendency of majorities to oppress minorities and individuals. Two hundred thousand will oppress one hundred thousand no less than two persons will oppress one. Three moral motives may be considered as restraints, but all are proved by experience to fail for the most part. Every person holding public office ought to have a prudent regard for the relationship between the individual's own good and "the general and permanent good of the Community," but it is all too often ignored. A person who is accountable for the trustworthy discharge of public duties ought to be restrained by respect for his own integrity. Unhappily, in "a multitude its efficacy is diminished in proportion to the number which is to share the praise or blame." Finally, it has been argued that a religious establishment ought to restrain the behavior of civil majorities. It cannot be "pretended," however, that religious instruction in morals does so in the case of individuals, and it certainly does not do so when people act collectively as in a legislature whose members are bound, supposedly, by an oath. Even in its "coolest state," religious conviction supported by civil authority is more likely to become "a motive to oppression" than it is to be a restraint upon injustice. When religious belief is "kindled into enthusiasm," its force, like that of the other "passions," is multiplied by mass support. Although this latter condition is temporary, the idea that religion be "at the helm of Government" at any time does not offer a pleasant prospect.[31]

These basic weaknesses of representative government can be reformed once it is recognized that "an extensive republic meliorates the administration" of a small one. A supplementary objective furthering this end would be "a process of elections" which extracts from society persons whose motives and abilities prompt them to pursue the common good and enables them to devise the best means for attaining it.[32]

A SCHEME OF REPRESENTATION

By March, 1787, Madison had developed the essentials of the constitutional reforms which he believed ought to be presented to the up coming Convention. He tried to convince Jefferson that reform was absolutely necessary because the political situation was precarious. There was no way of predicting the outcome of the "political experiment" of calling a constitutional convention, but the risk had to be taken. The "mortal diseases" of the existing Confederation were so evident as to frighten the timid and alarm even "orthodox republicans..." They were ready to make every concession to the advocates of stable government "not infringing fundamental principles, as the only security against an opposite extreme of our present situation." (Years later Madison explained that he was referring to monarchy as the extreme to which there was a real possibility of turning.) The first reform must "lay the foundation of the new system in such a ratification by the people themselves of the several states as will render it clearly paramount to their [state] Legislative authorities." Next, Congress should be given powers over trade and other matters in which uniformity of power is necessary, and authority to invalidate state laws in all cases. Third, there must be "a change in the principle of Representation." As long as the execution of Congress's acts *depends on the states,* their equality of votes in that body did not destroy the "inequality of importance and influence" among the states. An increase in Congress's legislative powers *without depending on the states* to execute them would leave the smallest state equal in power to the largest state. Any effective reform must eliminate both of these fundamental deficiencies. The solution, Madison cryptically argued, is a change in the distribution of representation which would appeal initially to the "Eastern States by the actual superiority of their populousness, and to the Southern by their expected superiority" of population in the future. If this change should occur, a majority of the states will see themselves as "gainers" so that the small states should have to yield. With the matter of representation settled, the existing objections of the large states to giving up any of their powers should "vanish."[33]

The essentials of this sketch were repeated and fleshed out in letters to Edmund Randolph and George Washington a few weeks later. Madison envisioned radical changes in the structure of the federal government and enlargement of its powers. Congress was to become bicameral with representation in one house chosen by the people every "(___) number" of years with a smaller number in the second house required to be rotated periodically. Executive and judicial branches were to be added with appropriate powers. This plan of government, "well organized and balanced," should be ratified by the authority of the people and operate without intervention of the state governments. These changes would ensure its republican form by deriving the government's authority from the people and distributing its powers among the three traditional branches. Although some important details remained to be worked out, Madison wanted it understood that he favored a new system occupying a "middle ground" between the existing confederation and "consolidation...into one simple republic..."[34]

When the proposal to create a new Congress was introduced for debate at the Convention, Madison urged the delegates to create a national House of Representatives whose members would be apportioned according to an "equitable ratio" so as to make it analogous to the popular branches of the state legislatures. By this same analogy members of the House should be chosen directly and frequently by the voters. However, Elbridge Gerry of Connecticut wanted choice by the state legislatures in order to stem "the excess of democracy..." George Mason disagreed with Gerry on the ground that members of the legislature ought to be taken not only from "the whole republic," but also from "different districts" of its large members because it was very well known in Virginia that they had "different interests and views" depending upon the local economy and other matters. Madison supported Mason and opposed Gerry because the legislature in some states already had members chosen indirectly, and this practice carried the process of "refining" public opinion too far. According to Rufus King of Massachusetts, James Wilson and Madison said that "if the election is made by the Peop. in large districts there will be no Danger of Demagogues."35

On 6 June 1787, when Gerry repeated his belief that popular election places the "worst men" in the legislature, Madison responded with a long speech defending direct popular election of the House. It is "a clear principle of free Govt." and it will secure "better representatives." This result will follow because it has been admitted already that in a very small state "faction & oppression wd. prevail," but it should be conceded that they have existed in "the largest as well as the smallest" states. Are "we not thence admonished to enlarge the sphere as far as the nature of the Govt. would admit?" This is the only defense against the "inconveniences" of democracy consistent with that "form" of government. As founders we must accept as given the proposition that "all civilized societies would be divided into different Sects, Factions & interests" engaged in incessant efforts to oppress each other. If the sphere is enlarged, however, the community will be divided into so many "interests and parties" that a majority having a common and immediate interest is unlikely to form, or, if it should do so, to pursue its objectives successfully at the expense of a minority. Slavery, based on the mere difference of color, was a striking example of this truth. The remedy, therefore, is to frame a "republican system on such a scale & such a form as will control the evils wch. have been experienced." According to Rufus King, Madison said: "The election may be safely made by the people if you enlarge the Sphere of Election—Experience proves it—if bad elections have taken place from the people, it will generally have been found to have happened in small districts."36

Some of Madison's very acute colleagues perceived that he was referring to at least three anticipated effects to follow from the popular election of representatives in large districts. First, that such a choice will secure better representatives, an improvement which Madison earnestly desired. Second, that representatives chosen directly from every part of the nation would introduce into Congress's legislative deliberations a new and greater diversity of interests and opinions than had been the case hitherto. Third, that the effect of such diversity would be to moderate rule by legislative majorities because they would have to be coalitions.

Roger Sherman of Connecticut denounced the idea that representatives ought to be elected in large districts directly by the voters. The people would not much interest themselves in the elections, because "a few designing men in the large districts would carry their points and the people would have no more confidence in them than in [the present] Congs." According to Alexander Hamilton's notes, Madison said that republics ought to be constructed on two principles: 1. enlarge the extent to make combinations grounded on interest difficult; and 2. employ a process of elections to refine representation. The first claim, Hamilton thought, overlooks the certainty that a popular assembly, even one drawn from half the globe, will be liable to all the passions which actuate every such body. If more *"minute links"* are missing, others will supply them; the old regional conflicts as well as those between the commercial and non commercial interests will continue to operate. Madison's second claim, that "large districts are less liable to be influenced by factious demagogues than small" is true to some extent, but small areas of large districts often carry elections and demagogues may influence the whole. After all they are not always *"inconsiderable* persons–Patricians were frequently demagogues."[37]

These objections were probably unknown to Madison, but he was made aware of Hamilton's line of attack later, when the latter rose to oppose both the Virginia and New Jersey Plans. He expressed doubt that a republic can be established over an extended territory. The difficulty of drawing representatives from the extremes to the center of the country discouraged him. What inducements, he asked, can be offered that would attract men of standing and talent? The "moderate wages for the 1st. branch, would only be bait to little demagogues." The Senate would be filled with "undertakers who wish for particular offices under the Govt." This view of the subject "almost led him to despair that a Republican govt. could be established over so great an extent." Robert Yates and Rufus King corroborated Madison's account, reporting Hamilton as saying that Congress would not attract "gentlemen of fortune and abilities" or "men of first consequences."[38]

Governeur Morris later repeated this charge later in order to oppose a requirement that Congress be constitutionally obliged to reapportion members of the House on the basis of a periodic census of population. Morris wanted wealth to be added, and he arrogantly dismissed future representatives from the new states which would be included in reapportionments through the operation of this requirement. "The Western Country," he complained, would not be able to furnish representatives as "equally enlightened," as others to share in the governance of our common interests. The "Busy haunts of men [and] not the remote wilderness was the proper school of political Talents." Morris predicted candidly that if "the Western people get the power into their hands they will ruin the Atlantic interests" because the "Back members" always oppose the best measures.[39]

Madison rejected this implicit appeal to southerners to place confidence in the willingness of a future northern majority to add western representatives in the future. Neither American nor English experience justified any such expectation. Therefore, no "unfavorable distinctions" should be made between the original and new states regarding either "justice or policy." Madison argued, also, that population, rather than wealth, would serve as a proper basis of representation. The probable extent of the western states' contributions to the nation's treasury had been underestimated, he believed. Initially, the fertility of their soil should make them exporters of agricultural commodities with a concomitant stimulus to commerce augmented by their need to import manufactured goods through the Atlantic states. With the opening of the Mississippi River to trade, this commerce ought to result in the collection of increased revenue at its mouth from import taxes. Population alone provides the proper standard for apportioning representatives, despite the fact that population and wealth are not exactly interchangeable measures "of each other." Nevertheless, they are sufficiently so in the United States because, with the free movement of people among its parts, "population, industry, arts, and the value of labor" will continually tend to become equalized among them. The value of labor will become the chief criterion of wealth and the ability to pay taxes, and this value will tend to find its level in the various parts as long as intercourse among them is unobstructed. People will move to places where labor will cost the most until competition destroys the initial inequality among them at any given time. Consequently, people are moving constantly from the "more to the less populous places," from Europe to the United States and from the "Northern and Middle parts of the U.S. to the Southern and Western." They go to "where land is cheap because labor is dearer." This axiom will eventually equalize the value of labor on both the Ohio and Delaware rivers.[40]

This speech explains what Madison meant when he said in March, 1787, that he had a scheme of representation expected to appeal in 1787 to the northern states because of their existing superiority of population and to the southern states because of their anticipated advantage in this respect in the future. It illuminates, also, his exhortation to enlarge the sphere by incorporating interests from areas not previously represented directly.   Third, it relates the full political incorporation of the Trans–Allegheny West to his theory of moderate majority rule, the germ of which he expressed to Jefferson and Lafayette in 1784–85. Finally, this exposition linked Madison's vision of constitutional reform with the natural laws which he believed defined and justified the unique destiny of the American republic as an independent nation.

His success in this endeavor was not complete, however. When the Convention voted to fix the number of members of the House at 65 until the first census should be taken, Madison moved to double the number for all states. He argued that a bare quorum of 65 was too small to possess the necessary local information, and the small number limited the opportunities for popular candidates to seek election. Twice the number proposed, even with the addition of new states, would not be too many, he contended, but his motion was defeated 10 to 2 with only Virginia and Pennsylvania voting for it. Jacob Broom announced at once that he would seek equal votes in the Senate for his state, Delaware.[41] On 8 September Madison vainly supported one more motion to reconsider the intitial size of the House.[42] These votes left him disappointed, but certainly not defeated. This much of his plan had gone very well, indeed. Broom's declaration of intent, however, was an ominous portent of an impending, crushing defeat for Madison's vision of a national Senate.

Madison sketched no model of the Senate before attending the Convention, so that it is necessary to extract and develop one from his speeches. These sources reveal that he wanted a senate which would be national because it would have the same popular foundation as the House, except that the latter would choose senators from an unspecified number of persons nominated by the states' legislatures. The number of senators should be small in order to exercise certain exclusive powers which Madison did not elaborate in his Notes of Debates, except for a veto of undefined limits over state laws. This objective could be reached only by creating what he called an equilibrium of northern and southern interests in the upper house. He was well aware that this condition could be established only if his theory of the movement of population proved to be valid, although he never specified how the growth of the western states would affect an equilibrium designed to relate to the conflicts between northern and southern states existing in 1787.

Before elaborating these main characteristics of his model, one should note that he explicitly rejected at the outset of the Convention the use of large districts for the selection of senators. When this arrangemenent was proposed on 31 May 1787, he opposed it on the ground that this mode would destroy the influence of the small states associated with large ones, as they would have to be in order to form a few very large districts. Experience in Virginia had demonstrated that local pride in the choice of members from large counties had often triumphed over the "superior merit" of individuals from smaller ones.[43] On the supposition that the New Jersey Plan proposed this mode of electing the members of a single chamber in Congress, he said that such an "amalgamation and repartition" of the aggregate population of the United States into "13 equal parts" was unacceptable. It would destroy the differences among the states concerning "rules regulating property...manners, habits and prejudices..." to the danger of the small states.[44]

Opposition to the choice of senators by the popular branch of Congress was voiced by some delegates who claimed that this arrangement was intended to give preponderance to the "landed interest" in the Senate. Elbridge Gerry of Massachusetts admitted that he favored election of senators by the state legislatures because the "commerical & monied interest" would be more secure than in the "hands of the people at large." The members of these legislatures would possess a much better "sense of character" than the voters. Therefore, indirect elections by these bodies would result in more "refinement" of choice. Madison opposed this degree of refining "popular sentiments" through legislatures, some of which had indirectly elected branches. The "necessary sympathy" between rulers and ruled would be lost. There would be quite enough refinement if the popular branch of Congress were to choose the upper branch, the executive, and the judges. Indirect choice made this way would eliminate the "agency" of the state legislatures in the operations of the "general" government.[45]

Madison was roused next by a threat to the small size which he advocated. On 7 June John Dickinson of Delaware argued for a large number, "80 and twice 80," so that an American senate might be analogous to the British House of Lords as much as possible. This proposal reused Madison to say that, if this idea were to carry, the delegates must either give up "proportional representation" or provide a very large number of members. The first choice was "unjust" and the second one was imprudent, if the Senate were expected to proceed with more "coolness... system...[and] wisdom" than the popular branch. Enlarge the number of members in a legislative body and "you communicate to them the vices which they were meant to correct." The power of individual members in such an assembly is in "inverse ratio to their number," as long as they are elected to take care of their constituents' interests. The larger the body, the more its members mirror the numerous interests of their constituents and become divided among themselves from either their own "indiscretions" or the "artifices" of opposing factions. These divisions render them incapable of fulfilling their public trust. When the "weight" of a legislative body depends "merely on their personal characters," the greater their number, the greater their weight. However, when their weight depends on their "political authority," as it must in the United States, "the smaller the number the greater the weight." He concluded that these considerations "might" be combined in the proposed Senate.[46]

When Dickinson persisted with his arguments, Madison responded again. He said he could not understand in what way "family weight" would be transmitted to the Senate through elections by state legislatures. The question concerned the best method of choice to provide an "uncorrupt & impartial...preference for merit." He could not understand how choice by state legislatures would produce such senators. The great evils which delegates complained of were that the state legislatures had enacted "schemes of paper money etc." sometimes because the people wanted them and on other occasions without any demand from this source. Why, Madison asked, would anyone believe that this tendency would not be replicated in a national legislature consisting of one branch chosen by the very legislative bodies in which these so-called evils were perpetrated? "Nothing can be more contradictory than to say that the Natl. Legislature without a proper check will follow the example of the State legislatures, & in the same breath, that the State legislatures are the only proper check [on the Senate]."[47]

Despite the power of Madison's logic, which was lucidly supported by James Wilson, Oliver Ellsworth of Connecticut responded with a direct attack on Madison's exhortation to enlarge the sphere. The Framers, Ellsworth insisted, must maintain the "agency" of the states in the new government. Without their cooperation it would be "impossible to support a Republican Govt. over so great an extent of country. An army could scarcely render it practicable." This prediction rested on experience. Virginia had conceded that it could not govern Kentucky. Massachusetts could not maintain "peace one hundred miles from her capitol." Pennsylvania must surely experience similar difficulties in the future. Therefore, if the "principles & materials of our Govt. are not adequate to the extent of single states, how can it be imagined that they can support a single government throughout the U. States?" The issue was settled with the vote on 25 June to vest the power of choosing senators in the state legislatures.[48]

This decision prompted Madison to make one more appeal for a senate composed of members likely to have a national perspective. He chose the ensuing debate over the proper term for senators, although he had already stated his position on this subject on 12 June. He then said that a seven-year term would give the legislature stability, the absence of which the enemies of republican government attributed to it as an incurable disease, although he admitted there was no experience in the states to confirm this prediction.[49]

On the twenty-sixth he spoke for a senate in terms which give a superficial plausibility to the belief that he advocated an aristocratic body. Placed in the existing context of debate, however, it appears that he was directing an appeal particularly to the delegates from Massachusetts and Connecticut. He said the Senate should be given a form which would protect the people from their rulers and the people from artful manipulators. Hence, two branches are required to "watch & check" each other. All public business "liable to abuses" should pass through separate bodies which are the means of checking each other. The Senate should be small, the members' terms long enough to acquire the requisite knowledge of public business, and service should start only at an age when disqualification from reeligibility would be consistent with the public good and the members' private interests. These provisions should engender respect for the "wisdom & virtue" of the members and enable the senate to secure the "preponderence of justice by throwing its weight" into the conflicts arising out of the heterogeneity of American society. He shrewdly added the prospect that such a body would serve, also, to curb all those who might in the future wish for an equal division of property. Indeed, there was already a "leveling spirit" abroad in the land, but, he admitted, no attempts had been made to pass "agrarian" laws equalizing the ownership of land. Therefore, a people calmly deliberating on a constitution to last for ages to come would provide such a senate as the proper republican guardian against these prospective dangers.[50]

A bit later on the twenty sixth Madison opposed the motion by Oliver Ellsworth of Connecticut that would pay members of the senate out of the state treasuries. This branch ought to be a "firm, wise and impartial body," Madison said, to stabilize the federal government's operations on individuals and to balance the interests of the different states. If the Convention persisted in its existing course of decisions, however, it would make "the Senate, like Congress, the mere Agents & Advocates of State interests and views instead of...impartial guardians of justice and the general Good."[51]

Both Robert Yates and John Lansing of New York understood Madison to be pleading for long-term protection of the "landed interest," which was then prevalent. In the long run, however, it would become comparatively small as it had already in Europe. In future elections this interest will be overcome by "trade and manufactures..." In England at this time, if elections were open to all classes of people, the property of landowners would be insecure as ours will be if laws are enacted to secure an equal distribution of property. Our government ought, however, to secure the "permanent interests" against such changes by giving landowners "a share in the government, to support these invaluable interests and to balance and check each other." They should be constituted so as to protect "the minority of the opulent against the majority. The Senate ought to be this body..."[52]

It is true that Madison anticipated a long-term decline in the political power of landowners, but he was unwilling to give them control of the new government. When George Mason moved to require the ownership of land as a qualification to hold office in Congress, Madison vigorously opposed him on several grounds. He had seen individuals having unsettled accounts with governments secure election to legislatures for the "sinister" purpose of serving their own personal financial interests. Furthermore, the ownership of land was no evidence of "real wealth" nor of devotion to the public good. He had observed individuals who had bought land on credit and then secured their elections to legislative office for the private purpose of enacting laws which unjustly protected them from their creditors. Furthermore, if the amount of property required to qualify were great, then the "proper representatives of those classes of Citizens who are not landholders" such as the "monied interest" (public creditors) would be excluded, as other critics of this qualification noted. The prudent and just policy is to represent and protect the "interests and rights of every class" in the legislative branch. It is for this reason that their members are chosen from districts which are distributed throughout a given political system. Representatives are taken from each one not only to understand and sympathize with the interests of all groups, but also to be responsive to them. At the moment of these deliberations the United States consisted of three major classes, "the landed, the commercial and the manufacturing..." The first one is larger than the other two, but daily the latter will increase in proportion to the whole as the experience of Europe demonstrates. Members of these three interests understand each others' affairs much less than persons of the same interest who live in different districts of the country. Therefore, it is necessary that the interest of any one group should not be left to the "impartiality" of a third one as would be the case if the ownership of land were required to serve in Congress. His motion to strike this requirement carried by an overwhelming vote.[53]

On this occasion Madison demonstrated his determination to block any provisions which would give any one interest full control of the reformed government at the expense of others. On the other hand, he failed completely thereafter to secure adoption of any provisions likely to give each major interest a constitutional power of self-defense. This combination of results helps explain in part the complex argument which he made subsequently in his first contribution to *The Federalist*, number ten.

The overwhelming vote to allow the state legislatures to choose senators thwarted Madison's hope that this body would consist of impartial guardians of the nation. In addition, this vote made it almost impossible by the logic of numbers for him to secure a Senate of small size apportioned to the whole population of each state. If each state were to choose no more than one Senator, the total number would always have to equal no fewer than the number of states in a growing union. If, on the other hand, the number were to be small in harmony with Madison's axiom that the body's weight would be inversely proportional to its size, delegates must have asked themselves: will every state be authorized to choose a senator? Madison hinted at a breathtaking answer to this question in a speech on 28 June. He opposed John Lansing's motion to limit each state to equal representation in the House in accordance with the plan of New Jersey. It proposed to aggregate the population of the United States and then redivide it into thirteen equal electoral districts without regard for the boundaries of states, their laws or their social systems. There was no need for such a remedy on the suppostion that a proportional representation would result in domination of the small states by the large ones. Virginia, Massachusetts, and Pennsylvania shared no common interest which distinguished them from any other three states. Their "manners, Religion and other circumstances which sometimes beget affection between different communities" were no more "assimilated" than those of any other states. Their economies were as materially dissimilar as those in any other three states. Equality of size had never produced political combinations in either Congress or the state legislatures where counties of varying sizes were represented. The histories of Europe's monarchies and the Dutch Republic demonstrated this truth. The inference is that "among individuals of superior eminence & weight in Society, rivalships were much more common than coalitions." The choice facing the Framers at this moment was between "a perfect separation & a perfect incorporation of 13 states." If the first option were chosen, the states would become independent nations subject only to the law of nations. If the second choice were made, they would become "mere counties of one entire republic, subject to one common law." Make the first choice and the small states will have every reason to fear the large ones. It is in the formers' interest, therefore, to choose the system which will "most approximate" them to counties within a state. If, on the other hand, the government is left feeble, the large states will distrust it and, "foreseeing that their importance & security may depend on their own size & strength," they will not submit to a partition of the whole union into thirteen equal parts. A government endowed with sufficient "energy & permanence," however, would remove their objection. "Gradual partitions of the large & junctions of the small states will be facilitated." Time may "effect that equalization" of power which the small states desire, but such changes will not occur at once.[54]

This aggressive and audaciouss speech resulted in a threat of disunion on a sectional basis. Oliver Ellsworth insisted on proportional representation in the House and equality in the senate. The former accorded with "the national principle" and the latter with the "federal principle." If this compromise were *not* agreed to, he predicted, the Convention would have met in vain; if "the Southern States contend for this plan of a popular instead of a State Representation we shall separate; the political body must be cut asunder at the Delaware."[55] This report, corroborated by Rufus King, casts strong doubt, once again, on the familiar claim that Madison's scheme of representation was intended to create a senate of oligarchs.   Madison was then forced to reveal that his goal was a senate in which proportional representation of states would create a sectional equilibrium of interests.

Madison was not surprised that sectionalism was interjected at this time because it had long been evident to him in the old Congress, much to his dismay.[56]   Ellsworth, however, proposed to "repair the roof" instead of "razing [*sic*] the foundations..." of the government properly. On the other hand, his contention that every "peculiar interest whether in any class of citizens, or any description of States ought to be secured as far as possible" by a constitutional defensive power had great merit. It was not the size of the states which created material and conflicting differences among them and the resulting need for defensive powers. The "great division of interests" was between the northern and southern states, with slavery accounting for the greatest measure of differences. If any "defensive power were necessary, it ought mutually to be given to these two interests."   For this reason he had been trying to think of some defensive power for both regions.   The one which had occurred to him was to apportion representation in one branch to the number of free inhabitants and in the other to the whole population of each state, counting slaves in the ratio of five to three.   This arrangement would give the southern states the voting advantage in one house and the northern states in the other one (as he had hinted to Jefferson in March). He had been reluctant to urge this solution, however, because of his "unwillingness to urge any diversity of interests...when it is too apt to arise of itself..."   Furthermore, "the inequality of powers that must be vested in the two branches would mutually destroy the equilibrium of interests." He did not at this time specify the powers which would be unequal, although he had already spoken in favor of a veto over state laws which he wanted exercised by the Senate exclusively.[57]

On 7 July Elbridge Gerry tried to change the subject from a discussion of the rules by which the states would hold power in Congress to the scope of the latter's legislative powers.   Madison objected immediately to any discussion of the quantity of power until the distribution of its control had been decided.   It would be impossible to decide what powers could be "safely & properly vested in the Govt. before it was known in what manner the states would be represented in it." If this basic decision were not "just, the states would refuse to grant some important powers so that the new government would be as weak as the existing one and or the same reasons."   Virginia has objected to every addition of powers to Congress because it had only "1/13 of the Legislature, when they ought to have 1/6."   This issue was complicated, Madison argued according to the notes of Rufus King and William Paterson, by the supposition that the Senate would be given "certain exclusive powers such as the appointment to offices, etc."   If the states were to have equal power in this branch, "a minority of the people or an Aristocracy will appoint the [great] officers.[58]   Apparently, Madison was convinced that Virginians would not give to other Americans a share of power to make federal laws totally incommensurate with their physical resources from which the nation would draw a portion of its strength.   Therefore, those who wished to "infuse mortality into a Constitution which we wished to last forever" would insist on equal votes for the states.[59]   They would do so, moreover, despite the vast increases in population, economic diversity, and social complexity which will make the United States in the future increasingly like the Europe of 1787.[60]

In a last and losing attempt to block equal votes in the Senate, Madison implored his fellow Framers to act on his basic proposition: "If the proper foundation of Government was destroyed, by substituting an equal in place of a proportional Representation, no proper superstructure would be raised, or ought to be raised, that would either fulfill the public wishes, or be a credit to the Convention."   The history of the Confederation confirmed this truth.   Should the delegations persist in acting contrary to his views, he predicted, five highly undesirable results could be expected.   A numerical minority in the Senate would be able to nullify the "will of the majority of the people" expressed in the popularly elected House, "extort" measures to serve the minority's interests as the condition for enacting necessary legislation, or force upon the majority certain policies because of the "peculiar powers which would be vested in the Senate."   All of these evils, instead of being "cured by time," must increase with the addition of every new state because all must be admitted on the principle of equality with the original states.   Finally, it now seemed to be pretty well understood that the "real difference of interests" lay not between the small and large states but between the northern and southern states, which were divided over slavery and its consequences.   There were eight of the former and five of the latter.   If representation were made proportional, the northern states would outnumber the southern, but "not in the same degree, [as they do] at this time;" and "every day would tend towards an equilibrium.[61]

Presumably, Madison based this expectation on the rapid increase in population which would occur in the southern and western states with the advent of free immigration, according to his theory of the mobility of population.   His hopes for such a senate were defeated as was his implicit appeal for southern solidarity by the grotesque vote of 5 states to 4 (New York, Massachusetts, and New Hampshire not voting).   Thus, this great issue was carried against him by an obvious minority of the thirteen states then in the union.[62]

The upshot was that Madison succinctly and pointedly expressed his dislike of the Senate to his fellow delegates, although he later hid it from the public.   It was "only another edition of [the former] Congress." The Framers' senate was "nothing more than a combination of the peculiarities of two of the State Govts. which separately had been found deficient."   Maryland provided the "model" for one of these defects and New York the other one.   Consequently, the United States Senate would provide the new federal government with none of the "stability" which had been so conspicuously lacking in the state governments.[63]

Today we may be put off by Madison's scheme of representation and dismiss it as a major constitutional reform, because representative government still seems to have all of the flaws which he observed in his time. It should be recognized instead as a bold and imaginative plan to improve on the American discovery that republics can be "unmixed and extensive..." If Americans were to adopt the reformed system, they would demonstrate the "full efficacy" of representative government when its sphere is truly extended.[64] It is easy to forget that Madison's plan successfully provided for the addition of a democratic branch of the legislature on which a small senate and the executive (as we shall see) would be dependent for election. It truly would have concentrated the will of the government in its largest and most popular body, the one which directs the force of society to the common good. This plan visualized the full political incorporation of the diverse interests of American society in a stable legislative equilibrium precisely because of the dynamic changes anticipated in population and the economy with the addition of new states.

Madison developed his complexity–diversity axiom to secure the support of Framers like Pierce Butler of South Carolina who wanted slaves treated as secure property and counted as persons to be represented because their labor contributed greatly to the nation's wealth; others like Elbridge Gerry and Governeur Morris who implored their fellow delegates to reject any provision which would "enable the poor and numerous inhabitants of the western country to destroy the Atlantic states," as they surely would do if power were transferred from "the maritime to the interior & landed interest"; still others like Alexander Hamilton, who predicted that the western voters would send only demagogues to the House and undertakers (office seekers and their agents) to the Senate; those who, like Roger Sherman, asserted that the voters would elect only designing men from large districts; and Oliver Ellsworth, who predicted that no republican government could be maintained over so great an extent of territory without using an army to compel obedience to its laws. In view of this forcefully articulated opposition alone, it is scarely surprising that the Framers would not give Madison the senate he wanted and, consequently, the degree of power which he originally wanted Congress to have.[65]

The effect of denying proportional power to the large states was recognized at once. Governeur Morris moved to reconsider the final vote on representation taken on the previous day. He made his motion, he explained, so that delegates might discuss "in the abstract" the quantity of power to be assigned to the "general government." He feared that the "vote of yesterday including an equality of the States in the 2d. branch" would become mixed either explicitly or unconsciously in the delegates' discussion of every question concerning the powers to be conferred. No one seconded this motion because everyone understood the significance of the decision determining control over the legislative powers of Congress.[66] As Madison told Martin van Buren in 1828, the *"threatening contest* of 1787 did not, as you supposed, turn on the degree of power to be granted to the federal government, but on the rule by which the States should be represented and vote" in it. The conflicts and compromises which turned on the grants of power to Congress were very important in regard to some matters, but they were "knots of a less 'Gordian' character."[67]

There was another equally noteworthy effect of the defeat of Madison's hope for a sectionally equilibrated senate exclusively possessing certain powers. It changed his conception of those which ought to be allocated to the President and the means by which this novel functionary ought to be chosen in order to insure accountability to the American people at large so as to compensate in part for the defeat of his plans for the Senate.

NOTES

1. *The Federalist*, 85, 226 (Nos. 14 and 37).
2. *PJM*, 2:127–34, passim, and *PJM*, 8:101. Madison appears to have used Locke's argument that sovereign power is forfeited by a government which does not use its powers to benefit its people; found in John Locke, *An Essay Concerning the True Original, Extent, and End of Civil Government*, ed. with an introduction by J. W. Gough (Oxford: Basil Blackwell and Mott, 1946), chap. 13, par. 149, cited hereafter as Locke, *Essay*.
3. *PJM*, 8:107–8.
4. Ibid., 9:76.
5. Ibid., 31–46, 49; 7: 422–23. Thomas Jefferson, *Notes on the State of Virginia*, with an Introduction by Thomas Perkins Abernathy (New York: Harper Torchbooks, 1964), 37–55, 157, 161, 164.
6. *PJM*, 14:100–104. This essay on the natural order was composed as early as 1785 and probably no later than 1791.
7. *PJM*, 8:105–6.
8. Ibid.
9. Ibid., 251–52.
10. Ibid.
11. Ibid. 6:492–94 passim; 11:97.
12. Ibid. 3:297, 307–8 passim.
13. Ibid. 6:286–87; italicized words encoded in the original.
14. Ibid. 8:334–35.
15. Ibid. 9:140–41.
16. Ibid. 182.
17. Ibid. 8:438–39.
18. Ibid., 503; italicized words encoded in the original.
19. Ibid., 505.
20. Ibid. 9:4–17 passim.
21. Ibid. 8:348–54 passim.
22. Ibid., 350–51.
23. Ibid. 9:231, 272, 276–79.
24. Ibid., 286, 294–95, 321.

25. Ibid. 6:147.
26. Ibid. 8:374.
27. Ibid., 335.
28. Ibid, 7:89.
29. Ibid. 9:354.
30. Ibid., 355–56.
31. Ibid.
32. Ibid., 357.
33. Ibid., 318–19.
34. Ibid., 369–71, 383–85.
35. Farrand, *Records*, 1:49–50, 56.
36. Ibid., 132–36 passim, 143–44.
37. Ibid., 342.
38. Ibid., 146–47.
39. Ibid., 287–88, 298–99, 303.
40. Ibid., 584–86.
41. Ibid., 568–70.
42. Ibid. 2:553.
43. Ibid. 1:52.
44. Ibid., 321.
45. Ibid., 48–50, 134.
46. Ibid., 150–52, passim.
47. Ibid., 154.
48. Ibid., 406–8.
49. Ibid., 218–19.
50. Ibid., 421–23.
51. Ibid., 427–28.
52. Ibid., 431–32; *PJM*, 10:78.
53. Farrand, *Records*, 2:122–24.
54. Ibid. 1:446–47.
55. Ibid., 468–69, 478.
56. *PJM*, 1:132; 3:124, 168–69, 262, 293.
57. Farrand, *Records*, 1:485–87, passim; see also 164–65.
58. Ibid., 551, 554.
59. Ibid., 464.
60. Ibid. 2:124.
61. Ibid., 8–10.
62. Ibid., 15.
63. Ibid. 1:490; 2:291.
64. *The Federalist*, p. 81 (No. 81).
65. Farrand, *Records*, 1:536, 542, 562, 580, 592, 604, 605.
66. Ibid. 2:25.
67. *LJM*, 3: 634.

Chapter 2

A Proper Energy in
the Executive

Five weeks after the Convention completed its work Madison reported to Jefferson that one the Framers' principal problems was to combine "proper energy" in the executive with stability in the legislative branch while maintaining the "character of Republican Government." They were impeded at almost every turn, however, by disagreements over the choice, structure, and powers of this branch because these issues all bore directly on "the independent exercise of the Executive power" and the "defense of the constitutional rights of [this] department" against the "incroachments [sic] of the Legislature..."[1] This definition of the Framers' problem revealed Madison's judgment that the Framers provided for a president so institutionally weak as to be either disinclined or unable to resist congressional erosion of the exercise of executive powers. It is a mistake, however, to leap to the conclusion that this judgment represented the whole of Madison's position. This letter reveals only that at this time and for the next three years or so, Madison's primary concern for the presidency was to strengthen and facilitate the independent exercise of executive powers prescribed by the Constitution.

This problem is endemic to a written constitution. It is peculiar to a republican chief executive–at least, Madison judged it to be so. In fact, the creation of the executive at the Convention provides a classic example of the kind of problems which the science of constitutions was supposed to solve in the eighteenth century. The Framers had to prescribe rules for choosing functionaries and allocating their powers so that each branch of the government would actually exercise in practice, as well as in theory, the powers prescribed in the constitutional text. Provisions granting and limiting powers were at least supposed to predict official behavior within known limits. Constitutional energy, the capacity for authorized action, is derived from this document. Expectations that official behavior would conform to these textual authorizations could be made with confidence, however, only on the assumption that there is an invariable factor, a constant, on which all prediction must rest. For the Framers this constant was, of course, human nature, which they believed to be universal, immutable, and given. This perspective, although not without some challenge, was voiced repeatedly by the more articulate Framers in the debates over the means of infusing the executive branch with the capacity to act. Indeed, it was apparently assumed that these debates would be pointless unless it was believed that political man is moved by either of two passions: ambition or avarice. Few of the Framers ever argued that patriotism, the desire to serve the public good without private gain, exclusively accounts for the behavior of those who govern. The executive branch was regarded as the arena in which human nature is given fullest scope for action because of the functions traditionally performed by it. Therefore, the Framers' problem was to devise a constitution providing both the source of legal energy and limits on it, while depending on natural energy to move rulers to actions calculated to gratify private motives and also serve the public good. The fact that maleable public opnion utimately must sustain the Constitution and simultaneously enforce accountability through elections, greatly complicated Madison's efforts to solve this problem.

Madison believed that it was especially difficult to create a republican chief executive and maintain the independence of this branch over time. His efforts can be divided analytically into three parts, which are best understood in the context of the debates, particularly in view of the fact that he provided no model before going to Philadelphia. As his letter to Jefferson suggests, the first problem was to create means of supporting the independent exercise of specified executive powers. The second task was to fashion controls over the use of these powers. A third challenge, one related to the first issue, arose when the convention voted for equality of power for the states in the Senate. Madison's expectation that the Senate would exercise certain powers to the exclusion of the House could no longer be fulfilled since the Framers refused to create a body controlled internally by a dynamic equilibrium of sectional interests. Therefore, Madison shifted his strategy by trying to make the president a counterweight to the Senate in the exercise of powers over domestic administration and, late in the Convention's proceedings, in the conduct of foreign relations.

CONTROL OF THE EXECUTIVE

Madison confessed to Edmund Randolph shortly before the Convention was to open that he had "scarcely ventured" to form his own opinion of the proper structure and powers of the executive. He was certain only that there should be a Council of Revision consisting of the chief ministerial officers. For the past few years he had thought that New York's Council served well to curb unstable and poorly drafted laws. Such an agency would protect both the public interest and private rights. The supremacy that he proposed to give the new national government presented some difficulties in framing the executive and endowing it with powers, he confessed to Randolph and Washington, because its officers should be appointed by the national government and the militia ought to be placed under its authority in some way. Aside from recommending a Council of Revision and choice of the executive by the national legislature, he offered no particular prescription for infusing the executive with energy. He did urge, however, that, if the

Convention wished to give "the new system its proper energy," it would have its work ratified by "the authority of the people."[2]

After arriving in Philadelphia for the Convention, Madison apparently discovered that some delegates wanted to imitate the British model. On 6 June, when the Convention was debating features of the executive branch, he found the time to report to Jefferson: "Mr. Adams' Book...has excited a good deal of attention." A printing in Philadelphia is soon to be followed by another one in New York. This book will be "much read, particularly in the Eastern States, and contribute with other circumstances to revive the predilections of this Country for the British Constitution." It is likely to have a powerful influence on "public opinion," and many of the remarks in it are "unfriendly to republicanism..." It is to be hoped that this trend will not be reinforced by "the operations of our Government.[3]

Madison disliked Adams' praise of the supposed balance of the British constitution achieved in fact, as Adams said, through the artful distribution of "loaves and fishes, honors and emoluments..." Neither did Madison like Adams' characterization of the British system as "the most stupendous fabric of human invention" ever known in the political world, surpassing even the Roman Republic in this regard. It was understood, of course, that the attachments created by these means enabled the executive to govern in reality, even if not in theory.[4]

Madison undoubtedly had this problem presented by Adams in mind when he explained to the Convention on 6 June the difficulty of establishing and maintaining a republican chief executive:

> The great difficulty in rendering the Executive competent to its own defense arose from the nature of Republican Gov't which would not give to an individual citizen that settled pre-eminence in the eyes of the rest, that weight of property, that personal interest against betraying the National interest, which appertains to an hereditary monarchy. In a republic personal merit alone could be the ground of political exaltation, but it would rarely happen that this merit alone would be so conspicuous as to produce universal acquiesence. The Executive Magistrate would be envied & assailed by disappointed competitors: His firmness therefore wd. need support. He would not possess those great emoluments from his station, nor that permanent stake in need therefore of being controuled [sic] as well as supported.[5]

The lack of established preeminence in the individuals elevated to this high public position only to be degraded to a private status by the working of the calendar would pit the reputation of a single person against that of the many members of an elective legislative branch. Madison assumed that egalitarian as well as parochial tendencies prevailed sufficiently to ensure that few persons would be recognized as being intrinsically worthy of holding the office and standing against a popularly elected assembly of their peers. Experience had taught him that rivalry rather than cooperation and coalition was the common relationship among the most visible and influential members of society.[6] Aspirants to the presidency would be likely to fall victim to this behavioral precept because they would probably not have continental reputations for prudence and integrity strong enough to enable them to overbear Congress. There could be no high status confirmed by heredity nor even the kind of exalted standing derived from the possession of wealth which is preeminent and public in source and function. Neither symbols nor titles nor ceremonies nor mysteries could inspire awe and veneration among the credulous. Unlike a British monarch, the president's person could not be sacred. There could be none of what Washington called "habitual distinction" nor the deference so often derived from it.[7]

Madison's desire to create an institutionally independent chief executive was prompted by his conviction based on experience, observation, and reading, that the tendency of elective legislatures is to accumulate power by encroaching on the other branches. It is a process of undermining the will of one of the other branches to exercise its powers independently. This strategy of gaining control over another functionary's powers is a subtle and largely invisible process. Madison distinguished encroachment from usurpation, which consists in exercising powers constitutionally allotted to another branch without changing the laws. There is nothing subtle or invisible about usurpation because the claim of power must be made openly. The question for the framers of a written constitution was how to avoid both kinds of constitutional change over time. For example, if the president claims the power to make as well as to enforce the laws, he clearly and publicly usurps power from the legislature. If he fails to veto a bad statute, to remove a worthless subordinate, or to perform any of his other constitutionally mandated duties because he fears retaliation by the legislature or has made a corrupt bargain with its leaders, then he permits the latter to encroach on his powers with a means of control almost impossible for the public to detect. Encroachment might lead, also, to collusive actions by the two branches for the personal benefit of some members of each one. Over the long run encroachment is more deadly than usurpation. It is by nature insinuating beyond the reach of the senses, and it operates to change the nature of the regime by altering the distribution of its governing powers in fact, even if not in theory.

Madison undoubtedly had the problem of encroachment in mind when he argued at the Convention in favor of giving the chief executive the power to veto laws. The prevailing wisdom now is that he favored the veto as a curb on plundering democratic majorities which ought to be replaced with a high-toned government.[8] In fact, he perceived better than his modern critics the need for creating institutions which would establish and maintain an equilibrium between the long-term, aggregate interests of an extended republic and the short-term and partial interests naturally released in a free society to seek their goals. In addition, in his memorandum called "the Vices," he noted that members of legislative bodies had all too often enacted laws which were claimed to serve the public good, but in fact served the purely personal interests of the legislators who enacted them. Furthermore, he had long been eager to devise some means of improving the technical quality of statutes. If the chief executive were to have the energy to share effectively in a legislative process calculated to produce stable and well-conceived laws to serve the common interest, then he must be provided with the constitutional means of exercising his judgment without fear of enfeebling retaliation. In 1785 he suggested that a state constitution might elevate the quality of legislation by appointing a standing committee composed of a "few select and skillful individuals" to draft bills for members. As an antidote to both the "jealousy & danger of their acquiring an improper influence they might be made incapable of holding Office Legislative, Executive or Judiciary." Madison liked this idea so much, he said, that he had thought of proposing it to Virginia's General Assembly "who give almost as many proofs as they pass laws of their need of some such Assistance."[9]

At the Convention he initially favored a qualified power to veto laws. The president's refusal to sign a bill should be overridden by a "proper proportion" of both branches of the legislature. It would be folly to give him an absolute power to veto because an executive "constituted as ours is proposed to be" would rarely have the "firmness" needed to resist the legislature unless he were backed up by a significant fraction of it. Not even the British king, despite his "splendid attributes" could withstand opposition to both houses of Parliament. To give to our chief executive such "a prerogative" as absolute as the veto enjoyed theoretically by the British King would "certainly be obnoxious to the (temper of the country; its present temper at least)."[10] In supporting a proposal for a Council of Revision joining the executive with judges, Madison exculpated it from the charge that it violated the doctrine of separated powers. He pointed out that the latter was drawn from the English example which mixed functions by giving the executive an absolute veto and the House of Lords a judicial power. The operative objective in the American republic, however, was to restrain the legislature from "encroaching on the other coordinate Departments...the rights of the people at large" and from passing laws "unwise in their principle or incorrect in their form..."[11]

When the Convention returned to this matter about six weeks later, Madison again supported a Council of Revision as an institution likely to inspire "confidence and firmness in exercising the revisionary power." In addition to helping the judiciary defend itself against the legislature, the firm use of the revisal power would give "consistency, conciseness, perspicuity & technical propriety to the laws, qualities peculiarly necessary and yet shamefully wanting in our republican Codes." It would certainly protect the community at large from the bad legislation which had resulted in the states from the tendency of their legislatures to absorb all power. It is not enough to oppose such an institution with the charge that the proposal violates the maxim requiring the three departments to be kept "separate and distinct." On the contrary, the proposal was an "auxiliary precaution" in favor of the doctrine. If a nominal constitutional prescription of it were sufficient to make it work in practice, then all other provisions would be superfluous. Experience, however, had taught the necessity of introducing such a "balance of powers and interests, as will guarantee the provisions on paper." So, instead of contenting ourselves with formal declaration of the theory in the Constitution, Madison urged, give these two branches the "defensive power" needed to "maintain theory in practice." To the few delegates who objected to this union of powers Madison answered that, if this union violated the doctrine, or if judicial review were inconsistent with the theory of free government, then it was improper to give the president a share in making laws. On 15 August Madison's motion to join the Supreme Court with the President in exercising the veto power subject to a complicated congressional override also failed, but not due to doctrinal objections. Had such a council been created, Madison pointed out many years later, it would have "precluded...judiciary annulment of legislative acts."[12]

His continuing support of a council of revision even at this late date in the Convention's proceedings reflected his doubt that the Framers would create a presidency independent of Congress. Yet, such a relationship was made even more imperative than it initially was once the struggle of representation was finished and the character of the Senate was established. The effect of the mode of choosing the president and the question of eligibility for reelection captured Madison's attention on 17 July. On the first day of debate after the compromise on representation was reached, he supported the motion of his colleague, James McClurg, to give tenure during good behavior in order to secure the executive's "independence" from Congress. Speaking for McClurg, Madison declared that it is essential in a "well-constituted Republic" to keep the legislative and executive branches, in particular, independent of each other. Whether the motion for tenure during good behavior was a "proper one was another question." It deserved a "fair hearing and discussion" until a better plan for avoiding the dangerous union of these two departments should be presented to the Convention. He wished, however, that no member should believe that in supporting this discussion he favored taking "any step towards monarchy" because his "real object was to prevent its introduction." He meant only that experience had demonstrated the tendency in the states "to throw all power into the legislative vortex" and thereby to reduce their executives to "Cyphers." If the federal executive were not enabled to restrain legislative "instability and encroachments" then a "revolution" of one kind or another would be "inevitable." The *preservation* of republican government required some means of attaining this objective. Therefore, in devising the proper expedient, the "genuine principles of that form should be kept in view."[13]

The tactical situation was greatly clarified two days later, when a move was made to bar reelection of the executive. This proposal prompted several delegates to say that the means of choice and reeligibility were linked inseparably. Some were spurred, further, to speak in favor of popular election at large because, as Governeur Morris put it, "the extent of the country" would secure a president's reelection against "factions and discontents" in particular states regardless of who agitated them. Rufus King agreed, despite the "improbability of a general concurrence of the people in favor of any one man." This line of argument prompted William Paterson of New Jersey to suggest that the choice be made by electors chosen by the states, giving one to the smallest and three to the largest. James Wilson was pleased to hear these sentiments in favor of popular election which he had urged previously. Elbridge Gerry, King's colleague who had opposed him by favoring equal votes in the Senate, again demonstrated his lack of enthusiasm for both republican government and a close union. He opposed popular election on the ground that the people are ill–informed and easily misled by a few "designing men." Let the state governors choose the federal executive. Madison interjected into this debate his firm adherence to the "fundamental principle of free government" that the three powers ought to be not only *"separately,"* but also *"independently"* exercised. Therefore, choice by the "people at large was in his opinion the fittest" procedure, one as likely as any other to produce a president of "distinguished Character." The people generally vote for a person whose merits have made him an object of "general attention and esteem." The only impediment to popular election was to be found in the more "diffusive" right to vote in northern than in southern states. The substitution of electors would obviate this difficulty, however.[14]

This discussion terminated in a unanimous vote to reconsider generally the creation of the executive with the result that it was decided to have the president selected by electors chosen by the state legislatures. Madison could only have regarded this turn of events with utter dismay, but there is no record showing that he spoke to these motions.[15] It is impossible to account for this turn of events from the record, especially since Oliver Ellsworth reversed himself on 25 July by moving that the executive be appointed by the national legislative branch and made ineligible for reelection. After Gerry repeated his contention that this mode of choice would be "radically and incurably wrong," Madison called, once again, for an independent executive capable of controlling any tendency which the federal legislature might have to enact bad legislation. To secure this objective, there were but two real options before the Convention: either selection by electors chosen by the people or direct election by the people. He liked the latter "best." This mode presented two difficulties worthy of note, however. First, the people would be inclined to prefer candidates from their own states and this disposition would work to the disadvantage of the smaller ones. The second problem arose from the disproportionality between voters and total populations in each state, especially between the northern and southern regions. This disproportion would gradually decrease, he predicted, under the influence of "Republican laws introduced in the S. States, and the more rapid increase of their population." Furthermore, local considerations ought to be yielded to "the general interest. As an individual from the S. States he was willing to make the sacrifice." Ellsworth's rejoinder was that the "largest States wd. invariably have the man." His motion was defeated so that resolution of the issue was put off for later decision.[16]

It is not surprising that Madison opposed any version of congressional or, worse yet, senatorial choice of the president. When it was proposed to leave the choice to the two houses by joint ballot in the absence of an electoral majority, Madison objected. This method would give the largest state, relative to the smallest, "an influence of 4 to 1 only, altho the population is 10 to 1." He charged that any such disproportionate allocation of voting power is wrong because the "President is to act for the people, not for the States."[17] On this supposition he objected, also, to choosing the president and vice–president from among the five persons receiving the highest number of electoral votes. He pointedly noted that any such permissive feature would focus "too much on making candidates instead of giving their votes to [make] a definitive choice." He believed that the "primary object" was to make the eventual choice of a president by Congress "improbable..." Any feature which turned the attention of people in the large states to the secondary business of nominating candidates instead of securing an "effectual appointment" to the presidential office ought to be avoided.[18]

The decision to allocate electoral votes to the states to be chosen according to their laws and to allow the House to choose the president should the electors fail to give a majority, settled the problem of eligibility to Madison's satisfaction. Reeligibility for election seems to have been implied from the vote which dropped words which previously declared the executive ineligible. This seems to be the proper conclusion to be drawn from an explanatory note subjoined to Madison's record of debates on 6 September.[19] He clearly favored this outcome because accountability is reinforced by eligibility for reelection. The chief executive's "ineligibility...takes away one powerful motive to a faithful & useful administration, the desire of acquiring that title to a reappointment." Also, it discourages "beneficial undertakings which require perseverence and system." Next, it "fetters the judgment of the Community," especially in "critical moments" when such a choice may be essential to "the public safety." Finally, if the chief executive is placed by the Constitution in the position of the "tenant of an unrenewable lease," then he may be likely to neglect the defense of his constitutional powers in favor of conniving "usurpations" by the legislative branch in order to serve his personal "future ambition or interest."[20]

The net result of the Convention's deliberations and votes on the matter of choosing a president left Madison satisfied that the President would be elected "by the people and for four years."[21]

CONTROLLING THE POLITICAL PASSIONS

In his speech of 6 June, Madison ended his remarks by noting that it is necessary to control the President of a republic in addition to supporting him. Madison had already sketched briefly the proper scope of the executive powers intended both to authorize and control the executive. Although "certain powers were executive in nature," he declared, they should be defined expressly. They should be those necessary to "carry into effect the national laws, to appoint officers in cases not otherwise provided for," and to execute other powers "delegated by the national legislature" from time to time. According to Rufus King, Madison joined James Wilson in saying that the "executive powers ex vi termini do not include the rights of war & peace." The extent of these powers must be defined overtly, not left vague in either substance or scope, if Americans were to avoid the evils of an "elective monarchy."[22] Some of the other leading delegates said that the new American chief executive should not have monarchical attributes. Edmund Randolph insisted that the British government would not serve as the "prototype" for the American republic. James Wilson refused to be guided by the "British model," which was inapplicable to this country because of both its great extent and the republican manners of its people.[23]

In the debates which followed it was the president's power to appoint to offices which brought into sharp relief the widely held view that government–more exactly the executive branch–must depend on nature's source of energy, the political passions. Benjamin Franklin deliberately and forcefully raised this issue on 2 June and thereby set the terms for the debates which followed over the degree to which the executive branch must depend for its energy on appeals to the ambition and avarice of the members of the legislature. He proposed that compensation of members of the executive branch be limited strictly and exclusively to payments for necessary expenses. In political life, Franklin declared, there are two motives: ambition and avarice, the love of power and the love of money. Either one of these motives alone has great force in prompting men to action. Combine them in pursuit of the same object, however, and they will have the most violent effects on many people. Hold before the eyes of such men a "post of *honor* that shall at the same time be a place of *profit* and they will move heaven and earth to obtain it." The struggle for the great number of such posts available in the British government was the source of all the factions which perpetually divided it, sometimes rushed it into fruitless and foolish wars, and often compelled it to submit to dishonorable terms of peace. Americans could avoid the same fate, he warned, if they were not to sow the seeds of "contention, faction and tulmult" by making our offices in the new government places of both profit and honor. If the Framers ignored this warning, he feared that they would "only nourish the foetus of a King."[24] This warning of covert constitutional change, corruption, or degeneration as it was then called, did not go unheeded.

Alexander Hamilton disagreed with this argument without elaboration until two weeks later when he mounted a far–ranging attack on the prospects of establishing republican government in the United States. In addition to doubting that good representatives would be chosen, he denied the possibility of founding a good executive on republican principles. A good executive is the supreme test of a good government, he asserted. The British model was the only one worth emulating in this regard and he thought some people outside the Convention were beginning to think so as well. The plans before the Convention offered none of the appeals to the motives which must be counted on to give government its energy by interweaving its success with the personal interests of those who hold its honorable and profitable offices. For a reformed government to succeed, Hamilton insisted, it must appeal to all the passions, "avarice, ambition, interest which govern most individuals, and all public bodies."[25] A week later he confessed again that he "did not think favorably of Republican Government," so he still hoped to prevail on the delegates "to tone their government as high as possible."[26]

Madison expressed his thorough disagreement with Hamilton over this matter. It is war, or the fear of it, he contended, which gives governments their high tone. Even the constant fear of other nations which breeds insecurity makes it certain that all regimes will be "transformed into vigorous & high toned Govts." which have "too much energy," an ingredient eventually fatal to internal liberty.

> The same causes which had rendered the old world the Theatre of incessant wars, and have banished liberty from the face of it, would seem to produce the same effect here...In time of actual war, great discretionary powers are constantly given to the Executive Magistrate. Constant apprehension of war, has the same tendency to render the head too large for the body. A military force with an overgrown Executive will not long be safe companions to liberty. The means of defense against foreign danger have always been the instruments of tyranny at home. Among the Romans it was a standing maxim to excite a war, whenever a revolt was apprehended. Throughout all Europe, the armies kept under the pretext of defending, have enslaved the people. It is perhaps questionable whether the best concerted system of absolute power in Europe cd. tame the people to the domestic yoke [alone].[27]

This speech, reminding all of the aggrandizement of executive powers during wars, like Franklin's warning against creating the institutional conditions which make war the supreme goal for gratifying the political passions, underlay the remaining debate over the the creation of offices and the president's power to make appointments to them. Madison did not address the matter again, however, until he published his *Helvidius* essays in 1973. Delaware's John Dickinson also, expressed at some length his fear that the kind of executive which some members had in view was not "consistent with a republic." A "firm Executive" could exist only in a limited monarchy such as Britain's where "the weight of the executive arises from attachments which the Crown draws to itself & not merely from the force of its prerogatives. In place of these attachments, we must look for something else."[28]

A full debate over motives was prompted by the Virginia delegation's proposal to limit these attachments to the executive by the simple expedient of paying "liberal" salaries to members of Congress and forbidding them to be appointed to any non legislative offices during the terms for which they are elected and for one year thereafter.[29] When this proposal was taken up, it provoked a sharp conflict over the propriety of relying on the political passions to give energy to the new republic. This division produced a distinct cleavage between those delegates who wanted to establish only the supports needed by a republican chief executive and others who saw no alternative to mimicry of the British model in this matter. When Madison rose to explain and defend this provision of the Virginia Plan, he was attacked at once by other members who believed that the sole operative motive individuals have for seeking legislative offices is to secure eventual appointment to executive offices. It was perceived with equal clarity that, if ambition is to be gratified ultimately only by the enjoyment of this prospect, hopes and expectations of gratification will constitute the kind of attachments which had enabled the British executive to control the behavior of a significant number of members of the House of Commons. A number of delegates divided by either appealing to the British model as proof that experience was on their side, or rejecting it on the same ground as an imitation inappropriate to the American republic. This choice was debated warmly because all the participants supposed that the legislative branch is the arena in which political talents are displayed initially, but that the executive branch provides the ultimate rewards to ambition and, perhaps, to avarice as well. They assumed, also, that the normal progression in a political career is from the legislature to the executive. The judicial branch did not figure in this debate at all.

Madison and Robert Yates both recorded the first discussion of this issue on 22 June and the two accounts are useful to the extent that they differ. Madison noted rather briefly that Nathaniel Gorham of Massachusetts moved to strike the words which forbid legislators to be appointed to other offices for a year after completing their terms. The provision, he said, was unnecessary and injurious. Rufus King and James Wilson agreed with Gorham, pointing out that able commanders might be ineligible to serve in Congress during time of war. Pierce Butler of South Carolina and George Mason supported the motion to prevent "corruption" of the sort practiced with unashamed "venality" in the British government. Hamilton replied that Founders must accept human nature as it is given. If a person is expected to serve the public, "we must interest his passions in doing so." In commenting on the British system, one of "the ablest politicians (Mr. Hume)" had concluded that the Crown's influence, called corruption, provided the weight essential to maintaining the equilibrium of the constitution.[30]

According to Yates' account, James Wilson admitted that "avaricious" individuals sometimes serve in legislatures out of the desire to gain executive office eventually, whereas we ought to rely exclusively on "honorable inducement" which is "truly a republican principle." Madison is reported to have favored the exclusion to eliminate the practices he had witnessed in Virginia's legislature. Mason pointed out that because of the corrupt trade in offices, the influence of the Crown had materially increased, although this change could not be detected by reading British laws. Without the exclusionary clause to serve as the cornerstone of American liberties, he like Franklin, warned that the new constitution would be "a fabric for our destruction." Hamilton, according to Yates' account, expressed his dismay that Americans had been "taught to reprobate the danger of influence in the British government without reflecting how far it was necessary to support a good government." Americans had accepted criticism of the British practice to the point where it was accepted as a truth beyond question. "Hume's opinion" confirms the observation that there will always be a few committed "patriots" who will seek office out of "worthy motives" and shake up a corrupt administration, but the majority of mankind will not do so unless they are moved by their "prevailing passions...ambition and interest " Therefore a soundly constructed government will appeal to these passions which "ever induce us to action." A few persons may be prompted by "patriotic motives" to seek office in order "to display their talents, or to reap the advantage of public applause," but this exclusionary rule will "destroy the motive" for legislative service. The Convention then divided on Gorham's motion to strike the restrictive language. The issue was left ripe for further maneuver and deliberation.[31]

As the result of this vote, Madison rose on the morning of 23 June and proposed new language which he hoped might distinguish the passions appealed to as the source of governmental energy and limit it to patriotism and honorable ambition. He chose words precisely so as to prevent the legislature from creating unnecessary offices or increasing their salaries to make them attractive objects for exchanging service in the legislative for the executive branch. He offered his motion as a middle position between total exclusion and none at all. He did not intend for the new language to bar eventual service in "honorable offices." Neither did he believe that the desire for such appointments necessarily constituted a dishonorable motive for serving first in Congress and subsequently in the executive branch. After all, its members would have to travel great distances in order to serve, and their financial rewards for doing so would be limited. His sole objective, he insisted, was to "fill offices with the fittest characters and to draw the wisest and most worthy citizens into the legislative service," an objective he had pursued since at least 1784. According to Yates, Madison said that patriotism could be relied on as the sole inducement as long as most people regarded legislative service as "the road to public honor." He certainly wanted Congress to be as "uncorrupt as possible," and he did not believe that all the support which legislators gave each other and their friends among the public was invariably given from "the base motives of venality." James Wilson reinforced Madison by saying that it was a mistake to use the word venality to stigmatize "laudable ambition" in view of the fact that legislative service was perhaps the most difficult and the least profitable form of public service.[32]

The proponents of total exclusion would accept none of these arguments. George Mason admitted that the ablest people probably would not serve out of patriotism, but he was certain that there were enough talented Americans to serve without encouraging "virtue" with this "species of venality." Pierce Butler pointed to the actions of George II to prove the case. He pensioned some supporters, gave others offices, and in some instances "to put them out of the house of commons, he made [them] lords." Therefore, the "great Montesquieu" was correct in warning against the abuse of power by those who, entrusted with power, abuse it. Elbridge Gerry, also, thought Madison's revised proposal would fall short of its intended purpose because of an apparent decline in the ethics of *public office holders* since 1776. At the beginning of the Revolutionary war, Americans possessed "more than Roman virtue," but it appeared that it had been lost since then because of the increase in the number of speculators in land and public securities. Here we have "constantly endeavored to keep distinct the three great branches of government, but if we agree to this motion, it must be destroyed by admitting the legislators to share in the executive, or to be too much influenced by the executive, in looking up to him for offices."[33] Obviously, conflicts of interest among officeholders were assumed by the Framers to be commonplace and a serious threat to maintaining the separation of powers in practice.

The subject was postponed until 14 August, long after the decision on representation, when the delegates debated a proposal modified to exclude members of Congress from appointment for one year after their elected terms were completed. Even this discussion turned out to be inconclusive, although the deliberations are instructive in relating the discussion of energy to the popular themes of virtue and corruption in government. On this occasion Charles Pinkney tried his hand at supplying completely new language which was intended to exclude avarice, but to admit ambition as an energizing motive for public service. He proposed to forbid members of Congress to be appointed to any office from which they or other persons would receive any benefit in the form of salary, fees, or "emoluments of any kind." His stated purpose was to make the Senate a magnet attracting persons of first rate talents and serving as a "school for Public Ministers." George Mason, predictably, could not think of any provision more likely to produce corruption which might not otherwise thrive in America; it would provide the aristocracy which some members apparently wanted and would, finally, give "premiums to a mercenary and depraved ambition."[34]

John F. Mercer of Maryland then made an uncommonly blunt speech in which he unequivocally revealed what he and his colleagues meant in saying, as Alexander Hamilton had in his first speech at the Convention, that the proposed national government must provide its members with an "active and continuing interest" because governments derive their energy from those motives which political moralists have always deplored the most.[35] Mercer appealed to "political science" for affirmation of the proposition that all elective governments necessarily became aristocracies because the rulers who are the few can extract "emoluments for themselves from the many. Public measures are calculated for the benefit of the Governors, not of the people." The interest of those who rule is "plunder." A change of rulers by the people results in nothing more than new schemes of "emolument to the rulers." Governments can be maintained only by force or influence; deprive the executive of the latter and he becomes a "phantom of authority." The legislative branch will necessarily be composed of persons of wealth and abilities who will easily overcome an executive without influence. Nothing less could protect the people from an aristocracy in government such as those "speculating Legislatures which are now plundering them throughout the United States." Elbridge Gerry confirmed Mercer's argument with further illuminating points. When the legislature of

Massachusetts instructed its delegates to the Constitutional Convention, he noted, it forbid them to agree to any reforms which made members of Congress eligible to hold "offices under the Government." Gerry, too, lamented the conditions described by Mercer and imputed the low state of public ethics to "the faults of those in office, not the people. The misdeeds of the former," he predicted, "will produce a critical attention to the opportunities afforded by the new system to like or greater abuses." After James Wilson pleaded, once again, for constitutional language which would not discourage from public service the kind of talented persons who would give "weight" to the new government, Mercer replied scornfully: "the paper we propose will [not] govern the United States. It is the men it will bring into the Government and interest in maintaining it that is to govern them. The paper will only mark out the mode and the form..." Six other speakers added heat to the subject, but agreed without dissent to postpone resolution of the issue until it was determined "what powers would be vested in the Senate." Only then, Madison noted, could the delegates judge the "expediency of allowing the Officers of State to be drawn out of that body."[36]

The Committee of Eleven tried to settle the issue with language reported on 1 September and debated on the third, when three different members offered amendments before the final language was adopted by the vote of five states to four with Georgia divided. One last murmur of protest was voiced on 14 September against the provision now in article one section six of the Constitution, but it was ignored. As Madison noted drily: "nor did anything further pass on the subject."[37] The wording of this section was intended to prevent chicanery between the legislative and executive branches of the sort which the Framers had observed as commonplace and the public had denounced before and after 1776. Members of Congress could have no personal, beneficial interest in passing laws multiplying unnecessary offices or increasing the salaries of existing ones; neither could they hold multiple offices, a practice from which pecuniary benefit was ordinarily expected. Neither could executive influence be generated by these well known means, especially since the delegates accepted Madison's motion on 24 August to restrict the president's power to appoint to offices only after their creation by statute.[38] The president, unlike the British monarch, could not become the "fountain of honor" by creating and filling offices at will.[39]

Public sensibilities toward this matter were so strongly felt, however, that Madison was constrained to point out during debates over ratification of the Constitution in Virginia that the Framers deliberately barred the multiplication of unnecessary offices, but not the eligibility of able persons to serve their country in existing offices. No state constitution, he insisted, had done as much to guard against the well-known inducement to legislators to create new offices or to increase the monetary benefits of old ones as means of self-aggrandizement. The provision leaves every citizen the opportunity of "enjoying, in common with other citizens, any of the existing offices which they may be capable of executing." If members of Congress were to be excluded from this common privilege, then citizens with the "greatest fidelity and ability would not be on a par with their fellow citizens who would be eligible for appointment to judicial and executive offices because they had not served in the legislative branch."[40] To this assurance ought to be added his remark made five months later that the "re–eligibility of members [of a legislature] accepting offices of profit is so much opposed to the present way of thinking in America that any discussion of the subject would probably be a waste of time."[41]

Such was the climate of opinion about ethics in government which guided Madison's discussion of the separation of powers in *The Federalist*. These debates also explain precisely what was meant by corruption as a moral issue in the debates over the framing of the Constitution.

A FRESH STRUGGLE

According to Madison, once the Convention settled the contest over representation, "a fresh struggle" broke out among the delegations. All tried to organize the government in ways which would increase the importance of the branches in the creation of which each had obtained the greatest share of influence. This conflict constrained them to sacrifice "theoretical propriety" to the force of other circumstances.[42]

In the struggle over the powers to be allotted the Senate, Madison opposed constitutional provisions which might enable it to obstruct presidential control of domestic administration. On 21 July he moved that federal judges be nominated by the president and that their "nominations shall become appointments unless disagreed to by 2/3 of the 2d. branch." Three considerations support this proposal, Madison contended. It will secure the "responsibility" of the president for selecting "fit characters" with a greater likelihood of success than if the whole legislature "or even the 2d. branch" had the power..." In the latter case the members would be able to hide their "selfish motives" behind the sheer number of persons participating in such decisions. Next, if the president were to make a nomination which was flagrantly partial or erroneous in the judgment of two–thirds of the members of the second branch, they would block appointment. Finally, the second branch is now to be "very differently constituted" from what it was proposed to be, when the appointment of judges was formerly referred to it. Since then, it had been decided to represent the states equally in one branch and by population in the other. "The executive magistrate would [now] be considered a national officer, acting for and equally sympathizing with every part of the United States." If the Senate alone should have the power to appoint judges, they might be the choice of a minority of the states–a totally unjustifiable principle. Moreover, it would "throw the appointment entirely into the hands of ye Northern States, a perpetual ground of jealousy & discord would be furnished the Southern States."[43]

Madison's message was clear. The president ought to be responsible to the nation for the quality of his judicial appointments and not to the partisans of interests which would undoubtedly dominate the Senate. In regard to other matters as well Madison sought to limit the Senate's power over the President with one notable exception. At a time when it appeared that the Senate would choose the president, should the electoral vote fail to provide the choice, he moved without success to require two–thirds of the members to be present in order to vote on this issue.[44] His next move was to require that a quorum of the senate consist of two–thirds of all the members, but this effort failed, also, on a strictly sectional division of votes without New York's participation.[45] Undaunted, Madison then objected to the trial of impeachments of the president by the Senate for treason or bribery because such vague terms would be the equivalent to a tenure during the pleasure of the Senate; next, he objected with equal vigor to trials for misdemeanors, because they would make the president "improperly dependent" on that body. His attempt to eliminate all trials of the president by the Senate failed.[46] When it appeared that either the president or the Senate might be given exclusive power to pardon treasons, he objected. He preferred that the Senate be made a "Council of advice" to the president for the latter's exercise of this power.[47]

The position he took concerning the relations between the president and the Senate concerning control of foreign relations was somewhat mixed. Except for the opening remarks about the extent of the executive powers already noted, nothing of any importance was said about the Senate's powers over foreign affairs until the first week of August. In fact, until this late date the full extent of comment had consisted of James Wilson's musing aloud that because every nation has "wars to avoid & treaties" to be made, the "Senate will probably be the depository of the powers concerning the latter objects."[48] Perhaps Madison was expressing his agreement with this observation when he conjectured four days later on 30 June that the "2nd branch will probably [sic] exercise some great powers, in which the 1st will not participate."[49]

These conjectures were confirmed when the Committee of Detail proposed that the legislature should have power to "make war ..." and the Senate shall have power to "make treaties and to appoint ambassadors..." The "President" (so named for the first time) shall "receive ambassadors" and have other specified powers. Some of these had been mentioned earlier, and none fitted even remotely into Locke's definition of the federative power or the prerogative.[50] When this report was debated on 15 August, there were scattered objections, but no votes were taken until the seventeenth when Charles Pinkney objected to the word "make" war; in addition, he said, the Senate is the "best depository" of knowledge about foreign relations and it represents the states equally. Madison and Elbridge Gerry then moved to substitute "declare" for "make" war so as to leave the executive free to "repel sudden attacks." Roger Sherman wanted to keep the word make so that the executive could resist invasions, but he did not want him authorized to "commence war." Gerry then said he never expected to "hear in a republic a motion to empower the Executive to declare war." The danger was purely hypothetical. No such motion was before the house. Oliver Ellsworth agreed that it ought to be easier to get out of war than into it. War is begun with a simple declaration, whereas peace follows from complex and secret negotiations. George Mason did not want to give the power to commence war to either the president or the Senate. He was all for "clogging war & facilitating peace." At this point Madison's motion carried, and Congress was authorized to "declare" war.[51]

When discussion of the power over treaties was resumed on 23 August, Madison made a very interesting observation, but not a motion. He said: "As the Senate represents the states alone, and for this as well as other obvious reasons, it was proper that the President should be an agent in treaties." There is no recorded comment on this hint of a departure from the position of the Committee of Detail which left the president in the position of a passive conduit of ceremonial exchanges with foreign nations. He would receive ambassadors, but the senate would send them. It is impossible to deduce from anything Madison had said to this moment just what he had in mind. Some indication that he visualized a more active role for the president as the organ of communication with other nations is found in the remark he made at the end of the day's debate on the main issue: to what degree, he asked, will treaties create obligations which are binding domestically without the aid of statutes? After several delegates revealed some differences of view, Madison "hinted for consideration" a distinction allowing the president and the senate to make treaties "eventual and of Alliance for limited terms," while requiring the concurrence of the "whole legislature in other Treaties."[52] Once again, Madison made no motion, so no debate ensued and no vote was taken. This fact is remarkable in view of the next step in the development of the Constitution. On 31 August Madison was appointed a member of the Committee of Eleven to deal with such parts of the Constitution and reports not yet acted upon.[53] When this committee reported on 4 September, it proposed wholly new language which incorporated Madison's new preference for executive agency in making treaties. The president was proposed to have, by and with the advice of the Senate, the power to make treaties to be affirmed by a vote of not less than two–thirds of the members present. Also, the power to appoint ambassadors was shifted from the senate to the president subject to senatorial confirmation of nominations.[54] These provisions appear to make the president a more active agent in the exercise of the treaty–making power and in serving as the organ of communication with other nations.

Madison did not make his final move to regulate the division of powers between the president and the senate concerning foreign relations until after the final votes were taken determining the mode of choosing the president. On 7 September Madison tried to limit the senate's share of the power to make treaties. During debate over the requirement that two–thirds of the members present must give their assent he proposed an amendment saying that "treaties of peace" should be exempt so they could be made more easily than other kinds. This motion was accepted initially without objection or recorded vote. Madison then overreached himself by moving that the senate be authorized to conclude treaties of peace "without the concurrence of the President." Otherwise, Madison argued, the latter officer who would necessarily derive "much power and importance from a state of war" might be "tempted, if authorized, to impede a treaty of peace." Not even Virginia's delegates supported him as he lost both of his proposals.[55]

Madison explained to George Nicholas on 17 May 1788 the reason for adding the president as an "agent" in the process of making treaties. The Constitution makes the "concurrence of the President necessary to the validity of treaties." This advantage over the Articles of Confederation is "conclusive" because treaties can be concluded only with the "joint consent of two individual wills." This result will follow because the president is to be chosen by a mode different from the one used for senators. Therefore, the president will be under a "different influence from that of the Senate, and will be more apt and more free to have a will of his own." As the single person who is "responsible for the events of his administration" the president will more "naturally revolt" from approving treaties which might bring down on him the charge of partiality or the dishonor of surrendering a "national right." The length of the president's term and each incumbent's reeligibility ought to add further security against these dangers. Consequently, Madison predicted to his correspondent in Kentucky, no president in the foreseeable future would be likely to yield the American claim of right to navigate the Mississippi River, a right on which the harmony and growth of the republic would depend so heavily.[56] This clear evidence shows not only the great importance which Madison attached to making the President a counterweight to the Senate, but also, the precise effects to be anticipated from joint responsibility for making treaties. The President's perspective would necessarily be national, even if the Senate's were local.

POPULAR ELECTION OF THE PRESIDENT

The record of Madison's speeches and parliamentary maneuvers which followed after the final decision concerning representation reveals that his support for an independent executive was greatly increased by the decision to leave the states with equal votes in a senate possessing important powers exclusive of the House of Representatives. Thereafter, he and many other delegates recognized the strategic importance of making the choice of each president the focus of national politics through popular elections. The president had to be made the great counterweight to the disequilibrium of interests represented in the House and Senate, respectively. Madison's grand strategy of creating what was initially called a national government now required that the president and the House serve as the popular branches of the government. This strategy had its difficulties and perils of execution. It required, for the first time in American history, skillful efforts to ensure what he called previous combinations (political parties) to prevent electors from merely nominating candidates and leaving their choice to the House of Representatives in which each state was given one vote contrary to the ideal of proportionality of votes on which a single nation ought to be founded. Without doubt, the adopted provisions permitted considerable variation of interpretation and experimentation in practice.

In October, 1788, Madison reported to Jefferson that Pennsylvania had adopted a law providing for elections of members of the House of Representatives and presidential electors by having all voters choose the whole number of electors alloted to the state. This method of choice, the general ticket, had the advantage, he thought, of confining the choice of a President to persons who were generally well known. For that reason elections by the general ticket should be favorable to "merit." This method is liable, on the other hand, to some "popular objections agst. the tendency of the new System. I am inclined to think the State (Virginia) will be divided into as many districts, as there are members." Some other states, notably Connecticut, will probably follow the example of Pennsylvania. Yet other states may adopt a "middle course... It is perhaps to be desired that various modes should be tried, as by that means only the best mode can be ascertained." Regardless of the ones chosen, there "is no doubt that Genl. Washington will be called to the Presidency" and several candidates are spoken of for the vice–presidency.[57]

Madison's prediction was fulfilled in Virginia. The first presidential election was conducted during January, 1789, one month *before* the choice of members of the House of Representatives was made. In mid–January Madison reported to Washington that the returns from "the Electoral districts" were coming in slowly, but he was able to report the number of votes cast for electors in some of them. Many, he was pleased to say, were of the "federal party," unlike a good many members of the legislature who opposed the Constitution and would probably choose like–minded senators. "Among the bulk of the people," very little attention had been given to "the vice–president" because "the choice of a president has been regarded as the sole object of the selection."[58] A month later he reported to Tench Coxe that the choice of electors in Virginia was largely profederal, the voting for Washington was "unanimous," and the votes cast for vice–president went to Adams except for two given to John Hancock and John Jay, "solely with a view I presume to keep Mr. Adams in the place really allotted to him."[59] One correspondent reported to Madison that "the preceeding [*sic*] choice of Electors" showed so much antifederal sentiment in his county that he would not try "getting into the House of Representatives" in the elections under way in February.[60] This situation made Madison think that these elections would be a better gauge of "the sense of the community" regarding support of, or opposition to, the new Constitution than the legislature provided. The decided "repugnance" of Virginia's General Assembly to the Constitution stood in contrast to "a very different temper in the body of the people" insofar as the issue could be gauged from his lack of "diffusive knowledge of what is passing in the State."[61]

The election of 1796 further confirmed his understanding of the function of presidential electors and alerted him to the failure of the Convention to include in the Constitution a procedure for overcoming an "equilibrium of votes." between a candidate for president and another meant to be vice–president.[62] In March, 1800, he expressed to Jefferson his alarm over a bill pending in Congress to regulate the actions of the electors. The Federalist party had proposed a bill to deprive the House of Representatives of its constitutional function of choosing a president in the case of a tie in 1801. The bill provided for a committee of thirteen members who were to canvass and determine the validity of electoral votes cast in the presidential election of 1800. The committee was to be chaired by the Chief Justice and six members chosen from the Senate and House equally. Despite the existence of a Federalist majority in both chambers, this brazen bill failed to pass both houses in the same form. Madison admitted that the Constitution ought to have been more complete in prescribing the election of president and vice–president, but the proper remedy for its omissions is a constitutional amendment, not a statute which is a form of legislative interference in the executive branch. The latter was "meant to be" and ought to be prohibited as much as possible because of the constitutional principle prescribing their independence of each other. The danger of the pending legislation was that the president may be "bribed into the usurpations by so shaping them as to favor his re–election. If this licentiousness of constructive perversions of the Constitution continues to increase, we shall soon have to look to our code of laws, and not to the charter of the people, for the form as well as the spirit of construction" of the constitutional barriers against "usurpation."[63]

He expressed himself more fully on this subject a quarter of a century later, when the breakdown of extracongressional party agencies raised the specter, once again, of the choice of a president by the House. In response to questions seeking his views of reform, he admitted that the inadequacy of the process originally provided was keenly felt by the members of the Convention, but they were not exempt from the fatigue and impatience which is felt in all such bodies as a long session draws to a close. They allowed the House to vote by states in choosing a President in order to accommodate the demand of the smaller states for equality and to assuage the "jealousy of the larger towards the cumulative functions of the Senate." There were other considerations, as well, but they do not compensate for violation in the present rule of "the Republican principle of numerical equality, and even...the Federal rule which qualifies the numerical by a State equality..." The best remedy is "election of presidential electors by districts." This method was "mostly, if not exclusively, in view when the Constitution was framed and adopted." It was "exchanged for the general ticket and the legislative election as the only expedient for baffling the policy of the particular States which had set the example." A constitutional amendment should restrict the choice of electors to districts. Each one should give two votes, naming his first and second choices for president. In the absence of a majority of electoral votes, the choice should be made by joint ballot of the two houses of Congress. A majority, rather than a plurality of electoral votes, ought to be required to avoid the choice of "a very inferior candidate." Next to the "propriety" of having a president who is the "real choice of a majority of his constituents," it is important that he "inspire respect and acquiescence" because his qualifications do not suffer by comparison with other persons voted for. The requirement that electors distinguish between their choice of president and vice–president is intended to emphasize their relative merits in the "consciousness of the of individuals" concerned, in "the public estimate of their comparative fitness", and in their capacities to perform "different services." One great benefit of this reform would be the rupture of the "string of beads" produced by the general ticket and state legislative choice of electors. In the event of election by districts, some would differ in sentiments from each other; yet others would sympathize with each other regardless of state boundaries so as to break the force of those "geographical and other noxious parties which might render the repulsive too strong for the cohesive tendencies within the political system."[64]

Despite this temporary breakdown in the popular election of a president, Madison must have marveled at the Framers' decisions which made this source of the executive's energy so thoroughly consistent with the characteristics of republican government.

NOTES

1. *PJM*, 10:207–09 passim, 211.
2. Ibid., 9:370, 384–5.
3. *PJM*, 10:29–30.
4. John Adams, *The Works of John Adams*, ed. Charles Francis Adams, 10 vols. (Boston: Little, Brown & Co., 1850–56), 4:197–8, 296, 358–59, 468, 559.
5. Farrand, *Records*, 1:138.
6. Ibid., 448.
7. *PJM*, 9:342.
8. For a review of scholarly literature expounding this interpretation and one rejoinder to it, see George W. Carey, "Separation of Powers and the Madisonian Model: A Reply to the Critics," *The American Political Science Review* 72 (March 1978): 151–164.
9. *PJM*, 8:351–52.
10. Farrand, *Records*, 1:100.
11. Ibid., pp. 138–9.
12. Ibid. 2:74–80, 298; *LJM*, 3:56.
13. Farrand, *Records*, 2:34–36.
14. Ibid., 54–57; italics in the original.
15. Ibid., 58–59.
16. Ibid. 1:108–11.
17. Ibid., 403.
18. Ibid., 500–501.
19. Ibid., 525.
20. *PJM*. 11:289.
21. Farrand, *Records*, 2:587.
22. Ibid. 1:65–67, 70, 72.
23. Ibid. 1:65–66, 83.
24. Ibid., 82–83 passim; emphasis in the original.
25. Ibid., 82, 87, 284–86, 289, 296, 302.

26. Ibid., 424.

27. Ibid., 464–65.

28. Ibid., 86.

29. Ibid. 20.

30. Ibid., 375–76. Madison's and Yates's reports of Hamilton's allusion to "Mr. Hume" is to his essay, "Of the Independency of Parliament." See David Hume, *Essays and Treatises on Several Subjects*, 4 vols. (London: T. Cadell; Edinburgh: A. Kincaid and A. Donaldson, 1770), 1:42–45.

31. Farrand, *Records*, 1:380–82 passim. On various occasions Madison used a theatrical metaphor to characterize the arena for displaying political talents; see *PJM*, 9:316; *LJM*, 2:158; 4:298.

32. Farrand, *Records*, 1:386–94 passim.

33. Ibid.

34. Ibid. 2:284.

35. Ibid. 1:284–85.

36. Ibid. 2:283–90 passim. The political science to which Mercer referred appears to have been suggested by Hume in his essay, "That Politics May be Reduced to a Science"; See Hume, *Essays*, 1:20–21.

37. Farrand, *Records* 2:484, 489–92, 613–14.

38. Ibid., 405.

39. The phrase is Hamilton's, used in *The Federalist*, 451 (No. 69).

40. *PJM*, 11:141.

41. Ibid., 288. In 1782 he was pleased by reports that a new ministry in Britain under Charles James Fox was "excluding contractors etc. from the Legislature–abolishing sinecure appointments–pruning the civil list–arming the Militia and even patronizing a scheme of equal representation." Ibid. 4:432.

42. *The Federalist*, 230–31 (No. 37).

43. Farrand, *Records*, 2:80–81.

44. Ibid., 526.

45. Ibid., 549.

46. Ibid., 551; see also 612.

47. Ibid., 627.

48. Ibid. 1:426.

49. Ibid., 486.

50. Ibid. 2:181, 183, 184.

51. Ibid. 297, 318–19.

52. Ibid., 392–94 passim.

53. Ibid., 473.

54. Ibid., 498–99.

55. Ibid., 540;; see also 548.

56. *PJM*, 11:48.

57. Ibid., 276.

58. Ibid., 417–18.

59. Ibid., 443–44.

60. Ibid., 448.

61. Ibid., 425.

62. *LJM*, 2:110.

63. Ibid., 157; see Dumas Malone, *Jefferson and the Ordeal of Liberty* (Boston: Little, Brown & Co., Inc. 1962), 461–62, cited hereafter as *Ordeal*.

64. *LJM*. 3:332–35; see also, 356–60.

Chapter 3

The True Principles of Republican Government

Before he opened his share of the public campaign to secure ratification of the Constitution, Madison reported to Jefferson on 24 October 1787. Among other things, Madison observed that the the the "mutability" and the "injustice" of the states' laws "contributed more...than those which accrued to our national character and interest from the inadequacy of the Confederation to its immediate objects" in fueling constitutional reform. Therefore, it was necessary to show why private rights would be more secure under the new government than they had been in the states. They are both founded on the "republican principle which refers the ultimate decision to the will of the majority." The difference in their capacities to protect rights requires a full exposition on the "true principles" of republican government. Such a discourse would prove, contrary to the concurring "opinions of theoretical writers," that this form of government "must operate...within...an extensive sphere." This axiom must be qualified however, because this doctrine holds only within "a sphere of mean extent." If the sphere is "too small, oppressive combinations may be too easily formed" against a weaker party. If it is "too extensive," a "defensive combination may be rendered too difficult against the oppression of those entrusted with the administration."[1]

The Framers and those who supported the Constitution faced another theoretical problem as well. That was the need to reduce to "practice the theory of a free government which forbids a mixture of the Legislative & Executive powers." The resolution of this problem had been difficult, however, because the "boundaries between Executive, Legislative and Judiciary powers, though in general strongly marked, consist in many instances in mere shades of difference."[2] Madison's attempts to explain these two theories in *The Federalist* are undoubtedly the best known of all his political writings, but they are also the most misunderstood.

Four weeks later Madison offered an extended proof of the correct theory in his first contribution to *The Federalist*, the Tenth essay. He claimed that representative government is most likely to secure the enactment of stable and just laws because of the restricting effect of its *form* on the tendency of popular majorities to act oppressively.[3] After demonstrating in the fourteenth essay that the territory of the republic was not too large, Madison met the Anti–Federalists' jeremiads against the small size of the House by arguing that the House of Representatives would meet all the requirements of accessibility, accountability, responsiveness and responsibility necessary to make it a democratic institution.[4] To these claims he reluctantly added a prediction that even the Senate would contribute responsibly to the moderation of majority rule. To these eight essays he added five more calculated to meet rhetorical attacks on the Framers for omitting a declaration that the Constitution embodied the separation of powers. In the course of doing so, he clarified and adapted this European theory to fit an American conception of republican government.

A PROBABLISTIC THEORY OF REPRESENTATION

Madison opened the tenth essay with the claim that the utility of a "well–constructed union" would be its tendency to "break and control the violence of faction..." It is the source to which the instability and injustice of laws has been traced in both ancient republics and in "the American constitutions" despite improvements made in the latter over the former. Consequently, the enemies of "liberty" denounce rule by the force of an "interested majority" tainted by a "factious spirit..." A faction consists of either a minority or a majority within a government which combines to violate the rights of individuals or acts contrary to the aggregate and long–term interests of a society. This characteristic of popular governments can be dealt with by only one of two means. Its causes would have to be removed by either destroying liberty or giving everyone in society uniform opinions, passions, and interests. The second possibility, and the only one consistent with the enjoyment of liberty, is to control the effects of faction. First, however, it must be demonstrated that every modern society is necessarily heterogeneous. Therefore, the ideal of perfect unity and harmony of opinions, beliefs, and interests in a modern society is a mere utopian fantasy.

He opened his analysis with the the supposition that when people live under a government where liberty is acknowledged to be essential to political life there will be a natural diversity, rather than uniformity, of opinions and interests. This is because nature has endowed mankind with reason, passions, and unequal faculties. When reason is used freely, it produces varying and often opposing opinions about every subject contemplated by the human mind. Reason freely used does not lead to unanimity of opinion because it is fallible. In addition, as long as reason is connected with self–love, human opinions and passions will influence each other reciprocally; passion will be attached to opinion; opinion will be attached to passion. There is another "insuperable barrier" to uniformity of opinion, however. Nature has endowed humans with unequal faculties out of which the rights of property originate. It is the first object of government to protect these faculties. From governmental protection of these faculties the possession of different degrees and kinds of property follows. From the influence of "these" on the opinions of their owners there follows a division of society into "interests and parties."[5]

The conclusion is that the "latent causes" of faction are rooted in human nature and, therefore, are original, necessary, universal, and immutable as far as the founders of a constitution are concerned. These latent causes become manifest socially in "different degrees of activity" according to the varying circumstances of "civil society." The zeal with which people express opinions about the theory and practice of religion and government are one form of this activity. Others include attachment to leaders contending ambitiously for power and high status or to others whose careers arouse the passionate attachment of followers. Even "fanciful distinctions" have moved mankind to divide into parties and inflamed them with mutual animosity and the determination more to oppress each other than to cooperate. The most enduring and common type of hostile activity is found among those who own different amounts and kinds of property as well as between such persons and others who have none.

The founder of a constitution must deal with factions rather than their latent causes, because faction is a governmental phenomenon. Factions exist because it is the function of modern governments to regulate diverse and hostile interests and to protect the unequal and varied faculties in which they originate. It is impossible, therefore, to eradicate the "spirit of party and faction" from the "necessary and ordinary *operations* of government."[6] By its necessary actions government exacerbates the passionate divisions which exist naturally in every political society. At its best, government will moderate these conflicts. At its worst, it will reinforce or even create them. This truth is apparent from observing members of legislative bodies who invariably act as partisan advocates of narrow constituencies, contrary to the ideal of impartiality toward all. No one ought to be the judge in his or her own case because self–love biases judgment and may corrupt personal integrity. This is the reason why an assembly is unfit to serve as both judge and advocate simultaneously, determining the rights of large bodies of people. Yet, legislators are advocates of the interests whose causes are to be regulated by law. Regardless of whether the people are creditors, debtors, landowners, or manufacturers, their respective causes are supposed to be decided by legislators on the basis of "justice and the public good." Distribution of the burden of taxes should require "exact impartiality," but there is probably no legislative act which provides greater opportunity and propensity for the numerically superior party to overburden the minority and thereby to violate our conceptions of justice. Immediate and particular interests prevail over remote, indirect, and general consequences affecting society because "enlightened statemen" are not often in control of affairs.[7]

Once it has been conceded that Locke's ideal of a perfectly impartial government arbitrating private conflicts according to fixed and known laws cannot be achieved in a free society, it must be recognized that moderation of governmental parochialism and partiality is all that can be hoped for.[8] It must be agreed, *a fortiori*, that the body politic is not a mystical communion which transforms human nature by an act of self–renunciation so complete that political equals become perfectly assimilated in their understanding of the general will and prefer it always to their particular wills. Such a society exists only in the speculations of advocates of popular governments.[9] Therefore, any means devised for moderating inevitable factional conflict must be consistent with the "spirit and form of popular government" in the real world. Since the causes of faction cannot be eradicated without losing liberty, only its effects can be controlled. This object can be attained by only one of two means. Either the existence of the same passion or interest in a majority must be prevented from existing at any given time, or a majority of persons having such a basis of union must be made unable by their "number and local situation" to execute their schemes of oppression. We "well know," however, that if both the impulse and the opportunity to oppress a minority or individuals "coincide," then "neither moral nor religious motives can be relied on as an adequate control." These motives certainly do not restrain the "injustice and violence of individuals," and they lose their supposed effectiveness "in proportion to the number combined together." Unfortunately, the greater the need for such restraints on the behavior of public bodies, the less efficacious they become. The means of controlling effects of faction are available, however, once it is recognized that the ease with which single interests or coalitions become ruling majorities depends on *the form of government itself.*[10] This critical factor does not prevent the formation of interested or passionate parties, but it may be devised so as to render them unlikely to act oppressively.

From this proposition it follows that "a republic, by which I mean a scheme of representation ... promises the cure for [faction] which we are seeking." For two "obvious" reasons representation, rather than direct participation by citizens in the conduct of government, offers the prospect that a large republic will be better than a small one in securing the election of representatives with the "virtuous sentiments" and wisdom needed to pursue the true long-term interests of the whole society. First, the number of representatives does not need to hear bear the same ratio to the population in the large and small political societies. In a large republic the ratio may be determined by adhering to the "mean" between too many (a multitude) and too few (rule by a cabal). Consequently, there will be a larger pool of "fit characters" for office and a "greater probability" that they will be chosen. It is equally obvious that "each representative will be chosen by a greater number of citizens in the large than in the small republic" with the probable result that use of the "vicious arts" of campaigning will be inhibited. Clean elections are likely to result in the choice of meritorious persons instead of those who get into office by "intrigue, by corruption, or by other means" only to "betray" their constituencies' interests. By limiting the number of representatives to a mean, twin evils are avoided. A representative is neither ignorant of local circumstances and lesser interests nor so attached to them as to be unfit to pursue great national objectives. The federal division of representation is a happy one because it avoids both evils, assigning local interests to the states and the "aggregate interests" of the nation to Congress.[11]

This institutional advantage of a large republic over a small one is supplemented by a sociological one: the relatively greater population and territory which can be included within the former. It "is this circumstance principally which renders factious combinations less to be dreaded" in a large republic than in a small one. "Extend the sphere," and a greater variety of parties and interests may be included, making it less "probable" that "a majority of the whole will have a common motive" to violate the rights of others; or, if such a "motive" exists, it will be more difficult for "all who feel it to discover their own strength and to act in unison with each other." The conclusion which follows from this analysis is that the "Union" will have the same advantage "over the states composing it" as any large republic has over a small one. These two inseparably related advantages will consist in "representatives whose enlightened views render them superior to local prejudices and schemes of injustice" and in the security provided by a relatively greater number of parties and interests who will be unable to "outnumber and oppress the rest." Consequently, the government of the union is likely to be insulated from "factious" leaders who inflame narrower constituencies within their states. The conclusion is that *both* "the extent and proper structure of the Union" provide moderating restraints on majority rule. This prospect should make all Republicans "Federalists," that is, supporters of the proposed Constitution.[12]

This essay is not only an original contribution to the theory of representative government, but also, brilliant example of advocacy. It is the flowering of a theory of restraints on majority rule resulting from the operations of representative institutions reflecting social diversity, which Madison first stated in germinal form in 1784.[13] To be sure, the tenth paper only implied that the choice of better representatives will result from their election in large districts, but this conclusion follows from more than his explanation of the effect of enlarging the ratio of representatives to population. The record at the Convention and thereafter explicitly supports this element of his theory. Also unstated at this point in his demonstration of the efficacy of representation as a restraint on governing factions is any mention of an important reason why we might expect members of Congress to be more inclined than state legislators to serve as impartial arbiters of conflicting interests rather than their advocates. The reason is that they are not required to own any kind of property in order to hold their offices. His argument would have been clearer and stronger had he made this point in this essay as he did at the Convention, instead of merely noting this important fact in the fifty–second paper.

The tenth paper's rhetorical power followed not only from this theory, but also, from four other elements. First, it offered reassurance to the critics of the Confederation that the reformed union would surmount the acute crisis of the times as many of the Framers perceived it: the instability and injustice of state laws adversely affecting the rights of all interests, but some in particular, as was clearly the case in Massachusets. His contention that demagogues would be limited to small theaters of operations served this purpose and, also, to deflect critics of full political incorporation of the trans–Allegheny West into the Union. Second, Madison sought to preempt discussion of the theory of large republics being used by some Anti–federalists to discredit the proposed Constitution with the contention that monarchy is the only form of rule proper to a polity of extended territory. Third, he sought to discredit the charge that the House of Representatives was too small to represent all of the interests which exist in a large nation. Finally, his claim that ruling majorities would be moderate because they would probably consist of coalitions rather than single interests was intended to appeal to all groups who feared control of the new government by a dominant, hostile interest. This essay was a remarkably skillful transformation of his ideal of representatives who are impartial toward all interests and faithful to their public trust into a prediction to be realized once the Constitution was ratified.

Subsequent essays confirm the conclusion that Madison was *not* relying exclusively on the territorial extension of the United States to moderate majority rule. In his second paper, number fourteen, he continued his efforts to counter the "prevailing prejudice" against republican government because of "the great extent of country which the Union embraces." He offered to prove that it does not exceed the natural territorial limits of a republic. In addition to following the errors of two unidentified European theorists, Americans were failing to note that they had already discovered how to make "representation...the basis of unmixed and extensive republics." The United States does not exceed "the natural limit of a republic" determined by the distance from its center which will "barely allow representatives to meet as often as necessary" to conduct public business. The mean distance between the Atlantic and the Mississippi, Canada and the Spanish colonies on the Gulf is 750 miles. The distance to be traveled from the farthest outposts has no bearing on the quality of representatives. This was an ingenious adaptation of Montesquieu's axiom to the effect that the size of a republic is proportional to the speed with which its troops can move from any point with equal facility to repel invaders on all borders. Madison paralleled this argument, too, saying that new states will be organized, and Americans will have the incentive to defend themselves because almost all states will be bounded by a frontier. The defense of borders will be facilitated by roads, canals, and inland navigation of rivers, all of which will increase "intercourse" among the regions of the country as well.[14]

In subsequent papers he reminded readers that this entire territory had been governed by Congress since the treaty of peace. Indeed, it even had enacted legislation to form new states in the trans–Alleghany West, to erect their temporary governments and to prescribe the conditions to be met for their full political incorporation into the union–all of this without "the least color of constitutional authority."[15] In short, *The United States was already an extended Republic*. He further reminded his readers of the fact that it had been governed by a representative assembly, but badly. "What is the spirit that has in general characterized the proceedings of congress?" The members have too frequently been "partisans of their respective States" rather than "impartial guardians of the common interest." The great interests of the nation had suffered on a hundred occasions because of undue attention paid to the "local prejudices, interests and views of the particular states." He did not mean to predict that the representatives of the "new federal government" would be totally free of these attachments, but neither would their views be as "confined as those of the State legislatures" and their predecessors in Congress had been. Members of the new Congress will be moved by both local and national views, he predicted, but at the same time they will be "disinclined to invade the rights of the individual states."[16]

His claim in the tenth paper that a legislature composed of a number of members based on a mean between excess and deficiency is the form of representative government which will control factions did not satisfy critics who asserted that the House would be too small. The need to counter this charge on which the validity of his theory depended prompted Madison to return to this subject in February, 1788, when he published four essays (Nos. 55–58) elaborating the reasons for expecting better representatives to be chosen from large districts necessitated by the small size of the House. They reveal Madison to have been an able advocate who could offer clever defenses of opinions which he did not necessarily entertain sincerely and completely.

First, he met the charge of one critic who insisted that "numbers alone could be a due security against corruption and partiality" in the House of Representatives.[17]   Madison repeated his contention that there are no arithmetical rules of political science to be applied except for the ideal of the mean. It can be said, however, that the number of representatives can be proportionally smaller as the size of the population increases. The guiding consideration is to secure the benefits of rational deliberation and to erect sound barriers to easy and interested combinations. It is equally desirable to avoid a number which turns the assembly into a mob. "Had every Athenian citizen been a Socrates, every Athenian assembly would still have been a mob."[18]

British experience demonstrated that an increase in the number of representatives will not necessarily protect the people against corruption and partiality among the former. The existing House of Commons was vastly larger in size than the proposed American House of Representatives and, yet, the former was notorious for the corruption and partiality of its members. A great proportion of the members of the House of Commons was elected by a very small proportion of the population. About one–ninth are chosen by 364 people and one–half are elected by not many more than 5700 voters. They do not reside in their districts and, therefore, cannot secure the rights and interests of the persons they represent because they lack knowledge of their local affairs. Indeed, it is "notorious that they are more frequently the representatives and instruments of the executive magistrate" than they are guardians of the peoples' interests and rights. Representatives are made servants of the government because they are subjected to "the whole force of executive influence" extending to every kind of legislation.[19]   To be more blunt about it: "the electors are...corrupted by the representatives and the representatives are...corrupted by the crown," although the House of Commons nominally possesses unlimited power.[20]

The American House would be unlikely to betray "the public liberty," however, because the Constitution provided no "fund of corruption" by which a president or the Senate could form a "mercenary and perfidious combination" in the House. The restriction on the eligibility of members of Congress to be appointed to civil offices will bar any such organization. In addition, Republican government presupposes some qualities higher than "depravity" in those who hold its offices. If there is not in fact enough "virtue" in mankind for self-government to function, then despotism is the only alternative.[21]

A truly beneficial effect of small size on the behavior of representatives, Madison argued next, is that their knowledge of public policy will be proportionally enlarged and improved. Members chosen in relatively large districts will tend to have a proper knowledge of the affairs and interests of all their constituents, whose concerns with federal legislation will be primarily "commerce, taxation and militia." Representatives "diffusively elected" in no more than ten or twelve districts in even a large state will possess the necessary knowledge of local interests and state laws because they probably will have served in their respective legislatures and may continue to do so while serving in the House. In addition, they should have knowledge of affairs beyond the boundaries of their respective states. They certainly should be acquainted with the "great dissimilarity" in the laws and circumstances of other states. Unquestionably, they will have much to learn about such matters as well as others on which they must act. Fortunately, this need will be met to an increasing degree in the future by the "assimilating effect" on the internal affairs of all states. In 1787 some were still almost wholly agricultural, but others had already developed the branches of industry which give "complexity and variety to the affairs of a nation." Increases in population will inevitably accelerate this process so as to minimize sharp economic and social differences among the states in the long term.[22]

A representative's need for knowledge does not end with local affairs. The public concerns of the United States, unlike those of the individual states, "are spread through a very extensive region, and are extremely diversified by the local affairs connected with them." Knowledge of both kinds can be acquired from both private and public sources, but some of it can be gained only from the latter. Indeed, nothing distinguishes the novelty and complexity of national affairs from those of the states as much as the importance of regulating foreign relations. Some knowledge of this sort can be learned in "a man's closet; but some of it can only be derived from public sources of information." This process of acquisition requires "practical attention to the subject during the period of actual service in the legislature." To be sure, a few members of both the House and Senate will become "masters of the public business" because of their superior personal talents, frequent reelection and the lack of such skills in new as well as uninformed members.[23] Nevertheless, it is of vital importance for all members to be well informed to perform the legislative function properly.

This theorizing reflected Madison's long-standing conviction that most members of Congress in his time were inadequately informed about national and international affairs so that steps should be taken to remedy this deficiency. As a prediction of the future behavior of Congress, his claim was frustrated, however. As early as 1782 he complained to Edmund Randolph that the lack of information among congressmen made it difficult "to deduce the general interest from a just and fair comparison of particular interests." To repair this deficiency of ideas and information, he tried unsuccessfully in January, 1783, to get Congress to appropriate the funds needed to establish an official library. At the Convention he favored a term of three years for members of the House so that they might acquire the knowledge which will give the degree of stability which can be derived in a "government so extensive" only from representatives who know the various interests of states instead of their own exclusively because they are not good guides to the interests of all the others. Consequently, in 1789, he urged use of the first census as a means of yielding valuable information for Congress from an authoritative public source. He proposed to include a census of occupations in order to enable Congress to have reliable knowledge of the number, diversity, and distribution of interests throughout the country. It was the kind of information all legislators had "always wished to have," but had not yet obtained. Census data, he predicted, would be useful in "marking the progress of society; and distinguishing the growth of every interest." Unfortunately, opponents who dismissed his argument for being academic and of no practical value carried the day.[24]

The next charge to be rebutted has a familiar ring. On 19 February 1788, the day on which he published the fifty-seventh *Federalist*, he wrote to Jefferson about the subject of this paper. At the ratifying Convention in Massachusetts some of Shays's followers and other "ignorant jealous men" fancied that the Convention at Philadelphia was a "conspiracy against the liberties of the people at large, in order to erect an aristocracy for the rich and well-born and the men of Education." Their sole objective was to prevent ratification of the Constitution and then go home without offering any alternative to it.[25]

In the fifty-seventh essay Madison said it was predicted that the number of members of the House had been kept small so that its members would be recruited from an "oligarchy" unsympathetic to the people. If this denunciation were to be true, it would strike at the "very root" of republican government. It is false, however. The object of the constitution was to secure rulers who have enough wisdom to perceive the common good and virtue to remain faithful to it while they are in office. Elections are the "characteristic" means of reaching this end in republics. The means to prevent the "degeneracy" of rulers are numerous and varied, but the most effective one is a limited term which makes them accountable to the voters who will consist of the great body of the people. Those whom they elect will be the candidates whose merits justify this honor in the voters' judgment. The office of representative is open to "merit of every description": citizens native and naturalized, young or old, with or without wealth and with or without religious faith. None of these considerations is allowed to restrict the voters' judgment of candidates' fitness to hold office. The only disqualification is that no one may do so under the authority of the United States during the period of congressional service.

The Constitution provides, also, numerous means for ensuring that representatives will remain faithful to their public trust while they hold office. First, election is presumptive evidence of this quality unless its absence is later demonstrated. Second, elections produce some "affection" for constituents, even if it is temporary. Third, certain "selfish motives" such as "pride and vanity" attach them to the government which gives them a share of its "honors and distinctions." A few "aspiring characters" may hope to gain personally from "innovations subversive" to the authority of the people, but the great proportion of members will not entertain such projects because they depend for their advancement in political life on their "influence with the people" who elect them. These considerations are ineffective, however, without frequent elections which make representatives habitually conscious of their "dependence on the voters." In fact, the moment the former are elected they are "compelled to anticipate the moment when their power will close, and their exercise of it will be reviewed " When this happens, there is always the possibility of having to "descend to the level from which they were raised" unless the voters believe that they have discharged their duties faithfully. Therefore, the charge that the House will degenerate into an oligarchy depends for its credulity on minds closed to the language of the Constitution. Only such persons could believe that eligibilty for election is restricted to persons of "particular families or fortunes," instead of being a common privilege to which every citizen is entitled. The real issue, therefore, is the unreasonable supposition that five or six thousand Americans voting for members of the House of Representatives are less capable than five hundred in a state constituency of choosing fit representatives; or, that the former are more likely than the latter to be "corrupted by an unfit one." Our experience is to the contrary in the states where there are some large electoral districts. The voters there have not elected "traitors" to office and undermined the "public liberty."[26]

This series of rebuttals dealing with the small size of the House which Madison fought against at the Convention, ended on a grandiloquent note. This last paper contained assurances, given in brief previously, that the size of the House would be increased after the first census to as many as one hundred. With the prospect of a growing population so favorable and the requirement for decennial apportionment so specific, he predicted that the House would grow to 200 members within twenty-five years and to 400 within fifty. He justified this prediction by pointing out the practical considerations affecting the distribution of power, supplemented by commitment to constitutional principle, which should prompt Congress to enlarge the House to match the anticipated growth of population. Then he recapitulated briefly his previous arguments and ended by saying that the greater the number of members the more they will reflect the "infirmities incident to the collective meetings of the people; [i]gnorance will be the dupe of cunning; and passion the slave of sophistry and declamation." There is no greater error than the supposition that the barriers against a government of the few consist of an increase in the number of representatives. On the contrary, experience warns that after securing a sufficient number for the purposes of *"safety...local information, and...diffusive sympathy with the whole of society,"* every addition of representatives will give the government the "countenance of becoming more democratic," but the "soul that animates it will be more oligarchic. The machine will be enlarged, but the fewer, and often the more secret, will be the springs by which its motives are directed."[27]

From his final flight of rhetorical fancy in defense of a small House which he had opposed at the Convention Madison turned to a reluctant defense of the Senate. In the first of two essays he offered explanations and defenses of provisions which were objectionable to him personally. He devoted the second essay to arguments integrating his justification of the Senate into the general theory of representation which he expounded in the tenth and fourteenth essays as well as the others in which he imputed representativeness, responsiveness, and accountability to the House of Representatives.

In the sixty-second essay he said it was unnecessary to dilate on the provision empowering the state legislatures to appoint senators because it was "probably" in harmony with "public opinion," and it would give the states a protective "agency" within the structure of the federal government. The equal representation of the states clearly violated the theory requiring that every district have a *"proportional* share of the government," when a people are incorporated into one nation. The Constitution should not be tested by this theory in framing the Senate, however, because the Framers acted solely on "the advice of prudence" in creating a second chamber justified by the political situation then facing the United States. The small number and extended terms of members would enable the Senate combined with the House to reinforce the likelihood of a faithful discharge of public trust by the legislative branch and thereby to overcome some of the "inconveniences which a republic must suffer," if it lacks a bicameral structure. This feature provides a "double security" against the misconduct of members and the hasty enactment of legislation. Long terms should provide the "motive" for members to acquire the sound knowledge needed for legislation based upon a national perspective and to ensure its stability. Furthermore, it is the test of good government that it secures the happiness of its people through stable laws. This good quality secures the respect and confidence of foreigners for our "national character" and protects the people at home from frequent changes in laws regulating commerce and revenue. In this way, no "unreasonable advantage" is given to the "sagacious, enterprising and moneyed few" to reap a rich harvest from the labor of "the great body of their fellow citizens." Furthermore, stable laws provide the degree of certainty which encourages every kind of productive enterprise. These good qualities, Madison assured his readers, beget popular "reverence" towards a political system.[28]

In his sixty-third essay he added the revealing and arresting argument that the Senate's small size would secure its accountability in the absence of popular election of its members. This claim is notable since he argued emphatically at the Convention that the second chamber ought to consist of a relatively small number of members in order to give this chamber weight. In this essay, however, he contended that in such a small legislative body each member is aware of the ease with which individuals may be identified and held personally accountable for the collective actions of the whole body. The Senate's small size should secure that "due responsibility in the government to the people, arising from the frequency of elections which in other cases produces this responsibility." When this term is used to mean, also, the obligation to perform official duties for the public good, it is evident that, for it to be reasonable it must be limited to objects within the power of the responsible party; and to be effectual, responsibility must be related to the use of that power in ways which allow constituents to make easy and proper judgments of governmental conduct. Some legislation has effects which are immediate and visible, whereas other acts have results which are both more remote and less visible despite their importance in securing the long-term interest and welfare of the nation. A legislative body chosen for a short time is unlikely to provide more than one or two links in the chain of actions needed to secure national objectives for which its members can be held properly "answerable..." Neither can "the people estimate the *share* of influence" individual members of assemblies frequently elected have on legislation. It is difficult enough to "preserve the personal responsibility" the members of a large assembly have for laws producing effects which are immediate and obvious to their constituents. It is almost impossible to secure accountability for the long-term effects of legislation in a large chamber having members elected frequently. The remedy for this defect is a second chamber with members having a sufficient "permanency" of tenure to be made "effectually answerable" for the consequences of legislative actions over the long term. Madison wished such behavior would be among the benefits of a "well-constructed Senate."

It may also serve, he continued, to defend the people from those temporary delusions and errors which experience demonstrates require the counterforce of the "cool and deliberate sense of the community..." to prevail over the "views of its rulers..." This body should be useful, too, when the people are "misled by the artful misrepresentations of interested men." Indeed, it has already been demonstrated in a "previous paper" that a people spread over an "extensive region," unlike the "crowded inhabitants of a small district," are not likely to be led into oppressive combinations by such demagogues. It is this advantage which recommends a "confederated republic" to the American people. Indeed, if the history of ancient republics provides guidance, it is evident that they included representative bodies in their constitutions, but they differed significantly from modern American governments. The latter exclude the direct participation of the whole body of the people acting in their collective capacity, but not their representatives, in the administration of the government. This difference gives a most decided advantage to the new American republic. Its purely representative nature will be given its full effect by its "extensive territory," for no one can believe that "any form of representative government could have succeeded within the narrow limits of the democracies of Greece." This argument incorporated as far as possible his justification of the Senate into the general theory of representation which he developed in the tenth and fourteenth essays. Finally, he claimed that the Senate, although to be chosen indirectly and for six years, would not gradually become preeminent in the government and "transform" it into a "tyrannical aristocracy." Before such a "revolution" could be effected, Madison countered, the Senate must corrupt itself, the state legislatures, the House of Representatives, and the people at large. Reason condemns this charge, and experience corroborates its denial Furthermore, the Senate is unlikely to be transformed into an "independent and aristocratic body" because the House, with the support of the people, will "at all times be able to bring back the Constitution to its primitive form and principles."[29]

Anyone familiar with Madison's private judgments of the Senate has to be struck by his deft and ingenious reasoning in support of it. By his rhetoric he transformed the fundamental structural flaws of the Confederational Congress into the virtues of the Federal Senate. His focus on the personal accountability of its members to the exclusion of reference to its actual accountability to the ruling factions of the moment in the state legislatures is a monument to his skill as a political advocate. His prediction that senatorial terms of six years would tend to stabilize legislation is no less wonderful to behold in view of his repeated charge that bad and unstable laws were the consequence of the frequent alternation of ruling factions in the state legislatures. There is a ring of truth to two of these claims justifying the Senate. Personal accountability for collective actions probably can be identified and judged more readily in inverse proportion to the number of persons making decisions. Also, his claim that the Senate would probably be more insulated than the state legislatures from the influence of demagogues and immoderate majorities was grounded on the congressional experience which led him to germinate his theory of representation in 1784–85: that is, the mixture of a complex structure of government with the social heterogeneity of people living over an extended territory is likely to produce rule by moderate majorities.

A POSTSCRIPT TO *THE FEDERALIST*

After publishing these ideas in *The Federalist*, he made a few further remarks about the representation of diverse interests and the effects of elections from large districts. In a letter to a correspondent in Kentucky, Madison predicted in May, 1788, that there were two circumstances in the "structure of the House of Reps." which will influence policy materially. Members will be selected more widely from each state than the delegates to the old Congress who were chosen by the state legislatures. They usually had little or no regard for particular local situations, and representatives were taken in most states "from the commercial and maritime situations which have generally presented the best choice of characters." The House, however, "must consist by a large majority of inland and Western members. This is a difference of some moment in my opinion" for it will increase proportionally the share of representation among Americans interested in securing the western territory to the union.[30]   A month later at Virginia's ratifying convention he pointed out that the new House "will have a material influence on the government." The commercial interests will have "little or no influence" in that body whose members will be taken from "the landed interest" and will include many from the western country rather than the Atlantic part of the continent. As population grows inevitably in the sparsely settled areas of the South and West, he argued, a majority in the House will favor the security of this area and use its not inconsiderable constitutional powers to secure this objective.[31]

In addition to this frank appeal for the support of delegates from the trans–Allegheny counties of Virginia, Madison used his argument for extensive districts to appeal to the self–conscious republicans among Virginians like George Mason who feared the replication of parliamentary corruption by the executive in the House to the disadvantge of the agrarians. British experience proves that "elections of representatives in great districts of freeholders" are "favorable to fidelity" in them, Madison asserted. In the British Parliament the members who forsake the public interest most readily have been found by experience to be those who are elected by the fewest voters. They are the least independent and the most easily manipulated by "influence." Who, he asked, are "the most corrupt members of parliament?" The answer is "the inhabitants of small towns and districts." The representatives of the city of London, however, chosen by thousands of voters, have supported "the peoples' liberty" and opposed "the corruption of the Crown." Almost continually

> the members of the ministerial majority are drawn from small circumscribed districts. We may therefore conclude, that our representatives chosen by such extensive districts, will be upright and independent. In proportion as we have security against corruption in representatives, we have security against corruption from every other quarter whatsoever.[32]

These remarks may explain what he had in mind in saying to Jefferson in October, 1787, that an extended sphere must be limited to a mean between deficiency and excess.

In some other remarks made in 1788 Madison reaffirmed his belief that the choice of representatives from large districts is beneficial. In this instance the likely effect will be the choice of representatives who have what he frequently called a diffusive sympathy with all interests in society. In commenting on proposals for a state constitution he said that senators ought to be chosen either at large by all voters or required to reside in different parts of the state, especially one which has large towns. Chosen by either of these arrangements, senators should be free of local bias and inspire "diffusive confidence" in them. This result, Madison concluded, is no less important than securing a broad perspective of the state's affairs.[33]

In January, 1789, before he was elected to the House, Madison called for a constitutional amendment to increase the size of the House so as not to leave this important matter wholly to the discretion of

Congress. He acted on this intention in June, 1789, when he included a constitutional amendment to enlarge the size of the House after the first census, using an increasing ratio starting with 1:30,000. Thereafter, Congress should regulate the ratio subject to a constitutionally specified minimum and maximum size. He defended this proposal by repeating the familiar argument that there may be too many members in a representative body, but a certain number is necessary to secure the major objects of representation. "Numerous bodies are undoubtedly liable to some objections, but they have their advantages also; if they are more exposed to passion and fermentation, they are less subject to venality and corruption." Furthermore, in this government where the House is connected with the smaller Senate, "it might be good policy to guard them in a particular manner against such abuse." It is evident from this debate that several large states desire more representatives, but in regard to "futurity, it makes little or no difference..." Congress thought so as well, and dropped the proposed amendment.[34]

All that one can say about this argument compared with those made in *The Federalist* in defense a small House is that Madison was consistent. He maintained repeatedly that in theory there is an optimum size for a representative body: it is the mean number between excess and deficiency. In practice the mean cannot be located with precision.

There is evidence from both the immediate aftermath of the framing and much later that Madison continued to be displeased with the Senate although he expected it to be an improvement in some ways over the old Congress. In May, 1788, he conceded privately that the senate would probably better than the old Congress in a few respects. First, the senate's power over treaties is exercised by two-thirds of the members needed to make a quorum, instead of two-thirds of the states as formerly required. Therefore, the "apprehension of an important decision in a thin [h]ouse will be a spur to the attendance of members" because these decisions will have "real efficacy." Second, policies ought to be more stable because of the members' term of six years with only partial renewal of the body every two years. This prediction supposed that the "probability" of any event "depending on the opinion of a body of men" is determined by the frequency of turnover among them. Finally, the allocation to each state of two votes to be cast by each member individually ought, also, to reinforce stability and secure accountability. In the old Congress votes on closely divided and important issues were often determined by the personal views of whichever members of the large delegations for each state happened to present to vote.[35]

Nevertheless, these improvements did not convince Madison that senators would generally be persons of superior talents. In November, 1788, he told Edmund Randolph that he wanted to see the new government put into "quiet and successful operation" and to contribute to this end he wanted to serve in "the House of Reps. rather than the Senate." It is possible, but doubtful, that he held this preference because he expected his own election to the Senate to be a most unlikely event in view of the power of the antifederalist majority under the leadership of Patrick Henry in the Virginia legislature. When Henry successfully led the opposition to the choice of Madison as a Senator and created an election district which pitted him against his friend, James Monroe, for election to the House, Madison brushed off the maneuver as the sort of thing to be expected in democratic politics. It tended to confirm his observation at the Convention that the Senate was simply a residue of the old Congress which had not been metamorphosed into an assembly of aristocrats by having senators elected by statehouse politicians.[36]

Despite the flaws which marred the senate's initial composition, Madison reported to Jefferson in May, 1789, that the "spirit" of the House of Representatives is already "extinguishing the honest fears which considered the system as dangerous to republicanism." Madison was persuaded that the "biass [sic] of the federal is on the same side with that of the State Govts. tho' in a much less degree."[37]

Two months later he favored a measure proposing to pay senators one dollar per day more salary than members of the House on the ground that "men of ability and firm principles" would otherwise prefer the repose of private life to the burdens of public service. Representatives could be paid less because "men of enterprize [sic] and genius will naturally prefer a seat in the House, considering it to be a more conspicuous station." Later, when Madison was criticized for supporting a differential in the salaries of senators and representatives, he said that inducements to public service ought to be proportional to private sacrifices with a view to attracting persons having the required qualification: public respect. The rewards were not lucrative and incumbents had to renounce private employment almost completely. Only experience gained over time would tell whether the inducement of a higher salary for senators than for representatives is justified. The standard of measure will be "the permanent spirit & character" of the Senate.[38]

Madison's many references to the objections of the large states to the Senate's share of executive power, when the Constitution was being framed and adopted, explain his attempts to claim some power over treaties for the House in 1796. In justifying his claim that the House has a duty to judge for itself the extent of its obligation to enact legislation in execution of a treaty, he noted "with great reluctance" the interest of the smaller states in the Senate's exclusive power to validate treaties. He wished, despite this unassailable distribution of power, that the spirit of friendship and mutual compromise would guide constitutional construction in this instance. If it did so, it would "preserve ... mutual control between the Senate and House..." instead of giving the former exclusive powers which leave the House unable to act without the participation and control of the Senate. In addition, he wished that "whatever jealousy might have prevailed unhappily" between the large and small states could be ended, as it should be, by referring to the journals of the old and new Congresses. In neither body was there a single instance in which a question had been decided by a division of the states according to their respective sizes.[39] He did not add that at the Convention he had made this same point about the real source of legislative divisions which had revealed distinct regional conflicts. Neither did he mention openly in 1796 that the Convention's rejection of his plan of representation lay at the heart of his abiding objections to the

Senate's exclusive control over a president's domestic actions most likely to be entangled in considerations of party advantage and over the power to make treaties which affect the vital concerns of particular interests and regions of the country.[40]

It is not amiss to note that he adhered to his early views of the Senate late in life as well. In 1830 he said it was well known in 1787–88 that the powers committed to the Senate, "comprehending as they do, Legislative, Ex. & Judicial functions, was among the most serious objections, with many, to the adoption of the Constitution."[41] In 1835 he expressed opposition to any constitutional change which would strengthen the Senate's powers relating to the president. Any changes which would increase the weight of the Senate in this relationship, he predicted, are bound to be opposed by the large states for the same reason which explains why they were not easily reconciled to "that part of the Constitution when it was adopted."[42] Later in 1835 he repeated this last point, saying that the opposition of the large states to "the aggregate powers of the senate as the most objectionable feature of the Constitution" was well known in "both the Federal and State conventions" in 1787 and 1788.[43]

It is surprising that this low opinion of the Senate could be so well known in the federal and state conventions of 1787–88, but unknown to us. Perhaps we prefer myth to reality. The only consolation which Madison, if he were alive, might derive from the exalted reputation which the Senate now enjoys, is that popular election of senators probably confirms his theory that representatives elected in extensive districts are likely to be accountable to hetergeneous constituencies rather than single interests.

IF ANGELS WERE TO GOVERN MEN

The debates at the Convention over provisions intended to create a republican executive who would be both controlled and supported unlocks what Wood called the puzzling discrepancy which has been noted between "verbal" affirmations of Montesquieu's praise of the separation of powers, and its application to American constitutions after 1776.[44] This alledged gap was unknown to Americans of this era. It stems from our failure to observe that Montesquieu's doctrine was operational rather than structural. The framers of our early constitutions did not believe that they were obliged by theory to observe a strict separation of functions symmetrically distributed among the three branches. They did profess to believe, however, that the constitutional distribution should be maintained in the exercise of these grants once a government is established and functioning. Formal statements of this doctrine were exhortations to those who govern to exercise their own constitutional powers and no others. The doctrine provided, also, a normative test enabling the people to determine whether their governments conform to this precept in their operations. When they do not, they fail to secure political liberty and are for this reason in the process of degenerating from an established and authorized form to one which is neither authorized nor as good as the one made legitimate by the ratified constitution. In this sense a government was then called corrupted.

For example, in 1774 the First Continental Congress appealed by name to Montesquieu's definition and prescription to denounce as corrupt the manipulation of colonial assemblies by the royal governors' control of valuable benefits to its supporters in these goverments. All history, Congress declared, demonstrates the need for the separation of powers to secure political liberty. It is, Montesquieu had said, that tranquil state of mind among citizens who believe that their enjoyment of rights under the law is secure. This condition can be met, however, only if the legislative power is possessed and exercised exclusively by the people's representatives. The great influence which elections have on legislators' behavior ensures the responsiveness of the laws. If this power is ever located in any other branch of government, then the peoples' right to self-government is destroyed.[45] Actually, Montesquieu was very doubtful that the British people would continue to enjoy political liberty so defined much beyond his own day. Their representatives in Parliament were too eager to benefit personally from the property and status the monarch could distribute as recompense for doing its bidding rather than that of their constituents.[46] Rousseau, too, thought that the British people had lost their liberty through the corruption of their legislature, the members of which sold their civic virtue for personal gain. The executive was able "to buy" a Parliament every seven years, although the price of purchase would probably be too high were terms limited to a single year. Consequently, Rousseau urged the founders of a prospective Polish constitution to find some substitute for money and to provide frequent elections of its parliament so as to ensure the civic virtue of its rulers.[47]

As a normative test of the legitimacy of a government, Montesquieu's doctrine seemed to provide America before 1776 with an unambiguous test and code language for exalting the virtue of self-government and condemning its corruption by royal executives. In fact, this elevation of the struggle for power, wealth, and high status to the level of a moral passion play was a bit too neat, as many of the Framers' remarks at the Convention demonstrate. What was called corruption required two parties. Madison agreed. In 1784–85 he said that the chief grievance against the colonial legislatures "under the British Government" before the Revolution was the lack of "*fidelity* in the Administration of power..." The chief means for overcoming this deficiency in the new state constitutions was a declaration forbidding any person to hold office in more than one branch of the government simultaneously. He supported these prohibitions because Montesquieu had declared such a "union" to be "tyranny." Not even temporary deviations from improper mixtures of the three powers ought to be permitted. They became precedents, although they are really "pretexts" which support persons who become "interested in prolonging the evil." Deviations from this fundamental doctrine also diminish popular reverence for it and make the people "a more easy prey to ambition and self Interest."[48] Nevertheless, as noted previously, these strictures did not bar Madison from warmly advocating and repeatedly a mixture of legislative and judicial branches to form a council of revision authorized to examine, correct, disallow, or return bills to Congress before permitting them to become law. It should be recalled as well that he moved to include the president with the Senate in the exercise of powers over domestic administration and foreign policy.

The appeal of the doctrine of the separation of powers as a moral purgative of the legacy of British rule was powerful in 1776. Many of the state constitutions adopted thereafter contained provisions excluding from the legislature all persons holding offices from which they profited personally. Some explicitly excluded persons having contracts with the army or the navy as well as other persons holding lucrative offices in the other branches of government; but, however worded, even to exclude ministers of the gospel, the purpose was the one stated in the constitution of New Jersey: to preserve the legislative branch of its government from even the "suspicion of corruption."[49] If the testimony of Madison and his colleagues at the Convention is to be accepted as reliable, not even these constitutional limitations on legislators' pursuit of pecuniary aggrandizement were very effective. This is why the Framers thought that constitutional language intended to limit the source of governmental energy to honorable ambition was difficult to calibrate with the degree of precision required to suit all of the delegations at the Convention.

In the first of five essays on this subject in *The Federalist* Madison disposed of the "supposed violation" of the doctrine in the structural distribution of powers. The three divisions were supposed to be "separate and distinct," according to these disingenuous critics. By failing to give the government the "symmetry and beauty of form" needed to prevent the stronger part from dominating the weaker ones, the Framers had violated Montesquieu's political truth. It forbid the "accumulation of all powers...in the same hands," and called any violation of this precept "tyranny." If this charge against the Constitution were to be sustained, then the proposed government would deserve nothing but universal condemnation, Madison conceded. It cannot be properly denounced on this ground, however, because "the maxim on which it relies has been totally misconceived and misapplied." Adherence to the maxim does not require a perfect symmetry in the form and functions of a government. All that is needed to show that the "fundamental principles of a free constitution are [not] subverted" is that no one department exercises the *whole* power of another one. Neither the British constitution, which, Montesquieu regarded as the "mirror of political liberty," nor the state constitutions adopted since 1776 were formed on the principle of perfect symmetry demanded by critics of the Constitution. Powers were "by no means totally distinct from each other" in the former. In the state constitutions there was "not a single instance" in which the powers were kept "absolutely separate and distinct" from each other. Three of them stated the meaning of the doctrine clearly, however, by forbidding each branch to "exercise" authority vested in the others. Therefore, the only issue is to determine whether the means of "maintaining in practice the separation delineated on paper have been provided."[50] The "great problem to be solved" is that of giving each department security from encroachment by the others, especially by the legislature, which can make pecuniary dependents out of the other two. Experience had demonstrated conclusively that mere "demarcation on parchment" is not the solution.[51]

Before explaining the solution to this problem, Madison insisted that, because the three departments are "perfectly coordinate," no one of them can properly "pretend to an exclusive or superior right of settling the boundaries between their respective powers."[52] Neither would Jefferson's recommendation for protecting the "weaker" departments against the "stronger" one work. A convention called by any two branches to correct violations of the separation of powers by the other one would be a misuse of the republican theory that the people are the only source of legitimate authority to frame and alter constitutions. This power ought to be kept open for these "great and extraordinary occasions" when it is needed. This power is misused when it is appealed to in order to maintain the separation of powers. Such a procedure would inevitably embroil the issue in partisan conflict. Such disputes imply flaws in a constitution, and argument over them weakens popular veneration and reverence for even the most free and wisest governments because "all governments rest on opinion..." It is no less true, however, that the strength of each individual's opinions and their effect on his conduct depend on the number of other persons who seem to hold the same opinions. Left alone, human reason is "timid and cautious" so that it becomes firm and confident only in proportion to the number of persons sharing the same beliefs. When they are both "*ancient*" and "*numerous*," they have a double reinforcing effect. In a nation consisting of "philosophers," a reverence for law would be inculcated by enlightened reason and serve to support government by itself, but such a nation is no more to be expected than the "philosophical race of kings wished for by Plato." In every real nation even the "most rational" government benefits from having the added support of the "prejudices of the community on its side." Therefore, contests over constitutional interpretation, if settled directly by public opinion, are likely to produce divisions between either "preexisting parties, or parties springing out of the question itself." Notables in every community will be divided, and the issue will be decided by passion rather than reason. An appeal to the people is the only "legitimate" means of framing or amending a constitution, but it is not appropriate for enforcing it. Such appeals would probably be frequent and, therefore, undesirable.[53] Even Pennsylvania's Council of Censors had been invariably caught up in bitter party differences over constitutional interpretations. These are inevitable, for it can be neither "presumed nor desired" that there should be no parties. Their elimination requires the "absolute extinction of liberty."[54]

Madison's solution to the problem of maintaining separation in practice was original, subtle, and republican. He steered a careful path between the opposing appeals to Hume and Montesquieu made at the Convention by delegates favoring and opposing, respectively, executive manipulation of the legislative branch. Madison provided a new solution to Hume's paradox and Montesquieu's criticism of it. Hume contended that a free government ought to provide constitutional checks which make it the interest of all men to act for the public good. Therefore, in contriving a system of checks on the behavior of such a government, it is necessary to appeal to its members' "avarice and ambition..." The latter, however, drives all men to pursue power, even by encroaching on that of others. In popular governments the weight of the legislature naturally overwhelms the executive unless the power is so distributed among the branches as to make it the "interest" of the members of each to limit their grasp for the power allotted constitutionally to the others. This restraining effect was achieved in the British constitution, Hume had pointed out, by permitting the Crown to use the critical mass of property under its control to gratify the avarice of its supporters in the House of Commons. Members were induced to abandon their ambition to aggrandize institutional power in favor of gratifying their personal avarice by holding lucrative and honorable offices. In this way, the executive power remained wholly in the hands of that branch.[55]

Montesquieu was not convinced of the effectiveness of Hume's solution. He insisted that the corruption of Parliament by the executive made the former the latter's dependents. In this way the British people were doomed to lose their liberty. An independent legislature would not really make the laws. This was so because the government of England consists of two "visible" powers, the legislative and the executive. In Britain, because every citizen has "a will of his own," he enjoys the pleasure of asserting his independence by expressing "greater fondness for one of these powers than the other..." The executive alone possesses the power to give employment, however. Consequently, it can stir great hopes among those who wish to receive its appointments to offices, but it is attacked by those who "have nothing to hope from it." Therefore, "all the passions" operate without restraint and are fully displayed in "an ambitious desire of riches and honors" to be given by the government. Were the situation "otherwise, the state would be in the condition of a man weakened by sickness, one who is without passions because he is without strength."[56]

Madison obviously agreed with these shrewd insights into the sources of energy in the British system at this time. He certainly accepted Hume's contention that the legislature tends to control all power in a popular government especially because Madison feared that our Framers had created a dependent executive. Hume was correct, too, in prescribing an interior structure of the government which would makes its constituent parts the means of keeping each other "in their proper places" simply as the result of their working relationships. Madison assumed, also, that the foundation for the "separate and distinct exercise" of the different powers of government is "a will of its own" in each department. For this reason, each one should have as little agency as possible in selecting the members of the others. If this requirement were adhered to rigorously, then each department's members would be popularly elected. For various reasons, he explained, some deviations from this pure theory are inevitable, especially in the case of the judiciary. Given its permanent tenure, however, its members must soon lose all "sense of dependence" on those who appointed them. It is "equally evident" that the members of each department ought to be as little dependent as possible on the others for their compensation. Otherwise, their independence will be nominal.

The "great security" for maintaining functional integrity among the departments consists in giving to the members of each the necessary "constitutional means and personal motives" to resist the others' encroachments. If each one is to have a will of its own, then "ambition must be made to counteract ambition. The interests of the man must be connected with the constitutional rights of the place." Reliance on the people must be the primary control of government, but it is necessary, also, to invent secondary, institutional restraints founded on the relation between action and human nature. Throughout society, public and private, reliance is placed on the opposition of rival interests to compensate for the absence of better motives. In all the "subordinate distributions of power," the object is to arrange them so that it becomes the "private interest of every individual" to oversee "public rights." If this reasoning is sound and it is applied comparatively to the state and federal constitutions, the latter will not be found inferior.[57]

By enlisting ambition to support the separation of powers, and to energize government, Madison rejected Humes' solution to his paradox in favor of one more consistent with Montesquieu's commitment to the separation of powers. Madison's reliance on human nature as the guarantor of the functional independence of the three branches was consistent, also, with popular faith in the separation of powers as the means needed to channel the self-interested motives of political man to serve the public good. Madison's ingenious argument was a resourceful, creative and distinctly American reformulation of the well-known ideas of both Hume and Montesquieu on this subject. There can be no doubt that Madison wished to restrict the political passions to ambition, alone, and to exclude venality as a motive for public service. Undoubtedly this desire accounts for his numerous promises that the Constitution would prevent the corruption of the members of the government by the means made familiar in colonial and British practice.[58]

At Virginia's ratifying convention Madison again emphasized electoral accountability as the ultimate means of maintaining separation. He said he expected members of Congress to do their duty to their constituents, but not because they necessarily would be persons of "the most exhalted [sic] integrity and sublime virtue." Instead, he relied on the "great republican principle" that the people will have enough "virtue and intelligence to select men of virtue and wisdom." If these qualities are missing, our condition is wretched, and "no theoretical checks" nor form of government can secure our liberty and happiness. If these good qualities are possessed within the community, they will be used to select those who rule. Therefore, "we do not depend on their virtue, or put confidence in our rulers, but in the people who are to choose them."[59] If the voters were to require anything to maintain the new system of government, it would be a free flow of information about the behavior of its members.

Events which followed soon confirmed his general position that the separation of powers was a very imprecise organizational precept to which Congress paid very little attention. On 8 June 1789 Madison included in his proposed Bill of Rights a new article which declared that the powers distributed by the Constitution to the three departments "are appropriated" to them separately so that none of them should "exercise" the powers vested in another. He made this concession to the Anti–Federalists despite his publicly declared belief that such pronouncements are merely hortatory. Apparently Congress thought that this proposal was not worthy of adoption and dropped it. It is certain that Madison suffered no pained pride of authorship on this occasion.[60]

Three weeks later Madison demonstrated that the doctrine provided him with very flexible guidance in enacting legislation. While debating a bill before the House, he remarked that the Comptroller of the Treasury was to perform duties which were *not* "purely executive" because they would also be "judiciary" insofar as this officer was to settle claims between the United States and individuals. This officer should be made both impartial and accountable by allowing the president to appoint him subject to senatorial confirmation for a fixed term of years unless sooner removed at the pleasure of the president. In Madison's judgment, "the legislative power is sufficient to establish this office on such a footing." Moreover, this proposal was not novel because one like it already existed in two of the states, he added. When it was claimed that this arrangement would violate the separation of powers, he demurred. It would not violate the "spirit of the Constitution" simply because one officer performed both executive and judicial functions. There must be "some modification accommodated to these circumstances," including a statutory right of review by the courts to be granted to individuals aggrieved by Comptrollers' decisions. By these actions Congress would be exercising its power of "establishing offices at discretion" within the "true spirit and scope of the Constitution..."[61]

On subsequent occasions Madison again showed that he could be quite supple in determining the proper application of the doctrine to legislation. In December, 1791, he opposed a bill to grant the president discretionary authority to locate post offices and roads, although he conceded the difficulty of determining "with precision the exact boundaries of the legislative and executive powers..." The pending bill would obliterate the line completely, however, by blending these powers. He admitted that there is great difficulty entailed in exercising legislative power so as to accommodate regulations to "the various interests of the different parts of the Union." Nevertheless, in this instance it was clear that "the Constitution has not only given the legislature the power of creating offices, but it expressly restrains the executive from appointing officers, except such as are provided for by law." Furthermore, there is no necessity for "alienating" this legislative power.[62] In this instance he had the undoubted advantage of express provisions of the Constitution to support his position.

In 1800, however, he opposed the Alien Act of 1798 on the general ground that it violated the principle of the separation of powers, among other things. Once again he conceded that the three powers cannot be clearly and easily distinguished from each other in every case. However, power conferred by statute on the executive and judicial branches may be "so general and undefined" as to be legislative and for that reason unconstitutional. "Details are essential to the nature of...a law" and especially so in criminal matters concerning which the determination of applicable rules should be left as "little as possible to those who are to apply and execute the law..." If Congress were to grant "a general conveyance of authority" without "laying down any precise rules" by which it is to be carried into effect, it would follow that "the sole power of legislation might be transferred by the legislature from itself, and proclamations might become substitutes for laws." A delegation of "this latitude would not be denied to be a union if the different powers." Proper delegations require "details, definitions and rules, as appertain to the true character of law; especially a law by which personal liberty is invaded, property deprived of its value to the owner, and life itself indirectly exposed to danger." This Alien Act vests in the president statutory discretion to deport "dangerous" aliens, makes his "will law," his "suspicion...the only evidence...to convict," and his order the only "judgment to be executed" and all of this simply because he believes them to be "dangerous..." to the peace and safety of the United States, or if he has reason to "*suspect*" that they are engaged in "treasonable or secret *machinations*" against the government of the United States. No delegation could be "less definite...particular...precise" than this one. Therefore, the conclusion is that this particular union of legislative and judicial powers with those of the executive "subverts the general principles of free government."[63]

Even if Madison's thought was tinctured with partisanship on this occasion, his definition of the legislative function was sound. To this extent, he provided some general precepts indicating the limits beyond which Congress ought not to divest itself of the power to make law. At the same time, he exposed the weakness of the argument he made in the fifty-first *Federalist*. He understood perfectly well that the ambition to remain in office easily moves legislators to trample on the rights of potential rivals and even to cooperate with the executive in the process. Neither the form of government nor appeals to justice prevail over self-interest on such occasions.

The Framers'-and certainly Madison's-rejection of any rigidly doctrinaire application of the dogma of functionally separated powers was both an important element of their political science and a precept of enduring value. What is equally striking is their deep skepticism toward a written constitution as a restraint on the exercise of governmental power. The record of debates reveals no unrealistic and, therefore, misplaced faith in the power of words to restrain the natural human drive to power, fame, and even wealth through public service. Almost every speaker showed an awareness that the formal distribution of powers and restraints in a written Constitution may mask the real distribution of power in a political system. As keen students of the British political system in their day, they could not fail to be aware of this distinction between appearance and reality. Consequently, they perceived a fundamental and inescapable tension between the two sources of energy in government: its constitution and the nature of political man. It is a conflict between art and nature which not even a common commitment to a Constitution established by the people and theoretically unalterable by the government can secure against violations of the terms of the former. While government founded on a constitution depersonalizes ruling power based on what Madison called personal character or the weight of family, the exercise of power is confined to this original agreement only with great difficulty, if at all. Nature has given every government energy by supplying those who exercise its powers the two great motives–ambition and avarice–which regulate the behavior of all public bodies in the opinion of the leading Framers.

The greatest difficulty the Framers faced in reconciling a due energy in the executive with stability in the legislative branch arose from the values which they believed commonly induced individuals to serve in the two branches, respectively. The Senate in particular was looked to by some Framers to serve as the nursery of statesmen, and service in either branch was only to spend time on the way to the Temple of Fame, to use Charles Pinckney's grandiloquent language. Even Madison conceded that ambition properly drives legislators whose labors are arduous and rarely rewarded with either wealth or fame so that they must look ultimately to the pursuit of the latter in the executive branch. Nevertheless, he insisted that the legislative branch must attract talented and morally upright persons to its service. This need notwithstanding, there was no doubt in his mind that the terms of a written constitution cannot guarantee that the members of any of the branches will be driven by ambition to maintain their formally alloted shares of power or be restrained by patriotic motives to eschew violations of written guarantees of individual rights. As long as government is the greatest of all reflections on human nature, there will be an inescapable tension between the constitutional and natural sources of energy in government. Ultimately, Madison concluded, only the accountability of morally imperfect rulers to an alert electorate can maintain the ideal of constitutional government in practice. Events were soon to prove how fragile mere parchment is as a barrier to the exercise of power in the best of circumstances and, especially if this nation is faced with either the reality or the threats of war.

NOTES

1. *PJM*, 10:212.
2. Ibid., 209, 212.
3. Parts of this chapter were published in Robert J. Morgan, "Madison's Theory of Representation in the Tenth Federalist," *The Journal of Politics* 37 (November 1974):852–85.
4. Farrand, *Records*, 1:228, 296, 303, 309; 2:638.

5. *The Federalist*, 55 (No. 10) See also his essays, "Parties" and "Property," published in the *National Gazette*, January and March, 1792; *PJM*, 14:197–98, 266–68.

6. *The Federalist*, 55–56 (No. 10), italics added.

7. Ibid., 56–57 (No 10).

8. Locke, *Essay'* chap. 7, secs. 89, 91, 94; chap. 19, sec. 131.

9. Madison was probably referring to Jean Jacques Rousseau, *The Social Contract*, translated by G. D. H. Cole (London J. M. Dent and Sons, 1973).

10. *The Federalist*, 58 (No. 10), italics added. For a philosophical discussion of Madison's use of a theory of universal causation in linking motives to opportunities to commit oppressive acts see Morton White, *Philosophy The Federalist and the Constitution*, (New York and London: Oxford University Press, 1987), 203–4.

11. *The Federalist*, 59–60 passim (No. 10).

12. Ibid., 60–61 passim (No. 10).

13. See page 4 above.

14. *The Federalist*, 81–84 passim (No. 14); Charles, the second Baron de Montesquieu, *The Spirit of the Laws*, trans. Thomas Nugent with an introduction by Franz Neumann, 2 vols. (New York: Hafner Press, 1949), vol. 1, book 9, pp. 129–130; cited hereafter as Montesquieu, *Spirit*.

15. *The Federalist*, 241 (No 38).

16. Ibid., 307–8 (No. 46).

17. Ibid., 238 (No. 38).

18. Ibid., 359–61 passim (No. 55).

19. Ibid., 369 (No. 56).

20. Ibid., 265 (No. 41).

21. Ibid., 364–65 (No. 55).

22. Ibid., 366–68 (No. 56), 351 (No. 53) *PJM*, 11:112–13.

23. *The Federalist*, 348–52 passim (No. 53).

24. *PJM*, 5:357; 6:65–66; Farrand, *Records*, 1:214, 361; *PJM*, 13:8–9, 15–16, 30, 41.

25. *PJM*, 10:515.

26. *The Federalist*, 371 (No. 57); see also *PJM*, 11:141.

27. *The Federalist*, 377–82 passim (No. 58), italics in the original. For evidence of the popularity of the charges that the House was too small and the republic too extended, see Cecilia Kenyon, *The Antifederalists* (Indianapolis, Ind.: The Bobbs–Merrill Co. Inc., 1966), xlix–lxi, and Alpheus T. Mason, *The States Rights Debate* (Englewood Cliffs, N.J.: Prentice–Hall, 1972), 27–55. I do not believe that *anything* in the record of Madison's discussion of the need for better representatives between 1783 and 1788 and his theory that choice from large districts would probably have this desired effect supports the contention that he prescribed a "natural aristocracy" in order to change the "social character" of persons holding office under the authority of the new federal government. For this thesis see Wood, *Creation*, 499–508, 605–6. Madison's explicit definition of aristocracy was Aristotelian, not Jeffersonian, as we shall see in chapter 5 below.

28. *The Federalist*, 400–7 (No. 62).

29. Ibid., 407–16 (No. 63); *PJM*, 12:340–41.
30. PJM, 11:48–49, 430.
31. Ibid., 137.
32. Ibid., 114–15.
33. Ibid., 286.
34. Ibid. 12:200, 336–37.
35. Ibid., 11:45–47.
36. Ibid., 328–29, 362–63.
37. Ibid., 12:186.
38. Ibid., 293; 14:399.
39. *WJM*, 6:276–77.
40. Madison's claim of a share of power for the House over treaties was clearly prompted by objections to Jay's Treaty in Virginia; see *LJM*, 2:65–66.
41. *LJM*. 4:77–79 passim.
42. Ibid., 342–43.
43. Ibid., 368–69. Madison's views of the Senate give no support to the argument that he intended it to be an aristocratic body such as was argued in Paul Eidelberg, *The Philosophy of the American Constitution* (New York: The Free Press, 1968), 37–65.
44. Wood, *Creation*, 150–61, 446–63 repeated the familiar argument that evocation of the doctrine of the separation of powers was part of a reactionary movement leading to the framing of the Constitution; he cited as proof E. S. Corwin, "The Progress of Constitutional Theory Between the Declaration of Independence and the Meeting of the Philadelphia Convention," *American Historical Review* 30 (1925): 511–36.
45. Montesquieu, *Spirit*, vol. 1, bk. 11, ch. 6; bk. 12, ch. 2; and vol. 2, bk. 26, ch. 20.
46. Ibid., vol. 1, bk. 19, ch. 27.
47. Jean Jacques Rousseau, *The Government of Poland,* trans. Willmoore Kendall (Indianapolis, Ind.: The Bobbs–Merrill Co. Inc., 1972), 31–32, 69–73.
48. *PJM*, 8:78, 350–51.
49. Quoted in Wood, *Creation*, 158.
50. *The Federalist*, 312–20 (No. 47).
51. Ibid., 321, 326 (No. 48).
52. Ibid., 328 (No. 49).
53. Ibid., 327–31 passim (No. 49).
54. Ibid., 332–35 (No. 50).
55. Hume, *Essays*, 1:16, 42–45 passim.
56. Montesquieu, *Spirit*, vol. 1, bk. 19, ch. 27.
57. *The Federalist*, 336–38 (No. 51).
58. Ibid., 364–65 (No. 55).
59. *PJM*, 11:163; see also, 14:179, 218.
60. Ibid., 12:202.
61. Ibid., 265–67.
62. Ibid. 14:142–43.
63. *LJM*, 4:531–53

Chapter 4

Supporting and Restraining the Executive

Before the opening of Congress in 1789, Madison had no opportunity to expound publicly the need for the president to be both supported and restrained constitutionally, the position which he took at the Constitutional Convention. The pressure under which the debates over the executive took place during the fourth month of the Convention precluded all but fragmentary speeches defining and defending his conception of executive power and its proper distribution. The division of labor between Madison and Hamilton in writing essays for *The Federalist* was such that Madison contributed nothing to the explanations of the executive branch, whereas Hamilton provided thirteen essays on this subject. Madison's first opportunity to express any views on this subject was postponed until May, 1789, when the House debated bills to establish three executive departments. Subsequently, Hamilton's bills to fund the remaining war debts and to charter the Bank of the United States appeared to Madison to lay the foundation for rule by a minority consisting of military and financial interests, but the circumstances were such that Madison was constrained to deal suggestively rather than directly with this matter in a number of essays published in 1791–92. Finally, President Washington's Proclamation of Neutrality of 22 April 1793 and Hamilton's expansive justification of it gave Madison the occasion to expound rather fully his understanding of the constitutional restraints placed on executive power over foreign policy. These essays reflected his theory that the tendency of every government and especially the executive branch is to be self-directed because of wars or threats of them. This tendency toward autonomy is purchased, Madison argued, at the cost of both accountability to the electorate and strict adherence to the terms of the written constitution.

A RESPONSIBLE AND ACCOUNTABLE PRESIDENT

Two issues raised in May, 1789, illustrate the difficulties Madison faced in precisely calibrating the scope and limits as well as the supports and restraints on an institutionalized rather than charismatic presidency. One set limits on the sources of its authority and the other one secured its independent, but accountable exercise. On 11 May the House debated the Senate's proposal to address the President with an inflated honorific title. Madison ridiculed it, knowing that John Adams was one of the chief instigators of this charade. Such titles were not dangerous because of any power which they might confer, Madison said, but they could not be reconciled with either the nature of our government or the republican "genius" of the American people. His strongest objection was founded on "principle": such titles diminish rather than enhance the "true dignity and importance of a republic" and its chief executive. If they are borrowed from abroad "the servile imitation will be odious, not to say ridiculous as well." If we use our "fertile fields of luxuriant fancy and deck out an airy being of our own creation," the chances are that it will be an "empty fantom [sic], ridiculous and absurd." Therefore, we ought to avoid such folly out of the conviction that the more simple, the more republican, we are in our "manners, the more rational dignity we acquire."[15] Despite Madison's resort to ridicule, it is evident that he fought vigorously to stop this effort to endow the President with the irrational authority conferred by symbolism. This determination is more remarkable than it might seem at first glance. It was exhibited openly at a time when Madison was convinced that the Presidency was constitutionally weak despite the prestige which the hallowed Washington brought to the office. This condition prompted Madison to support a broad construction of the president's power to remove executive subordinates only a short time after this incident.

Madison was given an opportunity to enlarge the president's control of domestic administration while diminishing that of the Senate early in the First Congress because "a very interesting question has grown out of the silence of the Constitutions with regard to the power of removal from offices."[2] The issue arose when a bill to create the executive departments was under debate in the House of Representatives. Madison seized this occasion to continue from the Convention his strategy of making the president a counterweight to the Senate. He argued that the "genius" of the system required the location of this power exclusively with the President.

This debate was complicated from the outset by reference to Alexander Hamilton's defense in *The Federalist* of the mixture of the president's powers with the Senate's in regard to impeachments, treaties, appointments, and removals. Despite his long absence from the Convention, he undertook to depict these relationships between the president and the Senate in terms which were far removed from the views held by Madison, to say the least. Hamilton explicitly dismissed the "hypothetical dread of the too great weight of the Senate" in the performance of these functions.[3]   On the contrary, this mixture of power will contribute to "the stability of the administration. The consent of that body would be necessary to displace as well as to appoint." Consequently, a change of president is not likely to result in a violent or general turnover of executive personnel as would be the case if one person alone were to exercise these powers. Furthermore, an incumbent who has demonstrated his fitness to perform his duties is likely to be immune to removal by the president because the Senate's disapproval of such an action would discredit the president. Everyone who values "steady administration" will applaud this provision which connects the official existence of public men with the approval or disapproval of the Senate. Due to its greater permanency than the House, the Senate will in "all probability be less subject to inconstancy than any other member of the government."[4]

The opposition's argument that the Senate will "influence" the president is refuted by adhering to the proper definition of this term. It means "a power of conferring a benefit" upon someone. How, Hamilton asked, could the Senate confer any benefit on the president by obstructing his actions? It might acquiesce in choices of his favorites, when adherence to "public motives" would dictate different conduct, but these instances in which the president is "personally interested" are unlikely to occur often. It is not the Senate, but the president who possesses influence in the form of the "POWER which can originate the disposition of honors and emoluments"; they are "more likely to attract than to be attracted by the POWER which can merely obstruct." Influence in this case must mean only restraint, and its effect should be "salutary" because it cannot limit adversely the president's power to nominate candidates to offices.[5] These disingenuous arguments can be attributed, no doubt, to Hamilton's need to counter the influence of Anti–Federalists in New York such as his two colleagues, Robert Yates and John Lansing, who left the Convention at the end of the first week of July, 1787, and did not return because they opposed the nationalizing trend of deliberations.

In the House, Madison lost no time in challenging Hamilton's contention that stable administration is the great value resulting from the Senate's power to obstruct and discredit a president's removals from office. He did so because he thought that it was of the utmost importance to settle the matter at that moment before some other interpretation should be authoritatively and permanently established. The "genius and character of the whole government" will be determined by this decision, he insisted. Congress at this time will decide whether the "equilibrium" intended by the Constitution will prevail, or there will be a tendency toward "aristocracy or anarchy" among the three branches. Consequently, this decision affects not only "the fundamental principles of the government," but also the fate of "liberty itself."[6] The issue was not simply a lawyer's question of constitutional interpretation as juristically oriented scholars would have us believe.[7] Madison was concerned with the far broader question of the fundamental charateristics of the American Republic and the political impulses which give it its energy derived from the constitutional text and the motives of officeholders exercising its authorized powers.

Given the belief that Hamilton's seventy–second *Federalist* contains the classic exposition of the doctrine favoring an efficient and responsible executive said to have been established by "The Federalists," it is illuminating to quote Madison's position at length and to examine in some detail his reasons for supporting it.[8] On 19 May 1789, the day on which the House first took up bills to establish the departments of foreign affairs, treasury, and war, Madison declared that for "the well–being of the Government" it is necessary to determine the question authoritatively without the heat of factional conflict likely to arise in the case of an actual removal. One of the most prominent features of the constitution "a principle that pervades the whole system, is that there should be the highest possible degree of responsibility" in all its executive officers. Therefore, anything which tends to lessen this responsibility is contrary to "its spirit and intention, and unless it is saddled upon us expressly by the letter of that work, I shall oppose the admission of it into any act of legislature."[9]

If we are guided by text of the Constitution and say, as some members do, that impeachment is the only means of removing officers, the effect is to establish good behavior as the only lawful tenure for every officer of the government. If this is the meaning of the Constitution, "it is a fatal error interwoven in the system and one that would ultimately prove its destruction." This construction gives the government more "stability in the executive department" than is "compatible with the genius of republican government in general and this constitution in particular..." The danger to "liberty" following from maladministration does not lie so much with the ease with which incompetent individuals gain office as it does from the difficulty of removing them, when they prove themselves unworthy of public trust. This interpretation of the power of removal is "incompatible with the principles of free government" because it means that all judicial and executive officers "from the chief justice down to the tidewaiter" [a customs officer] would have firm tenure during good behavior.[10]

Second, the Constitution expressly provides that Congress shall have power to *create* offices and by implication to determine the tenure by which they are to be held. Aside from the power to limit the duration of offices, Congress is authorized, also, to set salaries and to appropriate funds for other purposes. These are means of exerting restraint on the executive independent of the president's power to remove his subordinates, and they are almost beyond the power of the Constitution to limit. This condition follows from the decided predominance of the House which consists of the "numerous and immediate representatives of the people." Once Congress creates offices, however, "the legislative power ceases" except for the obvious influence of the Senate which shares in the appointing power.[11]

Third, there was, perhaps, no argument "urged with more success, or more plausibly grounded against the constitution under which we are now deliberating, than the one founded on the mingling of the executive and legislative branches." In particular, it was objected that "the senate have too much of the executive power..." The question for us to decide, therefore, is whether by our actions we "strengthen the objection and diminish the responsibility we have in the head of the executive," or limit the former's agency in the latter's affairs. The danger of arguing that the Senate is joined with the president in the power to remove executive officers is that one of the latter who was appointed to office with the support of "his friends in that body" will be able to join with them in a cabal in resisting the president's efforts to remove him. Thereafter, such persons could be cleared out of office "only by a revolution in the government."

Furthermore, if we support this interpretation of the locus of power, where does the responsibility of the officers we create terminate? The answer is in a body made "permanent," because of the means by which its members are chosen and renewed, a branch of the government possessing "that proportion of aristocratic power which the constitution no doubt thought it wise to establish in the system," despite strong objections against it. The question is whether we shall trust the Senate which is "responsible to individual legislatures, rather than the person who is responsible to the whole community." It is true that Senators do not hold office for life as in the aristocracies reported in history books, but they will "not possess that responsibility for the exercise of executive powers which would render it safe."[12]

Madison then said he never considered the share given to the Senate in appointing officers to be one of the Constitution's "most meritorious parts." He was unwilling to abridge any of the power granted, but it is "proper...to reduce the Ex. agency of the Senate to the very minimum that will satisfy the Constitution" because the Senate is the "least responsible member of the government..."[13]

Privately, too, Madison disjoined himself from the idea that the Senate was an aristocratic body. The real reason for limiting the Senate's agency in executive affairs and making the latter as responsible as possible was political. If the heads of departments were to be made dependent on the Senate for tenure, one of its factions might support them against the president, distract the executive branch, and obstruct the public business. The danger of undue power in the president from an exclusive power of removals, he told Edmund Pendleton, is not formidable. "I see, and politicallv *feel* that [the executive] will be the weak branch of the Government." Even with a full power of removal, a president will be more likely to spare unworthy officers, thro [sic] fear, than to displace the meritorious through caprice or passion." A displaced officer having "influence would immediately form a party against the administration—endanger his re-election-and at least go into one of the Houses and torment him with opposition."[14] In subsequent private letters he added that the theory which joins the Senate with the president in making removals takes power from the president, the "most responsible member of the Government," and vests it in the Senate "who from the nature of that institution, is and was meant after the Judiciary & in some respects with that exception to be the most unresponsible branch."[15]

In support of his objective of making the President solely responsible for the conduct of executive officers and accountable to the electorate for his actions, Madison declared to the House, it is "absolutely essential" that the president, alone, should possess the removal power. This necessity is fully consistent with the Constitution once it is understood that this power is exclusively executive in nature. "I conceive that if any whatsoever is in its nature executive, it is the power of appointing, overseeing and controlling those who execute the laws." We deduce this conclusion from the clause which literally places the executive power in the president and interpret this language by the rule of construction according to which exceptions to general rules are "ever to be taken strictly." The particular clause of the Constitution which favors this construction of the document is the one requiring him to "take care that the laws be faithfully executed." By imposing this duty on him, the Constitution seems to intend that he should have the power needed to accomplish this end.

Constitutional exegesis aside, we must view this matter from a political perspective by asking whether this exclusive grant to him is dangerous. The answer is in practice, no. He will have no opportunity for appointing an unworthy person and no motives for displacing a worthy one only to face the prospect of trying to secure consent from the Senate to the appointment of a successor. If the person removed has considerable influence and is supported by public opinion, the community will take his side against a president and consider the latter's action as misconduct by "refusing to elect him" at the first opportunity. It is difficult to imagine that a president will abuse this power, when we consider that he is elected for only four years and is "dependent upon the popular voice." Furthermore, he is likely to be little, "if at all distinguished for wealth, personal talents, or influence" from the heads of departments whom he may remove. If we say that he must share this power with the Senate, we "abolish at once that great principle of unity and responsibility in the executive department."[16] Madison's position carried.

RESTRAINING THE MOTIVES GRATIFIED BY WAR

The partial success of Madison's support of constitutional reform in 1787 led to ironic consequences and dilemmas of a fundamental sort. The powers of the new federal government, he pointed out in *The Federalist*, were limited constitutionally to "external objects" which are "few in number." They will be exercised "mostly in times of war," whereas the powers of the states will be "exercised in time of peace. I hope the time of war will be little compared to the time of peace."[17] The irony in this statement is derived partially from his perception before 1787 that the Confederation was too weak to survive the threats posed by foreign powers seeking to destroy it through internal subversion or war. An essential ingredient of reform, it should be recalled, was the ability of a reformed government to attract to its offices persons of not only continental, but also, international vision. The irony of the situation facing Madison in 1789 was compounded further by the fact that he acted in the Convention and the First Congress to strengthen the president's power over domestic administration at the cost of the Senate, and he had spoken at the Convention in favor of giving the president a share of power with the Senate over the conduct of foreign relations with one notable exception. He moved to deny the president the power to conclude treaties of peace because war enhances the executive's power.

Given his vision of the American republic as a model breadbasket and workshop producing a bounty of goods for the well–being of humanity, he had agreed with those who said at Virginia's ratifying convention that "national splendor and glory are not our objects" as a nation. Nevertheless, every government must possess power to tax and to borrow money to wage war as all of them must do on some occasions. British and French experience had demonstrated that the burden of the immense public debts under which these nations labored had been incurred to pay the expenses of "war" only. The United States must have this same power despite the fact that speculators will seek to profit from public war debts. If such speculation were to be minimized and posterity were not to be burdened with the debts of past wars, then congressional powers competent to discharge war debts promptly were necessary. Madison hoped that there would be little need for either land or naval forces in time of peace, if our government were "respectable" in the eyes of other nations. This quality ought to secure us from attacks abroad so that we should be able to avoid the "affliction" of the heavy costs of armaments.[18]

Unfortunately, the Framers were powerless to change human nature, on which the operations of the government would depend. Public service must be made to appeal to motives which moralists have almost invariably denounced as defective because of their self–serving ends. Like many of his leading contemporaries, Madison was convinced that framers must accept human nature as they find it and then establish constitutional restraints on the political passions which are gratified by war more than by the administration of domestic affairs. In his essay, "The Vices," prepared just before the Convention, he had listed three motives for holding public office: ambition, "interest" and a devotion to the public good. Unfortunately, the last one of these motives rarely directed the behavior of persons holding public offices. He had noted, also, that, although power and right are vested in the majority of the community according to the theory of republican government, this theory is rendered inoperative, if such a government is ruled by a minority consisting of a military and financial elite. He repeated this observation in the forty–third Federalist.[19] How could such a system of rule be avoided as long as the powers of the federal government were confined to the regulation of domestic and foreign commerce, public finance, and the conduct of foreign policy including war? As long as Madison believed that it is war which produces the high–toned government which Hamilton preferred to a republic, the former was bound to believe that the latter and like–minded members of the new government would soon resort to war and the perpetual public debts it generates in order to establish power over the masses whom some of the Framers held in contempt. At the Convention Hamilton had argued that the new American government must be maintained by an "active and constant interest" in "debts" and "plans of finance." Avarice, ambition and personal interest are needed to support every type of government. It must also have the "influence" derived from dispensing "those regular honors & emoluments which produce an attachment to the Govt." The "English model was the only good one..." because no sound executive could be founded on republican principles.[20]

Madison obviously had good reason to be troubled well before 1790 with the possibility that a ruling military and financial elite could be established to operate behind the mask of the Constitution, but the occasion was not then ripe for him to develop fully his thoughts about this subject. Hamilton's financial bills introduced in 1790–91 provided Madison just the occasion he needed for a fuller, albeit indirect, exposition of his views on this matter.

He undoubtedly expressed his fear that these measures would lay the foundation for an imperial republic when he and Jefferson met at Monticello for a Christmas holiday after the latter's return from France late in 1789. It appears that they discussed a strategy for supporting legislation liquidating the war debts, but they must not have reached any final conclusion about the proper means of doing so. At least, this is the inference one may draw from Jefferson's letter to Madison dated 20 January 1790, asking the question whether "one generation has the right to bind another" so as to oblige a society to recognize the "*natural* right" of a creditor to claim payment for debts contracted to him and his successors as well.[21]

Because this proposition is contrary to the law of nature which limits the life of each generation, every nation forming a constitution ought to declare that neither the legislature nor the nation itself can validly contract more debt than it can pay in its own age. This limitation would put both lenders and borrowers on their guard by restricting the obligation of public debts within natural limits. It would "bridle the spirit of war, to which a too free recourse has been procured by the inattention of moneylenders to this law of nature..." For this reason, Jefferson urged Madison to subject this line of argument to searching scrutiny and to introduce into the House of Representatives this "solid and beneficial" theory. It would furnish "a fine preamble to our first appropriation law" because it would exclude the "contagious & ruinous errors" which have plagued Europe and have armed governments with the means of binding their fellow men in chains "not sanctioned by nature..." Americans had already set an example by transferring the power to declare war from the executive to the legislature, from "those who are to spend to those who are to pay." The doctrine of natural limits to war debts would add an "effectual check to the Dog of war..."[22]

Madison agreed that Jefferson's axiom ought to stimulate thought among lawmakers, "particularly when contracting and providing for public debts." As a "philosophical legislator," he would be especially pleased to see it first announced to the world in an American law and always remembered as a wholesome restraint on the propensity of living generations to impose *"unjust & unnecessary* burdens" on posterity. There is an exception in the case of debts that are just and necessary, however. They may be incurred with a "direct view to the interest of the unborn" as well as the living generation which contracts them. Included in this category are debts for waging war to repel conquest by a foreign nation, the results of which may affect many subsequent generations. Debts for the calculated benefit of posterity may include the one contracted by the United States (to wage war for its independence). In these two instances it may not be possible to discharge debts within the term of nineteen years (in accordance with Jefferson's actuarial calculations). He saw no prospect, however, of introducing Jefferson's precept at this time because the "spirit of philosophical legislation" had not prevailed at all in some parts of America, and it was not fashionable in either this part of the country (New York City) or Congress in 1790. The emphasis was on strengthening the powers of the new government, not on restricting them. Moreover, Madison added, it is much easier to detect all the small obstacles to carrying out every great plan than it is to foresee its "general & remote benefits..." He concluded that much more light would have to shine on Congress before "many truths seen through the medium of philosophy, become visible to the naked eye of the ordinary politican."[23]

Within a month Madison reported to Jefferson that venality was moving some members of Congress to support Hamilton's bill to assume the state debts and thereby to add greatly to the national debt. This addition, Madison warned, increased "a Trust already sufficiently great for the virtue and number of the federal legislature" to bear.[24] The bill to incorporate the Bank of the United States and fund it heavily with existing public securities also aroused Madison's suspicion that venality would motivate some members of Congress (and some did eventually become directors of the bank). In July, 1791, he complained bitterly to Jefferson about "members of the Legislature who were most active in pushing this Jobb [sic], openly grasping its emoluments."[25] A month later he told Jefferson he would suspend judgment about the relative injustices practiced under the Confederation and the new government. If events continue in their existing track, however, then "my imagination will not attempt to set bounds to the daring depravity of the times. The stockjobbers will become the pretorian [sic] band of the Government–at once its tool & its tyrant: bribed by its largesses, & overawing it, by clamours and combinations."[26] Madison openly told the House that some of its members apparently supported the Constitution because they expected its "energy" to be derived from sources different from those he had anticipated: that is, the "enlightened opinion and affection of the people..."[27]

In private notes made in November, 1792, Madison indicated his expectation that a perpetual public war debt would have the same effect on the American constitutional system as it had on the British model which Hamilton wanted to imitate. Madison noted first that among the sources of "influence" available to the Crown in Great Britain "the National debt, weighs much." Second, he was convinced that, if his proposal for discriminating between the two classes of public creditors had been decided by the "disinterested part of the people of the U.S.," then it "is fairly presumable the measure wd. have carried. If the *disinterested* part only of their Reps. had voted, it is at least a problem what the decision would have been." Regarding to the Bank bill, there may have been a "mercenary change of opinion" by members having a "private interest in the species of paper" provided by a revision of the bill during the legislative process. In any event, a "corrupt tendency of the Estabt." has been "evinced by experience." Therefore, "every investigation into the nature & effects of such institutions...may be judged proper." The whole tendency of events reveals a "policy of paving the way for British Govt. by plans of British administration."[28]

If members of Congress were attached to the executive by benefiting personally from lucrative treasury operations, executive influence would be established over the legislative branch, the separation of powers would be breached, and the republican character of the new government would be subverted. If members of Congress were to seek personal enrichment from public debts created by war, Franklin's warning voiced at the Convention against making public offices profitable from this source would be in vain. His "feotus" of monarchy would have been planted in the American republic.

Prompted by suspicion that such a pregnancy had been commenced, Madison, writing anonymously, denounced those who favored measures "pampering the spirit of speculation within and without the government" by unnecessarily increasing and perpetuating a debt which adds to the "causes of corruption in the government..."[29] In addition he drafted an amendment to the Constitution that would have forbidden the conflict of interest he suspected by requiring members of Congress to disclose their holdings of stock in the Bank of the United States on assuming office and to promise under oath not to acquire public property of any kind whatsoever during their tenure in office. He reasoned that the constitutional prohibition which applied to the executive branch ought, for even more cogent reasons, to apply to Congress whose members are in a position to "convert public trust to their private emoluments."[30] He prudently decided, however, to leave this unrealistic proposal in his files. He was well aware that the Framers had deliberately rejected a somewhat clumsy constitutional bar to conflicts of interest among members of Congress.[31] Madison probably decided not to offer his amendment in 1793 because it would have barred speculation in public lands no less than in public securities and bank stock. Therefore, it might have been embarrassing for him and his allies to speak out boldly in favor of "civic virtue" among officeholders in an open debate over an exclusionary rule as broad as the one he drafted.[32]

Instead, he appealed to public opinion which is the real "sovereign" in a free government.[33] First, he persuaded Jefferson to endorse an American edition of Thomas Paine's *Rights of Man* which attacked the British funded war debt on the ground that it provided the emoluments needed to hold the British system together by corrupting the House of Commons. This effort failed, to Jefferson's mortification, when leading Federalists, including Vice-President John Adams, attacked Jefferson for giving offense to the British government while he was serving as the American Secretary of State.[34] When this ploy failed, Madison assumed personal responsibility for appealing to public opinion. Between November, 1791 and December, 1792, he published seventeen essays of varying length and sophistication. Some were quite learned, but a few were mere partisan phillipics. Of particular relevance are those which warned against imitating British policies having a tendency in America to undermine the republican and federal characteristics of the Constitution.

In "Universal Peace" he published an alternative to Jefferson's axiom intended to curb war and the debts which it creates. This essay was offered ostensibly as a corrective to Rousseau's *Project of*

Perpetual Peace published in an English edition in London in 1761.[35] Unfortunately, Rousseau appealed more to the heart than to the head because he failed to account for the "allurements to war" felt by governments. He failed, also, to foresee the tendency of his plan "to perpetuate arbitrary power" wherever it exists. In doing so, he cut off the hope of ending oppression. It was benevolent, but visionary, of Rousseau to offer the prospect of universal and perpetual peace, but war results in so much folly and wickedness that "much is to be hoped from the progress of reason" to curb wars.[36] They are of two kinds. One follows from "the mere will of the government," and it can be prevented only by a reformation which makes the will of the government identical with society's. The decision to wage war by governments independent of society results from the "ambition," avidity, caprice, or vengefulness of a government which is unaccountable to the community or can contradict the latter's will. Wars are declared and directed by those who are to spend public funds and not by those who pay taxes to support them. The power of those persons who benefit from waging war is increased, whereas the people whose "chains are riveted" by this "disease" must bear its curse in perpetuity. The first reform to be undertaken, therefore, is to regenerate the government by making its will the same as that of society. Had Rousseau lived to see the constitutions of the United States (and France!) he might have understood this requirement and conceived of a praiseworthy plan.

Wars of the second type reflect the public will and, consequently, are not easily curbed unless it is by the "reason" of society. This faculty can operate to best effect by establishing "permanent and constitutional maxims of conduct" to prevail over momentary considerations. Therefore, a "republican philosopher" would recommend a model of government in which war is declared only by the authority of the people who are to bear its burdens rather than by "the government which is to reap its fruits." In addition, this model would contain a declaration that "each generation should be made to bear the burden of its own wars, instead of carrying them on at the expense of other generations." To Jefferson's precept stripped of natural law, Madison added the provision that the model ought to be given "energy" by imposing taxes heavy enough to alert people to "misapplications of their money." To the hypothetical objection that war sometimes benefits more than one generation, it should be answered that reasons can always be given for converting exceptions into general rules. Instead, we should observe that the expenses of "*necessary* wars" can never exceed the fiscal resources available to an "*entire* generation." This conclusion is demonstrated by the "*fact*" that in "every nation which has drawn on posterity for the support of its wars, the *accumulated interest* of its perpetual debts has become more than a *sufficient principal*, of all its exigencies." Madison's rejection of hypothetical exceptions justifying perpetual debts seems to be calculated to foreclose argument that our Revolutionary War debt might be entailed on posterity because the latter receives the moral benefit of self-government in exchange for the cost of paying interest on the debt over time, as he had pointed out to Jefferson two years earlier. Every nation which adopts a constitutional requirement that each generation pay the costs of its own wars will compel "avarice ... to calculate the expenses of ambition." In the presence of the "equipoise of these passions reason would be free to decide" whether to go to war or not. Every state would benefit by avoiding all of its wars of "folly" and conserving its resources to fight wars of "necessity and defense." Had Rousseau lived to witness the "progress of reason and reformation," he might have recommended the reform of governments so as to subject them to the will of their people and to require each generation to pay its own debts.[37]

Madison's argument in this essay permits the fair inference that he was a careful reader of Adam Smith's *Wealth of Nations*. The latter, also, had excoriated wars as the sole cause of public debts which are funded to pay interest, but not to retire their principal. The popularity of the sinking fund in Britain since the Glorious Revolution was due, Smith asserted, to the ease with which governments had avoided raising taxes to pay the real costs of war while being waged. Governments are both "unwilling and unable" to increase taxes in proportion to expenditures because they "fear...offending the people" who would quickly become "disgusted with the war" if they were made to feel its real fiscal burdens. By borrowing much and taxing little, governments wage wars for "great empires" so that the people feel little inconvenience, but derive much satisfaction from the exploits of their victorious fleets and armies. This pleasure "compensates" for the slight increase in the level of taxes over the requirements of peace by giving the people "a thousand visionary hopes of conquest and national glory from a longer continuance of the war." The cure for all the bad effects of war debts is to eliminate funding. Wars would be "more speedily concluded and less wantonly undertaken," if the people were made to feel the complete burden of war during its continuance. They would soon grow weary of it, and the government, in order to humor them, would not be under the necessity of carrying it on longer than was necessary. Foreknowledge of the heavy and unavoidable costs of waging a war would hinder the people from "wantonly calling for it when there was no real or solid interest to fight for." Preventive measures are needed because a sinking fund has "gradually enfeebled every state" which has adopted it, as the experience of the Italian republics demonstrates. Such a fund is "pernicious," also, because it fails to multiply capital and ends in either declarations of bankruptcy by a government or the devaluation of its currency in imitation of the Romans.[38]

Undoubtedly, Madison would have been delighted to appeal to the authority of Immanuel Kant. Unfortunately, he did not publish an English edition of his republican recommendations for limiting wars until 1796. His arguments are noteworthy, nevertheless, because they were addressed to the problem facing Madison and bore a striking resemblance to his reasoning. Kant specified that there shall be neither standing armies nor national debts contracted to maintain the interests of a state beyond its boundaries. Standing armies contribute to frequent wars of national rivalry and public debts are "the ingenious invention of a commercial people..." Public debts are dangerous means of creating "a political engine" and "a monied power," as well as a "treasure for war...which cannot be exhausted except by a default in the taxes..." This eventuality is postponed because of the beneficial "reaction credit has upon commerce and industry " The ease which *credit contributes to waging war* is coupled with the "natural inclination of men...for it as soon as they possess the power" to engage in it. The only preventive is to make the "civil constitution of every state republican." This form derives its authority from the people and separates the executive power from the legislative. In a republican government "the assent of every citizen is necessary to decide the question, 'Whether war shall be declared or not.'" The people are not likely to answer in favor of war because of the extensive evils which they visit upon themselves as a result of voting for it.[39]

Two points deserve emphasis here. First, Madison's arguments in the debate over funding and the Bank give no support to the contention that he was one of the many Americans who regurgitated the English "reactionary" opposition party's "shibboleths and diatribes against public debts, and 'money men' and corruption," with its glorification of the "gentry ethic as unvarnished truth."[40] There can be no doubt that some of the leading thinkers of the eighteenth century were deeply concerned with, and analyzed critically, the constitutional and economic effects of waging wars and funding them with perpetual public debts in order to create capital for investments. David Hume was not alone in noting that this change marked a significant break with earlier practice and caused a profound alteration in the moral foundations of governments relying on this means of expanding and maintaining their power. It was the novel practice of funding wars of imperial rivalry (as well as revolutions), not the growth of commerce and manufacturing, which corrupted the ancient ideal of disinterested public service in the eighteenth century.[41]

Second, it was awareness of this phenomenon which infused the debates over human nature, public ethics and governmental energy among the American Framers. Furthermore, these analyses deeply influenced Madison's understanding of political science and shaped his determination to avoid imitation of the British political system in America because of its special destiny as he conceived it. It is apparent that there was no single source of influence on Madison's political and constitutional thought. Therefore, it is misleading to interpret it by reference to any one thinker or to party doctrine.

Madison supplemented the argument in "Universal Peace" in an essay entitled "Spirit of Governments". In this paper he amended Montesquieu's theory of the passions moving each type of regime. The latter had resolved the operative principles of government into fear, honor, and virtue, and ascribed them to despotisms, monarchies, and republics, respectively. Without doubt, Montesquieu unmasked some old errors and he perceived some new truths, but only dimly. It is unlikely that any government may be explained by a "sole principle of operation" because "heterogeneous principles mingle their influence in the administration" of each type. Therefore, it is better to classify each kind of government by the "predominant spirit and principles" which "maintain" them. One type operates by a "permanent military force which at once maintains the government, and is maintained by it." This reciprocal relationship is the cause of the people's burdens and their submission to them. Most of Europe suffers under this form of regime. A second type operates by "corrupt influence." It substitutes the "motive of private interest" for public duty by dispensing either bounties to its supporters or bribes to its enemies. It enlists an army of partisans whose voices, pens, and intrigues are combined to support "the terror of the sword" so as to maintain the rule of the few despite the apparent liberty of the many. Americans will be happy if they do not mimic the expensive pageantry of its form and the "venal spirit of its administration." The third type operates by deriving its energy from the will of society and directs its policies to the latter's interest and understanding. The "republican governments of America" are of this sort. May their reputation be enhanced by every possible improvement in their theory which experience teaches, Madison hoped, and may they be perpetuated by a "system of administration corresponding with the purity of the theory" by which they ought to be maintained.[42]

The essay, "British Government," roughly followed Hume's argument that constitutional balances do not necessarily maintain the real distribution of power, if the energy of government is derived from avarice as well as ambition. The "boasted equilibrium" of the British system, if it is real, Madison said, depends on public opinion rather than the "forms" by which the various powers are distributed. If the nation favored an absolute monarchy, then the representatives would surrender their power of self–government. If opinion favored a republic, then the monarch could not resist such a change. If public opinion were indifferent or silent, then the ambition of the members of the House of Commons could move them to strip away the monarch's prerogatives. If they were moved by avarice, they would sell the legislative powers to the monarch. If the civil list were made annual instead of for life, the monarch's rule would be merely nominal unless maintained by "corruption" and public opinion favoring it. Those who believe that the form in which powers are distributed and balanced in the British system preserve it, forget all the changes that have taken place before 1688. If the constitution which has prevailed since that year is self–balanced, then all of its predecessors were not. In fact, all of these balances of power have been maintained over time and under varying circumstances by public opinion. Changes in the real distribution of power can occur regardless of constitutional forms, if they are maintained with the approval of public opinion or are allowed to happen because of either the indifference of public opinion or its silence due to a muzzled press.[43]

To these pointed lessons teaching about the tendency of political systems to be changed without *apparent* reasons, Madison added other warnings against perpetual debts, which encourage corruption within governments; the "moneyed" interest, which is the "most active and insinuating" of all in society; and all who seek to rule through the "tenor of military force..." All such ideas and actions reveal a desire on the part of some persons to *approximate* the American government to a hereditary form.[44] In other essays he pleaded the case for republics in general and the American federal variety in particular. If both the republican and federal features of the American system are to be maintained, the people who were the authors of the Constitution must be its guardians as well. In "Governments" he argued that a monarchy is subject to two dangers: the ruler cannot know all that should be known about affairs within the realm, and a bad one cannot be opposed by combinations formed to prevent oppression. Both of these evils increase in proportion to the size of the monarch's domains. They prove, contrary to common practice, that this form of regime is unfit for a "great state." Small ones are commonly aristocracies because they are needed to concentrate public force against external danger. A "representative Republic" improves on both of these types. It provides for the choice of wise rulers instead of the chance that they may be produced by heredity. A federal republic attains the military force of a monarchy, but avoids its twin evils. In order to secure the advantages of a federal, representative republic, every citizen must be a "sentinel" guarding the people's rights and the authority of both the federal and state governments.[45]

In "Charters" he argued in various ways that the "stability" of governments and the "security" of individual rights depend on the support of enlightened and committed public opinion. He grandiloquently reminded readers that only in America are constitutions solemn and authentic proclamations of the people's will, the only "earthly source of authority..." Therefore, Americans have unique motives for supporting the "energy of their constitutional charters." They should demonstrate a "more than common reverence for the authority which is to preserve order through the whole." As "republicans" they ought to oppose all "anti-republican" efforts to change constitutions which are political "scriptures" to be guarded with both enlightenment and "holy zeal..."[46] In "Government of the United States" this appeal to maintain the constituent authority as the only source of legitimate constitutional change was repeated. All persons who love their country and its republicanism were enjoined to maintain its complicated form of divided powers because the alternative is the "high road to monarchy." The people must be both authors and guardians of their constitutions.[47]

The extremely broad interpretation of Congress' powers justifying the Bank bill and its delegation of significant rule-making powers to the executive jeopardized federalism, too. Both of the distinguishing traits of the new system were already proving to be hard to maintain. Much of the problem, Madison admitted, arose from try ing to describe both grants and limitations on power in a constitution. It is difficult enough to separate by proper definitions the three kinds of power, which actually differ very little in nature. It is even more taxing to distinguish between different categories of legislative power and assign them to different governments. There is equal vexation in "maintaining the division." Nevertheless, the effort must be made. If it is not, then Congress will be unable to legislate in such a way as to accommodate the variety of local circumstances cared for by the state legislatures. Instead, it will delegate broad rule-making power to the executive. This change will intensify political passions in presidential elections. Furthermore, the "same space of country which would produce an undue growth of executive power would prevent that control on the legislative body...[which is] essential to the faithful discharge of its public trust." Given the size and social diversity of a population extended over a large territory, it is likely that the views of many interests would not be conveyed effectively to the government. Neither could they restrain it. The ultimate result will be a government left to that "*self directed course* which....is the natural propensity of every government."[48]

THE PAPERS OF HELVIDIUS

In 1793 Madison resumed his education of Americans in the spirit of the Constitution in order to maintain its republican character. He was disturbed in private by language in President Washington's proclamation of 22 April 1793, saying that the United States was impartial toward Britain and France as belligerents engaged in war. The text appeared to Madison to mean that the president had assumed "a prerogative not clearly found in the Constitution," one appearing to copy a "Monarchical model..." If it were made out that Washington embraced any such claim, then it would become an incurably bad precedent for future use.[49] His concern was heightened when newspapers began to comment on the "anglified complexion" of Washington's apparent claim of power which violated the "form and spirit of the Constitution..."[50]   Madison's anxiety turned to anger and action, when Hamilton, writing as Pacificus, confirmed Madison's sensitive and perceptive reading of the President's text. With some prodding from Jefferson, Madison responded under the name of Helvidius with five essays published between 24 August and 18 September 1793.

The papers of Pacificus, Madison charged, revealed a hatred of our republican government and, under the color of vindicating the President's proclamation, advanced doctrines which strike at the very "vitals" of our Constitution.[51] In essence, Hamilton contended that the powers of making war and peace are executive in nature and, as such, are vested in the president save for grants to Congress to be construed strictly as exceptions to what is otherwise executive power. Therefore, the executive is the organ of relations with foreign nations; it interprets and expounds the obligations of the United States which are incurred in treaties or by the law of nations, whether concerning war or other matters; and it pronounces the state of affairs arising from the executive's understanding of our obligations under prevailing circumstances. If there is any support for this construction, Madison said, it must be found in the treatises of writers who are considered authorities on public law, in the nature and operations of these two powers, or in the text of the Constitution.

The first possible source of instruction is of little use because our Constitution is the best guide and, also, because a proper understanding of the separation of powers cannot be found in the most commonly accepted jurists' works. They wrote with their eyes "too much on monarchical governments" where all powers are confused with royal sovereignty. Writers such as Locke and Montesquieu are among the authors who fail to qualify as authoritative voices. Their views are both "warped" by their affinity for the British government to which one owed allegiance and for which the other professed an admiration bordering on "idolatry." Locke, whose royalism biased his philosophic reason, might have had a much clearer conception of the executive powers, if he had not lived under a monarchy or had written by "the lamp which truth now presents to lawgivers." Montesquieu's distinction comes from the importance he attached to separating the three powers of government and the reasons for doing so, but not from his definitions and enumerations of the specific elements of each kind of power.[52]

The second possible source of support for Pacificus' argument, the nature and operation of the power to make war and treaties, is equally unavailing. The function of the executive is to execute the laws, whereas that of the legislature is to make them. Every act which is "properly executive must presuppose the existence of laws to be executed." A treaty is a law to be executed like all others by the president. To argue that the power of making treaties, that is, laws, belongs "naturally" to the department which executes them, is to claim that the executive branch possesses legislative power. In theory this argument is absurd; in practice it is "tyranny." The power to declare war is subject to the same reasoning. A declaration that war is to exist in legal contemplation is not an act executing a law. It is, on the contrary, "one of the most deliberative acts that can be performed," and it has the effect of repealing statutes which operate in a condition of peace, insofar as they are inconsistent with a state of war. The further effect of a declaration of war is that it enacts rules for the conduct of a society and its foreign enemy, and they are to be carried out by the executive. The conclusion of peace annuls all laws which are unique to a state of war and revives other laws which have been in suspension during hostilities. The conclusion is that, while the executive is a "convenient organ of preliminary communication" between this nation and others in matters concerning these two powers, and is the proper agent for executing the final determinations of "the competent authority," the executive does not give *validity* to these determinations. Even if these powers are not "purely legislative," they are more so than not under our Constitution. Therefore, the "rule of interpreting exceptions strictly," diminishes rather than enlarges the executive's claims to exercise these powers at its discretion.[53]

The third possible source of support for the argument contended against is the text of the Constitution. It cannot be pretended that the doctrine is derived from any direct and explicit provision of the Constitution. The power of declaring war is expressly vested in Congress along with all other legislative powers given. The document treats this particular power as a legislative one without any qualification whatsoever. The power to make treaties is vested jointly in the Senate and the President. The former is a branch of the legislature. This arrangement does not in itself justify the inference that this power is not executive in nature because the Senate is joined with the President in exercising the power to appoint to offices. There are other circumstances, however, which do justify the inference that the

Constitution treats the treaty-making power as being materially different from pure executive power and as being more legislative than executive in nature. One of these circumstances is the constitutional provision for signifying the Senate's consent to a treaty. It requires a vote of two-thirds of the members because this provision is a substitute for, or even a compensation to, the House of Representatives, which is excluded from the exercise of this power because it cannot under certain circumstances serve "conveniently as a party to the transaction." The conclusive circumstance, however, is that once ratified, a treaty has the force and effect of law; it is a rule to guide the courts in controversies between private persons as much as any other law; and, finally, treaties are expressly declared to be the supreme law of the land.

Neither does Pacificus's doctrine receive support from constitutional provisions vesting certain powers in the president alone. He is made commander in chief of the army and navy and, of the militia when called into federal service. This power is in no way analogous to that of *declaring* war. On the contrary, it provides a striking demonstration of the incompatibility of vesting the powers of making war and directing its operations in the same branch of government. The reason is that those who are to conduct the operations of war cannot "in the nature of things" be safe judges of whether a war ought to be started, continued, or stopped. They are barred from performing this function by a "great principle of free government"; namely, that the power of enacting laws is separated from that of executing them. Such specific powers as requiring the opinion in writing of the principal executive officers, to fill vacant offices during a recess of the Senate, to take care that the laws be faithfully executed-these and the power to remove executive officers constitute "the essence of the executive authority."[54]

These three sources lend no color to Pacificus' doctrines. What source does so? The answer is that it has been borrowed from the "royal prerogatives of the British government," which are classified as executive powers by British commentators. It is not supported, however, in the doctrine expounded by Pacificus in his explanatory commentary in *The Federalist*. There he said that, although several writers on this subject classify the power of making treaties as an executive one, this practice is evidently arbitrary. The power to make treaties is neither strictly legislative nor executive. So, this commentary, too, supports the conclusion that the power to make treaties is plainly not executive alone.[55]

Next, it is necessary to dispose of the argument that the executive has the authority to judge what is the proper exercise of its own functions despite the grant of power to Congress to determine whether or not this nation shall be at war as a matter of law. Even applying the rule of strictly construing the express grants to Congress concerning war and peace, Pacificus admits that the power to judge these questions is given to the legislative branch. The inescapable inference is that the executive is excluded from the exercise of this power. The difficulty in Pacificus's argument arises from the phrase "'in the execution of its [the executive's] functions.'" The Constitution has made this function legislative. Pacificus's escape from this situation consists in arguing that there is concurrent authority to judge the obligation to go to war. This defense must be the ultimate one, if the claim of executive discretion is to be sustained. It is an "obvious and essential truth of political science," however, that no function can belong to two different departments and be exercised by either one or both of them. Such an arrangement would be as awkward in practice as it is absurd in theory. The right to judge is the right to judge differently so that we could have the spectacle for other nations to behold of the executive issuing a proclamation declaring that this nation is at war to be followed by a legislative declaration that we are not.[56]

Pacificus supported this doctrine, nevertheless, on the ingenious ground that Congress has the authority to make war, but the executive has the duty to preserve peace by refusing to give a cause of war to foreign powers until war is declared. In the performance of this duty, it is contended, the executive has the authority to judge the nature and extent of this nation's obligations arising under treaties to which it is signatory. This power includes the lesser one of determining that its obligations to any other nation are, or are not, consistent with a state of neutrality toward belligerents. In addition, the province and duty of the executive are to enforce not only our municipal laws, but also, the laws of nations relative to this subject.

The implication of this argument is that it is the executive's duty to determine whether or not peace shall be maintained in view of the obligations assumed in existing treaties. Suppose the executive should decide that neutrality is inconsistent with our obligations assumed through treaties. This branch is then left to conclude whether war is "obligatory, absolute and imperative; and the duty to preserve peace, subordinate and conditional." Furthermore, merely substituting the word *neutrality* for the word *peace* does not change the principle in the least. The former word refers only to the position of one nation relative to others which are at war. It has no reference to the existence or nonexistence of treaties or alliances between the nations at war and those at peace. The existence of obligations which may have been undertaken in treaties can take effect only by a declaration of war by the legislative branch of our government. Without this action the actual state of the nation relative to others cannot be changed by the executive any more than it can by the judicial branch. Suppose, further, that an obligation incurred by treaty to join in a war is inconsistent with neutrality (for example, the American treaty of alliance with France of 6 February 1778). What laws are to be enforced in the interval between the executive's determination of the issue and a congressional declaration--shall they be the laws of war? If so, then affairs are in the same state as they would be without the existence of any obligation arising from a treaty. The proper conclusion is that the executive's duty to preserve external peace no more includes the authority to suspend the force of external laws than that branch's duty of maintaining internal peace authorizes suspension of municipal laws. The executive's discretion in this matter is exhausted by convening the legislative branch and giving it information, whenever circumstances require.[57]

Pacificus touched additionally on the degree of discretionary power vested in the executive to interpret and enforce treaties. He claimed that the duty of judging and interpreting the obligations of treaties necessarily entails the power to judge whether or not a situation gives the United States a cause for war. The authority to interpret is essential to the executive as long as it does not interfere with the authority of the legislative branch, since no obligation of law exists without prior creation by the latter. All laws are to be enforced regardless of the disposition of the executive toward any of them. Pacificus tried to deduce power, also, from the president's duty to receive ambassadors. The power to receive them, it is claimed, includes the power to refuse to receive one from a new government which has come to power through a revolution. From this alleged power, it is deduced that the President may refuse to enforce a pre-existing treaty with the nation involved. On the contrary, this clause of the Constitution was intended to provide only the mode in which this traditional form of communication among governments should be carried out. The clause named the department to which other governments should direct their envoys. The president's power is only to authenticate their credentials and to admit them to the privileges of envoys as sanctioned by the law of nations. This ceremonial duty cannot properly be magnified into a grant of executive prerogative as the sixty-ninth *Federalist* makes clear. The authenticity of an envoy's credentials is a matter to be determined exclusively by the nation over whom a government rules. This question is one of fact. Therefore, the constitutional duty to receive an ambassador is not the power to reject the legitimacy of the government appointing him to this office.

Certainly, there are some extraordinary instances in which it may be necessary to treat a government as an "illegitimate despotism" because it violates the "general principles of liberty, the essential rights of the people, or the overruling sentiments of humanity..." The executive is not the organ of the American national will for doing so, however. Its authority does not extend to the question whether a government is to be recognized or not, and neither does it include the power to refuse to give effect to a treaty with a preexisting government which an American president is disposed to disapprove of. If any principle ought not to be questioned in the United States, it is that every nation has a right to abolish an old government and to substitute a new one for it. This doctrine provides the "only lawful tenure by which the United States hold their existence as a nation." Included in the right of self-government is the principle that governments are the organs of the national will.[58]

A third rule follows from these last two, according to two writers on the law of nations, Vattel and Burlamaqui. A change in governments does not terminate the obligations assumed by its predecessors. For this reason, the executive of this government has no authority to suspend or hinder the operation of a treaty, when such a change has occurred. This conclusion is reinforced further by observing that *private* rights guaranteed by a treaty are subject to judicial cognizance no less than to executive agency. The courts are an independent branch obligated to enforce the laws, and they might not on a particular occasion follow the executive's interpretation of rights guaranteed by treaty. So, once again, there could be the contradictory spectacle of one branch of the American government holding a treaty to be in force and another one ruling to the contrary.   If Pacificus's doctrine of concurrent powers were to be sustained, then it would be necessary to show what is logically contradictory; namely, that the legislative branch is both free to pursue its own judgment with regard to matters of war, peace, and the obligation of treaties and constitutionally bound by the independent judgment of the executive.[59]

The fundamental doctrine of our Constitution is that the power of declaring war, including the power to judge whether or not there are causes for it, is vested *"fully* and *exclusively"* in Congress.   The president has no power in this matter except to convene and inform the legislative branch, whenever this question seems to call for a decision. No part of the Constitution is more prudent than this one which gives the ultimate authority to decide this question to the legislature. If it did not do so, it would mix "heterogeneous" powers.   In addition, the "trust and the temptation would be too much for one man" of the sort who may be expected to hold office in the "ordinary successions" to the presidency likely to occur in the future. We cannot rest assured that nature will always provide a genius for this office. The reason is that war is the "true nurse of executive aggrandizement." It requires the creation of physical force and gives the executive the direction of it. *War unlocks the public treasury* and it is *the executive* which *disburses its bounties.*   The honors and emoluments of office are multiplied and it is the executive which controls and distributes this patronage. This branch reaps the "laurels" of war. "The strongest passions and most dangerous weaknesses of the human breast; ambition, avarice, vanity, the honorable or venial love of fame, all are in conspiracy against the desire and duty of peace."[60]

It is one of the most "sacred" duties of a free people, therefore, to note the first sign of doctrines which encourage the normal inclination of the executive to go to war because personal gratification of the love of fame depends so distinctly on it. In particular, a free people will be prudent, also, if they do not forget the danger involved, when advocates of the "prerogative of war can sheathe it in a symbol of peace."[61]

There is equal prudence in the constitutional provisions which deny to the president the exclusive power to make peace. Such a grant would strain the wisdom, and it might tempt the "virtue" of a single person, as the author of *The Federalist* pointed out in the seventy–fifth paper. A President of limited wealth and term of office might be tempted to sacrifice duty to personal interest. An avaricious person might be tempted by foreign sources of wealth; an ambitious one might be tempted to aggrandize his power with foreign aid.[62]   Given the importance of "personal interest" in motivating persons who hold public office, it is obvious that every addition to the powers under the "*sole* agency and influence" of the president is dangerous when the decisions involve war and peace. The trust is equivalent in both cases. The power to say that war ought not to continue is not greater than the power to say that it ought to begin. Every danger of "error, or corruption" involved in one of these decisions is equally incident to the other one. For this reason the

Constitution has treated both kinds of decisions as equally unsafe in the hands of the executive alone.[63]

One final point deserves reiteration according to Madison. The phraseology used by Pacificus is as novel as his doctrines in regard to the Constitution. The source of the former may enlighten our understanding of the latter. "I allude particularly to his application of the term *government* to the executive authority alone." The Proclamation of 22 April 1793 is said to be a manifestation of the "'sense of the *government*.'" Indeed, this term is used in this same sense at several other points in these papers. This singular style shows either a greater familiarity with that used by a foreign government, or a disposition to propagate this term to make it familiar in support of the doctrine advanced. This criticism may appear to be trivial, but its tendency is not. The phrase, *the government*, undoubtedly means in the United States the entire three branches and not the executive alone, either exclusively or "*pre*–eminently; as it may do in a monarchy, where the splendor of prerogative eclipses, and the machinery of influence directs, every other part of the government." The words *executive* or *president* can be used, as they have been hitherto, instead of the objectionable new "dialect..." Pacificus's obvious fondness for the British phrase in opposition to our common usage justifies this notice.[64]

Twenty–five years later Madison looked back upon his Helvidius essays with a sense of satisfaction. In 1818, a year after he left the presidency, he told Jacob Gideon that, if he were to publish a new edition of *The Federalist*, including the the essays of Pacificus and Helvidius, he (Madison) would correct some errors of transcription before a republication, but he would not indulge in retrospective reasoning in order to improve his position. He could find no ground for disavowing the "Constitutional doctrine espoused, or the general scope of reasoning used in support of it."[65]

COMMENTS AND A COROLLARY TO HELVIDIUS

The arguments in the Helvidius papers invite three general observations. The first one concerns their fidelity to the existing record, slim though it be, of the debates at the Constitutional Convention. The second noteworthy matter is Madison's rejection of European treatises on public law and theory as authoritative expositions of the Constitution. The third is Madison's charge that the arguments in Hamilton's *Pacificus* reveal a desire to transform the American constitutional relationship between president and Congress into an analog of the British system.

When the constitutional interpretations in the Helvidius essays are compared with the record of the two state plans, committee reports, motions, debates, and votes, it is evident that Madison faithfully represented the outcome of the Convention's deliberations. At no time was there any dissent (Hamilton always excepted) from the belief that the prerogatives of the British executive provided no model for the Framers to imitate. It was equally without dissent decided that Congress alone has the power to declare the legal existence of war. It was agreed with apparent unanimity that the president should have an unfettered discretion to repel sudden attacks, but whether on our territory only or on military forces abroad as well, cannot be determined. Until two weeks before the end of the Convention, it appears to have been assumed that the Senate, like the old Congress, would exclusively possess and exercise the vital powers over foreign policy. The addition of the president as an "agent" in the exercise of the powers shared with the Senate certainly altered the equation of power to a significant degree. There is no evidence, however, supporting Hamilton's claim that the Framers empowered the president alone to determine the legal obligations of this government or of individuals arising out of treaties or the law of nations governing war and peace. Neither is there any evident intention to authorize the president to validate his own actions simply because he possesses the executive power. It is equally apparent, on the other hand, that the Framers chose to make the president the sole agent through whom communications must pass between the government of the United States and that of any other sovereign nation.

Madison's rejection of foreign treatises in general and those of Locke and Montesquieu in particular as authoritative guides to American constitutional interpretation is extremely pointed because these Locke and Montequieu assumed that the British system provided a universal model of the separation of powers to be imitated. On the contrary, Madison insisted, only the literal text gives any interpretive guidance.

Locke had argued that there is a federative power in addition to the legislative and executive powers. The first of these is "natural" to every commonwealth because it is analogous to the power of every individual in an original state of nature to execute the law of nature in his own interest. Every commonwealth bears this same relationship to all nations external to itself and, therefore, it must possess the powers of "war and peace" as well as all others needed to regulate its relations with both private "persons and communities..." This federative power is "always almost united" with the executive power which must be in a position to function at all times. The federative power is in the hands of the executive because the legislature is confined to determining how the "force" of the community shall be used. The subject of foreign relations is such, however, that it cannot be regulated readily by laws made in advance. The legislature is subject to all the infirmities which justify the prerogative; therefore, the exercise of the federative power must be left to the prudence of those persons in whom the public has placed it. If the federative and executive powers were not placed in the same hands, then the public force would be under the direction of multiple hands, with the likely result of disorder or ruin for the commonwealth on some occasion.[66]

As Madison said by way of implicit commentary on Locke's dictum, to argue that the power of making war and peace as well as that of regulating all other transactions with foreign nations belongs naturally to the department charged by our Constitution with the faithful execution of the laws, is to say that the executive branch possesses the legislative power of determining what the good of the community is. Every act which is properly executive, he said, presupposes the existence of laws to be enforced. Therefore, any attempt to incorporate Locke's conception of the federative power constructively into the executive power named in the Constitution would be a fabricated codicil to the original document in Madison's opinion.

He rejected Montesquieu's *Spirit of the Laws* as an authoritative source of interpretations of the Constitution for at least two obvious reasons. Although Montesquieu formulated a perfectly symmetrical separation of powers according to functions in one part of this treatise, he actually derived this theory from the British constitution which he praised partly because the government derived its energy from the executive's vast powers to reward its parliamentary followers with lucrative and honorable offices. These were sought passionately by those who wished to benefit from them. This struggle divided the people into parties contending for the executive's boons with such feverish determination that it gave health to the body politic. If it failed to gratify these passions, the state would be left in the weakened condition of a sick man, Montesquieu contended. He had failed to point out, however, that the government also enlisted writers and other sycophants to support military power so as to maintain the rule of the few despite the apparent liberty of the many. The result of this system of executive direction of the entire government, once corrupt influence was combined with the ancient prerogative in order to sustain the latter, was a constitutional system incompatible with republican government, according to Madison: rule by a minority consisting of the persons who possess the great wealth of the community allied with others who possess the skills and habits of military life. It cannot be emphasized too strongly that in rejecting the guidance of Montesquieu, the great oracle on the separation of powers, Madison was dismissing any contention that this general theory determines the allocation of functions between the president and the houses of Congress concerning foreign relations. It is the text of the Constitution, alone, which is authoritative, he insisted.

It is noteworthy, also, that there is no record of an appeal to the authority of either Locke or Montesquieu by a single one of the Framers when they discussed the distribution of power over foreign relations between the president and the branches of Congress. In short, Madison stood on firm ground with the assertion in Helvidius that European theorists, all of whom wrote in support of monarchy, provided no guidance in determining the intentions of the Framers or the meaning of the Constitution. Madison was in an equally defensible position in arguing *against* the notion that there is an abstract standard to which to appeal in determining whether the executive and legislative powers have been properly separated in the performance of various governing functions.

Madison's challenge to Hamilton for using the phrase, *the government*, to refer to the executive branch alone may strike some people as a semantic quibble, but Madison thought not and with good reason. The choice of words often has a powerful influence in shaping the meaning of ideas they are used to express. Neither can he be properly charged with obfuscation. He defined monarchy as he understood Hamilton did: a form of government in which the manipulative force of influence and the royal prerogative are used to direct the entire government in its domestic and foreign acts. Madison did not have to guess that Hamilton considered the British model to be the only good one worthy of imitation. He knew it. Madison's definition of monarchy on this occasion coupled with all that was said by delegates to the Constitutional Convention should make it clear that Hamilton, too, had in mind the British model and no other. Both he and Madison undoubtedly were aware of David Hume's definition of monarchy, and Hamilton wished to imitate it in America. Monarchy, Hume had said, is a system of rule in which those who control the supreme authority of government have the capacity to distribute the many honors and advantages which excite the "ambition and avarice of mankind." In a monarchy, the persons eager to gratify these two great political passions look "upwards to court the good graces and favor of the great." In republics candidates for official recognition of their merits must look downward to the people who grant this boon through elections.[67] At the Philadelphia Convention Hamilton said explicitly that the term *monarch* did not necessarily denote a hereditary form. In defending his proposal for a chief executive with life tenure in order to approximate the British model, "the only good one on this subject," he said: "*Monarch* is an indefinite term. It marks not either the degree or the duration of power." If listeners were to charge that he wanted a monarchy because he proposed life tenure, then he would reply that the Convention had already voted to create an "*elective monarch*" for a fixed term.[68] Writing as Pacificus, however, Hamilton revealed to discerning readers that the British model provided the meaning of the term without regard to the means by which the chief executive was chosen. If this interpretation of the Constitution were permitted to stand, governmental energy derived from this source and human nature would provide the executive with both the legal and practical means of not only controlling the entire machinery of government, but also creating the monied and military interests made dependent for their existence and expansion on a policy of war, or threats of it, under exclusive presidential control. Writing as Helvidius it was Madison's task to place the conflict in this light and thereby to warn Americans of the threat such a system poses for accountability to the electorate and the stability of the political and social system.

For the next five years, Madison continued to believe that the Federalists who favored close ties with Great Britain and imitation of its model of government wished to expand a standing army to be used both at home and abroad and refused to vote the taxes needed to retire the public debt in order to perpetuate the financial interest dependent upon it. Indeed, he complained incessantly to Jefferson in 1793 and 1794 about congressional opponents whom he decried on the ground that they sought to aggrandize military power and to use against their enemies both at home to enforce the laws and in Europe to wage war.[69] Ultimately these fears drove him to formulate a little-known corollary to the doctrine expounded in the Helvidius papers. First, however, he resumed his role of public tutor on 20 April 1795, when he published "Political Observations."[70] In this essay he warned against the dangers following from war which contains in itself certain inherent evils and nourishes others. The latter include armies, public debts, the domination of the few over the many, the expansion of executive power and influence, an exacerbation of social inequality, and a general degeneration of morals and manners. All of these calamities are "dangerous to a republican constitution."[71] Aside from these inevitable, even if unintended effects of war, there had been deliberate efforts to "alter the fabric of the Constitution" by delegating to the president the legislative powers of raising and calling into action a standing army of a size to be determined at his discretion. A legislative grant of this power cannot be justified on any grounds, not even out of confidence in the incumbent. The American people are too intelligent to be unable to distinguish between the "respect due to the man and the functions belonging to the office." In making this distinction they will look beyond the present moment to a time when other persons (that is, other than George Washington) will hold the office. Therefore, they will understand the significance of this precedent which will descend to his successors, and they ought to oppose it. It is a counsel of futility to sustain this precedent by arguing that it is too difficult to draw the line between different kinds of power. Of course there are difficulties in drawing exact boundaries between legislative and executive powers. It is equally true that "precedents may be found where the line of separation" has already been insufficiently observed by Congress. This admission does not prove, however, that the line of separation ought to be considered only imaginary so that the constitutional distribution loses its effect. The existence of this problem proves only the importance of establishing precedents with much deliberation and demonstrates how much caution ought to be employed in deducing conclusions from them subsequently to the point where they become "encroachments."[72]

His continuing fear that executive power might be aggrandized further with a consequent tendency to change the constitutional system prompted him to issue another warning in 1796. The American government ought to avoid all imitations of a well-known model in which certain parts possess "independent and hereditary prerogatives," and the whole system depends for its energy on its members having "a personal interest in the public stations" which they hold.[73]

This warning became particularly relevant to Madison as he left public service on 4 March 1797, the date on which John Adams became president. The former remained convinced that Adams was unsuited by temperament and constitutional doctrines to serve as a truly republican chief executive. Adams had openly agreed with Hume's defense of the British model of executive control of the legislative branches, especially with his assertion that patriotism is a "pernicious" foundation for any system of government because there are never enough talented and virtuous patriots to fill all of the necessary offices. Madison thought that Adams was still guided by the "maxims" of the British constitution and his words and actions were part of a "progressive apostacy [sic]" from American revolutionary principles since 1789.[74] Furthermore, the Federalists seemed determined to imitate the British model system by engaging in a war, in this instance with France, with the intention of creating a perpetual "alienation of the two countries [fostered] by the secret enemies of both." The immediate consequences would be bad enough, but the "permanent ones to the commerical and other great interests of this country form a long and melancholy catalogue."[75]

Throughout the next year Madison poured out to Jefferson and Monroe his conviction that Adams wished to go to war with Spain as well as France. Finally, he concluded that Adams' secret diplomacy was intended to achieve this objective in a way which threatened to erode the constitutional distributions of powers Madison had defended as Helvidius. In particular, Madison was thoroughly convinced that Adams was manipulating public opinion through a selective flow of foreign correspondence, conciliatory speeches toward France in public and secret patronage to a press which vilified France. What was needed, Madison told Jefferson, was a corollary to the doctrine he advocated as Helvidius. There should be an effort mounted in Congress to force a full disclosure of the diplomatic papers in the president's possession. Such a move would be proper under three circumstances: first, when nothing short of an open declaration of the president's peaceful intentions will quiet the fears of the "constituent body," or eliminate the uncertainty which subjects one part (of the government) to the "speculating arts of another." Second, a call for such reassurances may be a "necessary antidote to the hostile measures or language of the Executive Department." If the president expresses sentiments favoring war, and his views are susceptible of a direct answer when sentiments in Congress oppose war, it cannot be doubted that a president ought to express his counter–sentiments unless, of course, it is a special message which does not permit a like expression of legislative sentiments except by "an abstract vote" (because war is a fact). Finally, a president may properly be forced to reveal his objectives clearly, when "measures or appearances" may "mislead another nation" and cause it to distrust us. In our government "where the question of war lies with Congress, a satisfactory explanation cannot issue from any other Department." This constitutional rule stands in contrast with the one prevailing in governments in which the power of deciding to go to war is an "Executive prerogative." Among such nations it is not unusual for explanations of the national objectives of diplomacy to be given either on demand from foreign governments or in order to prevent them from being improperly suspicious. Should a demand of this sort ever be made on our government, the answer "must proceed, if thro' an executive functionary, from the [constitutional source of the] war prerogative, that is from Congress." As long as it is proper for a foreign government to demand a statement of intentions from the president, one may be made "with equal propriety" by Congress to compel the president to declare his intentions concerning the maintenance of peace or the initiation of war.[76]

This inference that Congress may compel a secretive president to disclose whether his communications with foreign governments reveal an intention to start war or to maintain peace appears to rest on any one, or a combination, of at least three assumptions. The first assumption, one very persistent in Madison's writings, is the belief that the motives which activate the behavior of the members of the legislative and executive branches, respectively, toward war and peace are different and, therefore, have differing institutional effects. A second assumption is that the two branches are under the control of opposing parties which differ over questions of policy, of principle, or both, or simply out of the normal contention to control the machinery of government. A third assumption is that some interests or coalitions of them–even within the executive branch–are better served than others by presidential or congressional control, respectively, over questions of war and peace. Madison's claim of congressional power to force a president to declare his intentions or the tenor of his negotiations with a potential enemy power is clearly a doctrine tailored to serve a congressional majority in opposition to the president's desired policy. It does not serve as well, however, as the normal operational rule requiring the nation to speak to others with one authoritative voice after all of our diverse domestic interests have been consulted and reconciled in support of a national position. This ideal presupposes that a constitutional sharing of roles requires adherence to the rule of law in the conduct of foreign no less than domestic affairs.

It is useful to recall Madison's explanation given in 1788 (see p. 48 above) that this sharing of powers was deliberately created by Framers guided by prudence, not pure political theory and not by imitation of the British model. They expected the two branches to have distinct and independent wills because of the different modes of their election as well as the variety of interests which would be reflected in their varied electoral processes and tenures of office. Even the House of Representatives was expected to have considerable influence on foreign policy, short of declaring war, because of its power over appropriations and the need for the House to give efficacy to treaties by legislation. With brilliant insight Madison anticipated the full effects on foreign policy of combining a complex structure of government with the great diversity of interests and opinions found in the American political system (see pp. 6–7 above). This combination makes it unlikely that any government can *plan*, much less *execute*, an aggressive foreign policy without widespread support. Thus, the general causes which operate to moderate the domestic policies of the government serve with equal force to restrain the character of its relations with other nations.

Clearly, Madison understood that the task of creating and maintaining an institutional rather than a charismatic presidency was a labor of Sisyphus doomed to eternal toil without enduring success. Nothing was more difficult to execute than the task of supporting the president in the face of centrifugal forces within America without making the office so strong that the incumbent can aggrandize power endlessly through foreign adventures gratifying the love of fame for a few and a love of wealth for many. It was difficult to create republican institutions likely to prevent the inevitable tendency of governments to assume self–directed courses of action using a series of well–timed and tendentious measures shrewdly chosen to increase power at the expense of individual liberty. This tendency would surely be accelerated, Madison believed, by following the public policies which had made imperial Britain into the new Rome of the eighteenth century. All the attendant redistributions in power among interests in society and within the government would then be masked by the appearance of an unchanged Constitution.[77]

NOTES

1. *PJM*, 12:155.
2. Ibid., 257.
3. *The Federalist*, 431 (No. 66).
4. Ibid., 496–97 (No. 77).
5. Ibid., 498 (No. 77).
6. *PJM*, 12:232.
7. See Edward S. Corwin, *The President: Office and Powers,* 3d ed. (New York: New York University Press, 1957), 16–17.
8. Leonard D. White, *The Federalists* (New York: The Free Press, 1948), 13, 28, ignores Hamilton's essays in *The Federalist*.
9. *PJM*, 12:172–73.
10. Ibid., 170–71, 233, 245.
11. Ibid., 170–71, 244, 252–253
12. Ibid., 174, 226–27, 236–37.
13. Ibid., 256, 291.
14. Ibid., 190 (31 May 1789) italics in the original.
15. Ibid., 252, 271, 281–82, 291, 295.
16. Ibid., pp. 233–36 passim.
17. *The Federalist*, 300–3 passim (No. 45) For Hamilton's parallel argument see ibid., 101–3 (17).
18. *PJM*, 11:86–87, 97, 125, 132–33.
19. Ibid. 9:350; *The Federalist*, 284 (No. 43).
20. Farrand, *Records* 1:284–87 passim, 289.
21. *PJM.*, 12:382–85, 469, emphasis in the original.
22. Ibid., 385–87, passim.
23. Ibid., 13:24–25, italics in the original. Madison appears to have used the language of David Hume who spoke of the need to study politics with "a philosophical eye..." in *Essays*, 1:33.
24. *PJM*, 13:95.
25. Ibid., 14:43.
26. Ibid., 69
27. *Ibid*, 13:386–87.
28. Ibid., 164, 398, 400, emphasis added. See Joseph Charles, *The Origins of the American Party System* (New York: Harper and Row, 1956), 12–46 and especially 28.
29. *PJM*, 14:274.
30. Ibid., 470.
31. Farrand, *Records*, 2:125–26.
32. *PJM*, 14:325, 330, 332. A narrower amendment to apply only to the moneyed interest (holders of public securities) was proposed and defeated in the Senate in 1794 under the leadership of John Taylor, Madison's ally at this time; Henry H. Simms, *Life of John Taylor* (Richmond, Va.: The William Byrd Press, 1932), 50–52.
33. *PJM*, 14:170, emphasis in the original. See *The Federalist*, 328–29 (No. 49) and 410 (No. 63).
34. *PJM*, 14:15, 18 n. 1, 19, 20, n. 4, 22–23.
35. *PJM*, 14:209 n.1 (31 January 1792).
36. Ibid., 206–7.

37. Ibid. pp. 207–8, italics in the original
38. Adam Smith, *The Wealth of Nations*, The Modern Library (New York: Random House, 1937), 872, 878–79, 881, 885. In 1783 Madison recommended that Congress purchase this work for the library which Madison wanted established; *PJM*, 6:86. He first commented on Smith's Doctrines in 1785 in a letter to Jefferson; ibid., 8:266. Madison cited the authority of Smith's treatise in debates in the House on two occasions during 1790 and early 1791; ibid., 13:255, 373.
39. Immanual Kant, *Perpetual Peace*, preface by Nicholas Murray Butler (Westwood, Calif.: U.S. Library Association, 1932), 16–18, 24, 26–27 passim, emphasis added. I am grateful to Adam Watson for calling my attention to the close similarity between the arguments of Kant and Madison in their two essays on war and peace.
40. Forrest McDonald, *Alexander Hamilton: A Biography* (New York: W. W. Norton & Co., 1979), 159. Yet two pages thereafter the author says that Hamilton was *probably* influenced by the English example and that he had read the treatises of Montesquieu, Hume, and Adam Smith, all of whom "vigorously denounced the very idea of public debts...", ibid., 161. In Madison's notes made during this period there is no reference of any sort to the ideologists of the English Country party despite an effort to link Madison with them as if they were the sole critics of funding and legislative corruption. For this latter claim see also Banning, *The Jeffersonian Persuasion*, 178. Madison's references and citations are to his notes from the Convention, his letter to Jefferson on 24 October 1787, and "Federalist X et alia," as well as Plato, Aristotle, Thucydides, Montesquieu, Jonathan Swift, Edward Gibbon, and other historians now less famous; *PJM*, 14: 132, 157–168.
41. J. G. A. Pocock, *The Machiavellian Moment: Florentine Political Thought and the Atlantic Republican Tradition* (Princeton, NJ: Princeton University Press, 1975), 522.
42. *PJM*, 14:233–34.
43. Ibid., 201–2, (28 January 1792); see also 159. For the evidence that Montesquieu and Hume recognized that Britain was a new form of "civil polity" by the 1740s see Morgan, "Madison's Theory of Representation," 870–72.
44. *PJM*, 14:274–75, ("The Union"), 370–72 ("A Candid State of Parties"), and 426–27, ("Who are the Keepers of the People's Liberties?")–all passim. Their respective dates of publication were 31 March, 22 September, and 20 December 1792.
45. Ibid., 178–79 passim.
46. Ibid., 14:191–192, "Charters" 18 January 1792.
47. Ibid., 218.
48. Ibid., 138–39, italics in the original; ("Consolidation") 3 December 1791.
49. *PJM*, 15:39.
50. Ibid., 33.
51. Ibid., 66.
52. Ibid., 68.
53. Ibid., 68–69 passim.
54. Ibid., 69–72 passim.

55. Ibid., 72. Madison's citation to *The Federalist*, 486 (No. 75) left the score even with Hamilton.
56. *PJM*, 15:81–83 passim.
57. Ibid., 84–86 passim.
58. Ibid., 96–98 passim.
59. Ibid., 98–101 passim. Madison alluded on this occasion to Emmerich de Vattel, *The Law of Nations, or the Principles of the Law of Nature Applied to the Conduct and Affairs of Nations and Their Sovereigns* (Neuchatel, 1758). Madison invoked the authority of Vattel on many occasions, starting in 1780; see *PJM*, 1:128; 8:157; 15:13, 68, 98; *LJM*, 1:578, 634, 650–51; 2:229–391, especially 249 and 257; 3:346–48; *WJM*, 6:210–11, 296, 394–95.
60. *PJM*, 15:108, italics in the original quoted.
61. Ibid., 109.
62. Hamilton was the author of this paper.
63. Ibid., 109–10, italics in the original
64. Ibid., 114–15, italics in the original.
65. *LJM*, 3:60.
66. Locke, *Essay* chap. 12, pars. 143–48 passim.
67. Hume, *Essays*, 1:147; see also, 48, 103.
68. Farrand, *Records*, 1:290.
69. *PJM* 15:23, 269, 284, 299, 337–41, 379, 465, 468, 474.
70. Ibid., 511–33.
71. Ibid., 518–19.
72. Ibid., 520–522 passim.
73. *WJM*, 6:264.
74. *PJM* 9:249; *LJM* 2:117, 121, 127, 131; Adams, *Works*, 4:296, 358–59; 5:183; 6:81, 118, 187, 358.
75. *LJM* 2:107, 124, 125.
76. Ibid., 134–35.
77. Morgan, "Madison's Analysis," 618–24 passim.

Part II
RIGHTS

Chapter 5

Political Liberty

Madison's discussion of the right to vote and to form political parties on which the enjoyment of political liberty depend shows that these rights were essential elements in his conception of constitutional rights. He had very little opportunity to discuss either at the Convention of 1787. He did offer, however, a brief defense in *The Federalist* of the Framers' decision to leave the regulation of this right to the states with only a minimal restriction on them. It is widely believed that his remarks in the tenth essay showed him to be an opponent of political parties as were his leading contemporaries. His apparent conversion to parties a few years later is commonly treated as a puzzle. A few scholars have concluded, however, that he accurately predicted the rise of political parties that would secure moderate majority rule because of the social diversity of their respective members. The tenth essay has been interpreted, also, to prove that Madison predicted the rise of political interest groups.[1] In fact, he regarded both the right to vote and to form political parties to be essential to the enjoyment of political liberty.

THE RIGHT TO VOTE

In discussing a constitution for Kentucky in 1785 Madison said that it is a matter of "great delicacy and of critical importance" to fix the right to vote in a constitution at the time of its original framing.[2] The people living under it will enjoy what Montesquieu called political liberty only if there is a proper distribution of powers within the government. They will enjoy a tranquil state of mind, if they believe that the law–making power is vested in a legislature in which they are represented effectively.[3] Madison apparently believed that the attainment of republican liberty is a special case which is made difficult because of the differentiation of interests in a modern society. Conflict between interests occurs in all societies, but more so in densely populated ones. In particular, there is class conflict between the rich who are few and the poor who are many. It has always occurred and will continue to do so into an indefinite future. This being the case, neither class can enjoy political liberty if all persons are given the right to vote and to be represented equally in the legislature, or if one class is effectively denied these rights. In a republic both classes have rights which government ought to secure. It must promote the "welfare of all." Given the critical importance of the right to vote in securing such a commitment, this vital right ought to be fixed in a constitutional declaration of rights so as to exempt it from legislative tampering.[4]

The problem for the framer of a constitution is that, if the right is limited to freeholders, this provision will "exclude too great a proportion of citizens." If the right is extended to all citizens "without regard to property," then they *may* place too much power in the hands of persons who will either abuse it themselves, or "sell it to the rich who will abuse it." Therefore, "I have thought a good middle course" would be to differentiate the right to vote for the two branches of the legislature. One should not be surprised, however, if at the "outset at least it should offend the sense of equality which reigns in a free Country." Nevertheless, there is no good reason why the "rights of property," which bear the chief burdens of government ought not to be recognized as well as "personal rights in the choice of Rulers." Admittedly, the possession of property gives its owners "influence," but it should give them "no legal priviledges [sic]." This arrangement of voting will be safe, if "the business of legislation" is guarded properly with a bicameral structure.[5]

At the Constitutional Convention Madison spoke on this subject only once, briefly and incompletely. On 7 August, long after the Framers had decided to leave the choice of Senators to the states' legislatures, he tried to counter a motion by Governeur Morris of Pennsylvania to require a freehold suffrage instead of the less restrictive proposal presented by the Committee of Detail. It was generally agreed that such a limit on the persons to vote for members of the House of Representatives would be popular in many states, but it was pointed out by some members that this requirement would exclude merchants and manufacturers who bore much of the burden of taxation in some states. Madison tried to mollify both sides by saying that it is of fundamental importance that the right to vote be fixed in the Constitution because aristocracies have always been erected on the abridgment of this right and not on a broad suffrage, as Morris had contended. Whether the right ought to be limited to freeholders could only be an abstract issue on this occasion, however, because this right has been extended to "every description of people" in several states. Madison agreed with Morris, however, that a freehold suffrage might be needed in the future to secure "Republican liberty" in a society in which the great majority of the people would not own property of any kind. They would be likely to jeopardize the rights of property owners or become the "tools of opulence & ambition..." Madison did not state his personal views beyond this point, apparently because he and the other members of his delegation opposed Morris's substitute. So did six other delegations which voted to leave regulation of the right to vote for members of the House to the states in accordance with the least restrictive provisions in each.[6]

Madison supported this decision, saying in the fifty–second *Federalist* that the Framers' decision to adopt each state's most democratic qualifications for electing the members of the House of Representatives met a fundamental requirement of the theory of republican government. Given the variety of rules regulating voting then prevailing in the states, the provision adopted by the Framers was the best one they could adopt. It denied both Congress and the state legislatures any power whatsoever to fix qualifications already established in the state constitutions. It "cannot be feared that the people of the states will alter this part of their constitutions in such a manner as to abridge the rights secured to them by the federal Constitution," Madison declared.[7]

He added a fuller statement of his beliefs to his notes of the speech he made to the Convention on 7 August, saying that, because the states were to make some of the "appointments" to the federal government, citizens in those states where voting was not limited to property owners would have "an indirect share of representation. But this does not satisfy the fundamental principle that men can not be justly bound to laws in making which they have no part. Persons & property being both essential objects of Government, the most that either can claim is such a structure of it, as will leave a reasonable security for the other." The "most obvious provision" in the structure of government to secure political liberty to both classes of citizens was ignored by the Framers. They failed to confine the right to vote for one house of Congress to the owners of property, the least secure class in "popular governments." They did so despite the inevitable tendency for class conflict to erupt in densely populated countries of the sort which the United States must become eventually. The Framers left this matter imperfectly attended to, although other modifications suggested by the practices of the states were available. Therefore, the "federal principle" would have to serve as a substitute. It "enlarges the sphere of Power without departing from [its] elective basis" and controls in various ways the "propensity in small republics to rash measures & the facility of forming and executing them..." Federalism, he predicted, "will be found the best expedient yet tried for solving the problem" of securing political liberty to all interests.[8]

In 1788 he reconfirmed this prescription, claiming that it is consistent with both the "theory of free government and experience..." Again he stressed the importance of taking a long-term view of social change and arming both property owners and other persons with a "defensive share" of power in a constitution. For "obvious reasons," he said, this matter was not attended to, when the state constitutions were formed at the time of the Revolution. Their framers knew that in all ancient governments which were once regarded as "beacons to republican patriots & lawgivers...the poor were sacrificed to the rich." In America, however, it was assumed that the rights of the two classes were to be so little distinguished from each other that a suffrage providing for the rights of persons would secure those of property as well. It was "natural to infer from the tendency of republican laws, that these different interests would be more and more identical. Experience and investigation have however produced more correct ideas on the subject." Like some parts of the union in 1788, all of America must eventually reach a stage of development in which only a minority will be interested in maintaining the rights of property. The time to guard permanently against interested and abusive majorities is when a constitution is being framed. In 1788 the bulk of the people either possess property or entertain the hope of acquiring it. The moment is propitious for linking the right to vote with representation to prevent a future in which a majority shall have become either the "dupes & instruments of ambition," or the dependent "mercenary instruments of wealth." In either case, liberty will be subverted by the appearance of either anarchy or rule by a corrupt oligarchy.[9]

In 1791 Madison explained in a private memorandum the full implications of what he meant by saying at the Convention in 1787 that a freehold suffrage had always been the foundation for aristocracies. Virginia and the other southern states, like the ancient popular governments, were aristocratic in fact, despite being democratic in name. Aristotle, Madison noted, reported that power was exercised in the aristocratic Greek democracies for the most part by the "rich and easy." Aristotle defined a citizen as a person who is free enough from private cares to serve in public office. Madison cited a "de rep: lib. 3. cap. 1 & 4." On the basis of Aristotle's classification of regimes and definition of a citizen, the states of the American South were aristocracies. Virginia was made one, Madison said, by a freehold suffrage which excluded "nearly half of the inhabitants, and must exclude a greater proportion as the population increases." If the "slaves were freed and the right of suffrage extended to all, the operation of the government would be very different." In the southern states slavery places power "much more in the hands of property than in the Northern states." For this reason, the "people of property" in the South are much more contented with their existing governments than their counterparts in the North.[10]

Between about 1821 and 1829, Madison prepared two memoranda dealing with this subject. Apparently he wrote them for use at the convention in which he agreed to serve in order to revise Virginia's constitution. In the longer of the two, he repeated the main arguments he had made in 1787–88. He repeated his predictions of the long–term decline in the political power of landowners, but he voiced for the first time a willingness to accept an equal, universal suffrage, if it became inevitable. He believed that the prevailing widespread ownership of land could not protect agrarians against the fate of becoming a minority even with the sub–division of the vast tracts of arable land then still available for settlement. European experience had demonstrated additionally that there would be a "dependence of an increasing number [of persons] on the wealth of the few"; that is, "wealthy capitalists and indigent laborers." Not even the laws of inheritance can prevent this outcome of the operation of free institutions, although their "equalizing tendency" may diminish the opportunities for accumulating wealth in the hands of individuals and "associations." These prospective changes must be viewed with a basic political maxim in mind: "No free country has ever been without parties, which are the natural offspring of freedom." One of the most obvious divisions of parties is between those who own land and those who do not. In a sense the country belongs to the former insofar as each landowner has "exclusive" property in his share of the whole amount within a society. This conclusion follows from the "principle of natural law which vests in individuals the right to portions of ground with which they have incorporated their labor and improvements." Other persons have rights derived at "birth" from their interest in all the lands left open for other common uses, in "national edifices and monuments...public defense," and in their support of government. Despite the scope of these important personal interests, it seems unreasonable to give them a right which will eventually enable them to become a majority empowered to legislate the concerns of landowners without their consent. The need to give them a defensive power left Madison convinced that the equal universal right to vote must be modified in some way.[11]

At this late date in the nation's development he thought that traditional laws linking the right to vote with representation left two equally unacceptable choices: either a freehold qualification or a right to vote based on a rigid distinction between property owners and others, each group voting for separate branches of the legislature. The latter arrangement would not be either "equal or fair" because the rights to be defended are not equal. Furthermore, a division of the population into two classes controlling "distinct and separate organs of power...without any intermingled agency whatever, might lead to contests not dissimilar to those between the patricians and plebians at Rome." If public opinion requires an equal suffrage "such as prevails generally in the United States," but not in Virginia, the grant of this right will not in itself give the landed minority the defensive power it will need as much in the future. The best solution to this problem would be an "enlargement of election districts for one branch of the legislature and a prolonged term of office. Large districts are manifestly favorable to the election of persons of general respectability and of probable attachment to the rights of property, over competitors depending on the personal solicitations practicable in a contracted theatre." Large election districts do not bar the choice of ambitious candidates of "personal distinction," but such persons are unlikely to be elected to "many districts at the same time." If this solution cannot be provided, reliance must be placed on the influence derived from the ownership of property, superior information, a popular sense of justice enlightened and expanded by widespread education, and, finally, from the difficulty of combining to execute unjust public measures.[12]

When everything has been said on the subject, he concluded, it must be conceded that it is "indispensable" for the mass of citizens to have a voice in choosing the persons who make the laws which they are to obey. If the only alternatives are either an equal and universal right to vote for members of both branches of a legislature or a limitation of the "entire right to a part," then it is better that the property owners who have a greater interest at stake be "deprived of half their share in the Government, than that those having the lesser interest, that of personal rights only, should be deprived of the whole." This conclusion is inescapable, if a government is to be framed to last through a long period of great social and economic changes, while securing republican liberty.[13]

This very limited record shows that Madison was certainly no crusader for an extension of the right to vote and that he did not consider such an event to be an essential element of constitutional reform in 1787. It is difficult to say what qualifications he favored at that time, although it is evident that he was concerned about the eventual loss of the political power of landowners. His conversion to a supporter of white manhood suffrage in the 1820s demonstrates only that he was willing to adapt to the felt political necessities of the times.

It is of some importance that in discussing the right to vote forty years after the event he reconfirmed his theory expounded in the Tenth *Federalist* that the election of representatives from large districts is likely to make them impartial defenders of all kinds of property interests. Although the right to vote is an integral element of democratic theory, Madison's failure to push for its extension in 1787 is not proof in itself that he was hostile to democracy. He was a strong exponent of the addition of the House of Representatives to Congress, and he made it clear that he thought it added a democratic institution to the new government. It certainly did so and it is astonishing that scholars have ignored this obvious fact for so long. Moreover, Madison pushed for the popular election of the president through the choice of pledged electors in districts by the qualified voters. This process paralleled that of choosing members of the House, at least in Virginia, in accordance with his expectations. His motive, to give Virginia access to the institution which he wanted to serve as a counterweight to the Senate, may not have been the most disinterested imaginable. The fact remains, however, that this strategy turned out, as he predicted at the Convention, to be the basis for making the presidency a popular institutition. Indeed, the strategy was so successful that his friend Jefferson reaped the fruits of it and became the mythical figurehead of the political phenomenon called Jeffersonian Democracy.

POLITICAL PARTIES ARE NATURAL

His reference to political parties as the natural offspring of free governments in 1829 was consistent with his remarks on this subject in the tenth and fifty-first *Federalist* essays more than forty years earlier. In the first of these two papers he predicted that a well-constructed constitutional system would control the tendency of alternating, competitive, and self-serving majorities to produce unstable and unjust laws. Natural parties arise out of the diversity of opinions and interests which exist where liberty is regarded as essential to political life. These are the latent causes of "factions," which exist in governments because they must protect the diverse human faculties in which both natural parties and the right to acquire different amounts and kinds of property originate. The inescapable conclusion is that parties, factions, are the "natural offspring of free government." Any deliberate attempt to suppress them "implies an absolute extinction of liberty." The existence of parties in every free society requires only that their component elements be numerous and localized so that the legislative majority in the federal government is unlikely to have the capacity for unjust action.[14]   In short, Madison recognized that the actions of governments inescapably divide instead of uniting society in the real world.   Madison firmly believed and explicitly said repeatedly that governments perfectly harmonize all elements of society only in Utopia. This is an unpleasant and very inconvenient fact to all speculative theorists who long to unify the particular with the universal in political life.   Of course, the divisive effects of governmental actions is a truth no less unpalatable to those who exercise public power.

Madison returned to this subject in the fifty-first essay and offered a prediction that parties at the national level would probably consist of coalitions united only on the most general and virtuous abstractions. This conclusion followed, according to Madison, from the proposition that there are only two political systems available to protect one part of society against the "injustice" of another one.   There must be either a "will in the community independent of the majority; or society must include so many different interests as to make unjust governing combinations into a "majority of the whole...very improbable." The first method of curbing injustice is used in "all governments possessing an hereditary or self-appointed authority."   This form of rule provides a precarious security, however, because any government independent of society may further the interest of an unjust majority quite as easily as it may protect the rights of a minority.   As long as the pursuit of "justice is the end of government" in any society where the stronger part can unite under the "forms" of government and oppress the weaker part, anarchy may be said to prevail as much as it does in "a state of nature" where the weaker "individual" is not secured against the "violence" of the stronger.   Even in a state of nature the stronger individuals are prompted by the "uncertainty" of their condition to "submit" to a government which protects the strong as well as the weak.   In a weak civil society an analogous move to a stable government independent of society will be made.   Gradually, the more powerful "factions or parties" will be motivated by their insecurity to "wish for a government which will protect all parties," both weak and powerful.   American society offers the prospect of using the second remedy, however.   It will be divided into so many parts, interests and classes, that none of them would be the likely victims of oppressive majorities at the national level.   The security for all rights, civil and religious, he insisted, must be found in the multiplicity of interests and sects which he expected to increase in proportion to the territorial extent and population of the United States.   In fact, he boldly predicted, if the new federal republic established in the Constitution were not adopted, then "combinations" of interested majorities would be formed in "exact proportion" to the division of the union into small confederations.   The instability of the laws so feared by even the friends of republican government would be "proportionally increased."   In the "extended republic of the United States," however, with its great variety of interests, "a coalition of the whole society" would rarely be formed on any grounds other than a commitment to "justice and the general good..."[15]

   This argument in the fifty–first essay was not only consistent with the discussion of parties in the Tenth paper, but also an addition to it. At the very minimum Madison explicitly predicted that parties controlling the federal government would be coalitions. Consequently, he insisted that they would provide the best defense of the rights of minor parties in a society organized on the precepts of free government. He appears to have had legislative parties in mind at this time, although he had already recognized the need for "combinations" outside of government to secure the election of the president and vice–president, separately, when he published these essays. It cannot be determined from the available evidence in his writings of this period whether or not he expected to combine both types of parties into a single one in order to secure control of the government as the Republicans did in 1800. It can be affirmed positively, however, that Madison expected and accepted the formation of natural political parties in 1787. Underneath this lofty rhetoric, however, there was also a use of the word *parties* which posed a thinly veiled threat. He referred to Rhode Island as a state of the kind most likely to suffer, if the Constitution did not replace the Articles of Confederation. The latter was so nearly a state of nature that the stronger parties (states) would be motivated by their sense of insecurity to submit to a government independent of society and energetic enough to do justice to the major parties (large states). This part of the fifty–first essay strongly echoed Madison's bitter denunciation of the Confederation to James Monroe in 1786 on the ground that it lacked the "protective energy" needed to do justice to the major part of American society. In that same year he observed in his notes on confederations that the stadtholder of the Dutch republic was granted powers over foreign relations because men are by nature too jealous of their equals to vest such powers in their elected representatives. At the Convention on 26 June 1787 he issued a warning to the small states against thwarting the large ones. All of these observations seem to have informed this passage in the fifty–first essay.[16] The chief point of these observations is that Madison used the word *parties* on some occasions to denote the parts of a whole rather than organizations created to select candidates for office, establish policy positions, and mobilize voters in support of them.

   With political divisions clearly emerging in Congress by 1792, Madison published two brief essays on political parties. The first one, "Parties," started with the theme stated explicitly in the tenth *Federalist*. "In every political society, parties are unavoidable." The most "natural" and fruitful source of them is a division of interest, real or imagined, among the people. The "great art of politicians" consists in making these "natural parties" of a society into mutual checks on each other so as to create a politicial "equilibrium." It is a great error to add to natural parties such artifical distinctions as official orders and inequality of property acquired through the actions of government. Furthermore, the evils arising from party conflict ought to be combatted by establishing "political equality among all..." This goal is to be achieved by limiting the opportunities for acquiring immoderate amounts of property; by laws which reduce the extremes of wealth and poverty so that all tend to enjoy a "state of comfort"; and by refraining from enacting laws which favor one interest at the expense of others.[17]

To this homilitic he added another essay, "A Candid State of Parties." It was his duty as a "contemplative statesman," he claimed, to trace the history of parties in the United States in order to counter the "effusions of designing men..." Since 1776 there had been three periods in which parties had been formed. During the Revolution they consisted of patriots and loyalists, a division which was superceded by the treaty of peace in 1783. From then until 1787 there were "parties in abundance, but being local rather than general," they are not the subject of this review. The debate over ratification of the Constitution gave birth to a "second and most interesting" division consisting of supporters and opponents of ratification. During this debate most Americans were undoubtedly advocates of "republican liberty," but there were those who were overtly or covertly attached to "monarchy and aristocracy..." The latter group hoped to make the "constitution a cradle for these hereditary establishments." Not all opponents fell into this group, however. The third major period in the history of American parties started with the establishment of the new government. The division it has produced is likely to be one of "some duration," he predicted, because it is natural in most political societies. There are persons who favor the rich over people of modest means and who discount the capacity of the latter for self–government. These same people believe that government requires official ranks, the "active and insinuating" influence of money, and the "terror" of military force. The other party wishes to preserve republican government and, in doing so, opposes the opposite party on all of these theoretical points. Which one of them will prevail cannot be predicted at this time. In politics, as in war, "strategem" often overpowers numbers. It should not surprise a dispassionate observer of human affairs, however, to witness in due time the triumph of numbers, shared sentiments, and interests administering the government in the "spirit and form" in which it was approved by the people.[18]

Despite the partisan rhetoric in these two homilies, they pointed to some obvious truths about American parties in the late eighteenth century. During the brief period of government under the Articles of Confederation, parties were local and numerous because there was no need to be organized on a national basis to send members to Congress. This situation was changed under the Constitution because of the need to combine electors' votes to secure the election of predetermined candidates for president and vice–president. It was essential to the interests of the large states to adopt this strategy, although Madison said nothing directly about this matter in the two essays just noted. They were published, however, after he talked with Washington in May, 1792, about the need for him to run for a second term in order to maintain republican government against the efforts of persons whom Madison regarded as its enemies within the government. Obviously, he considered parties as natural and legal forms of political association organized on a national scale needed after 1789 to elect members of both the legislative and executive branches, especially the later. The fact that Madison urged Washington to run for a second term in 1792 makes it clear that parties had still not become very cohesive organizations, except insofar as Madison and his allies thought that there was a division over the nature of the constitutional system which jeopardized its republican character. This fear was not completely erased with Washington's reelection, as we noted in the previous chapter.

In 1793 Madison complained that one party consisting of anglophiles in the government was attempting to establish a close commercial connection with Great Britain and to effect a "gradual approximation to her Form of Government."[19]   He groused to Jefferson about the maneuvers of the "anglican party" and sent him a sketch of resolutions to be adopted in Richmond in order to oppose all steps taken toward "assimilating our Govt. to the form & spirit of the British monarchy" by persons "disaffected to the American Revolution" and others of "known" monarchical principles.[20] A year later he repeated this identification of the division of parties in the federal government: it was between those who favored "Aristocracy, anglicism and Mercantilism" united against the supporters of "Republicanism."[21] Much later, in 1834, he explained to a correspondent that he had deliberately sought election to the House of Representatives instead of seeking an appointment to the Senate in 1788 because the "Constn. in its progress was encountering trials of a new sort in the formation of new Parties attaching adverse constructions to it."[22] This explanation certainly fitted his analysis of the division of parties during the third period after the government was formed in 1789.

From Madison's perspective it is erroneous to say that he was a convert to parties sometime after 1789. It is, also, an over simplification to conclude that parties arose exlusively out of recognition of the need for a loyal opposition, divisions over domestic or foreign policies, or simply out of the desire of ambitious persons to gain office for its own sake. They originated in real differences over the nature of the constitutional system as well.[23] Divisions over questions of policy often had constitutional implications which raised questions of their compatibility with the spirit and republican form of the government which Madison so earnestly desired to preserve. He was not only a witness to these events, but also a leading participant. It would appear, therefore, that great weight ought to be given to his perception of the nature of the parties, organizationally amorphous though they were, both before and during the third period of their development after American independence was established.

In the years following his retirement from national offices, Madison occasionally commented privately on parties. He was stirred by the Missouri question in 1819 to rejoice that Americans were not yet cursed with the worst of all forms of political division: parties based on "Geographical boundaries" and "embittered" by differences over the issues coinciding with them. "Political parties intermingled throughout the community unite as well as divide." Those founded on "local distinctions and fixed peculiarities" so as to separate the whole into "great conflicting masses, are far more to be dreaded in their tendency."[24] Soon thereafter he confided in another correspondent his feeling that the spread of slavery "fills me with no slight anxiety." Should parties, which must always be expected and accepted in governments as free as ours, ever be formed to coincide with geographical boundaries and to oppose each other on the question of slavery, there would be nothing to control the conflicting masses of each party from "awful shocks against each other." For this reason, it might be more "humane," he speculated, to permit the spread of this institution to all parts of the union. This development might at least promote a more diffusive sympathy with every interest embraced within the nation.[25]

After debate over the Missouri Compromise opened up this dreaded prospect, he shrewdly pointed out to President Monroe that the strategy of admitting new states linked with the question of slavery in the Missouri Territory was calculated to form parties which would divide the "Republicans of the North from those of the South..."[26] He denied at the same time the contention that the debates over this issue demonstrated the existence of a "Southern ascendancy" in Congress. There certainly was none at the time when the Constitution was put into effect; it then lay "elsewhere." If there ever has been an ascendancy in Congress it has been "Republican...as it was called by all wherever residing, who contributed to it."[27]

In 1821 he urged President Monroe to face the tribulations involved in holding office by recalling that in free governments the people always find subjects on which the diversity of human passions will be brought into conflict and stimulate the spirit of party. The most that we can hope for is that they will not threaten the "character & prosperity of the Republic" with permanent and dangerous consequences.[28] Fortunately for Madison, he did not live to witness the proof of his warning against parties divided on sectional grounds and inflamed with moral passion.

In 1823, when the first Republican party was accused of adopting the policies of their former adversaries after 1801, Madison denied the allegation. On the contrary, those who were called "Republicans or Democrats" were always in harmony with the "spirit" of the nation and the "genius" of its government. It is true, he conceded, that "foreign circumstances...doubled population and...resources" have reconciled Republicans to "certain measures and arrangements which may be as proper now as they were premature and suspicious" when the Federalists championed them. With the passage of time, people tend to forget their "overbearing and vindictive spirit, the Aprocryphal doctrines and rash projects" which they espoused. There was always a "deep distinction" between the two former parties concerning the capacity of mankind for self-government, and this difference provides the key to many political phenomena in our history, he insisted. This difference must be expected in all free countries and it is never dangerous in a "well informed community and a well constructed Government," both of which, "I trust," are found in the United States.[29]

On another occasion Madison said he thought that many people put too much "remedial power in the press over the spirit of party." They ignore the fact that party divisions are founded on the varied opinions which exist in all free states. For this reason, interpretations of the Constitution will be influenced by this cause which will be an "unfailing source of party distinctions." Nevertheless, the abusive spirt of party cannot be controlled for it is necessary to "fan the flame of liberty..." Partisanship can be diverted from its more "noxious channels" with the aid of time and habit so as to end the "more dangerous divisions which grow out of it."[30] He uttered his final, known words on this subject in 1827. He agreed with a correspondent that "party zeal" ought not to be used to alter the Constitution and make its interpretation a matter of party dogma. The maturity of public opinion had resisted previous efforts of this sort, but it still would be a sound and patriotic policy to wish that portions of "heated parties" might be so "intermingled as to strengthen, instead of weakening the political fabric."[31]

If the consistency of Madison's limited discussions of political parties demonstrates nothing else, it shows that he fully expected them to develop once the Constitution was ratified. He was not initially an enemy of parties only to become a convert to them out of necessity after 1789. He apparently meant it when he said in the tenth *Federalist* that parties form in the presence of freedom because the actions of government inevitably divide free societies in the process of protecting diverse and unequal human faculties. Like many of his contemporaries he did not think that parties of every description are beneficial to free governments. Religious parties tend to become deadly factions. Parties divided over constitutional issues can lead to passionate conflicts which may well call the legitimacy of even the best form of government into question. Partisan cleavages based on geographical lines and otherwise divided strongly, as over slavery, are no less to be avoided, if possible. Nevertheless, none of these differences nor others of equal power to divide a nation can be avoided where opinion is free, as it must be, if there is to be political life in the best sense.

NOTES

1. *PJM*, 10:519.
2. Ibid., 8:351.
3. Montesquieu, *Spirit*, 1: bk. 11, chaps. 1–3, 6; bk. 12, chaps. 1–2. Madison occasionally used the phrase, public liberty as a synonym; see *The Federalist*, 348, 362 (Nos. 53, 55).
4. *PJM*, 8:351, 353.
5. Ibid., 353–54.
6. Farrand, *Records*, 2:203–4; see generally 201–6.
7. *The Federalist*, 342 (No. 52).
8. *PJM*, 10:140–41 and editor's note.
9. Ibid., 11:287–88. In the text Madison wrote independent instead of dependent. I have taken the liberty of correcting what must have been a slip of the pen.
10. Ibid. 14:163–64.
11. *LJM*, 4:22–25.
12. Ibid., 26–27.

13. Ibid., 27–28.
14. *The Federalist*, 53–54 (No. 10); 280 (No. 43); 335 (No. 50).
15. Ibid., 339–41 passim (No. 51).
16. See Chapter 3, p. 59 above.
17. *PJM*, 14:197–98.
18. Ibid., 370–72.
19. Ibid. 15:88.
20. Ibid., 92.
21. *LJM*, 2:13. This item is not in PJM.
22. Ibid. 4:341.
23. See Noble E. Cunningham, Jr., *The Jeffersonian Republicans: The Formation of Party Organization* (Chapel Hill, N. C.: University of North Carolina Press, 1957), 20–22; and John Zvesper, *Political Philosophy and Rhetoric: A Study of the Origins of American Party Politics* (Cambridge: Cambridge University Press, 1977), 3–13.
24. *LJM*, 3:142.
25. Ibid., 157.
26. Ibid., 164–65.
27. Ibid., 185.
28. James Madison, *The Writings of James Madison*, ed. Gaillard Hunt, 9 vols. (New York: G. P. Putnam's Sons, 1900–1910), 9:97.
29. *LJM*, 3:318. He repeated this analysis of party divisions in a letter to Jefferson in 1823; ibid., 325.
30. Ibid., 441–42.
31. Ibid., 601.

Chapter 6

A Few Obvious Truths

Madison is commonly thought of as the author of the Bill of Rights, and with good reason. Most of the first ten amendments came substantially from his hand. Nevertheless, there is more than enough irony in this reputation. He made no known effort to incorporate any specific guarantees of individual rights into the Constitution at the Convention of 1787 beyond the few scattered through the text. He made no apparent effort to reinforce the very few efforts of others to add provisions as the work of the Convention was nearing completion. Until 1789, he defended this omission and was only slowly convinced that the movement for amendments would have to be satisfied after ratification of the original document, if public confidence in the new government were to be established. Furthermore, neither the final form in which the amendments were placed in the Constitution nor their substance nor their effects in some cases were fully consistent with his recommendations in 1789. Certainly, the two guarantees which he thought were most widely believed to be in need of protection from the new government, "the freedom of the press and the rights of conscience, those choicest privileges of the people," have not been construed as strictly as he wished.[1] Nevertheless, it is important to distinguish between Madison the reluctant architect of the Bill of Rights and the ardent advocate of the fundamental freedoms embodied in the First Amendment.

There was very little opportunity at the Constitutional Convention for Madison to support a bill of rights of the conventional sort. The Convention's charge was to enlarge, not to restrict, the powers of the federal government. Apparently, the Framers thought that the ninth section of the first article provided the only restrictions which were indispensable aside from the prohibition against religious tests for holding office under the Constitution. The propositions which Charles Pinckney proposed on 20 August to be considered by the Committee of Detail included two of the provisions later placed in article one, section nine, and a guarantee of free press, as well, but the latter was dropped in committee. There was no debate on Pinckney's motion to refer and it passed without opposition. On 12 September George Mason voiced his desire for a bill of rights and said that he would second a motion to refer to a committee the task of composing one in "a few hours" by cribbing from state bills of rights. Despite a motion supporting his position, Mason's proposal was rejected by the states unanimously. Madison did not speak on either of these two occasions.[2] After four months of sharp debate over the augmentation and allocation of power among the branches of the reformed government, the delegates were apparently in no mood to wrangle further in the heat of Philadelphia over the wording of a bill of rights.

At Virginia's ratifying convention Madison spoke to this issue, when goaded into it by Patrick Henry. The latter charged slyly that the Constitution contained no bill of rights to secure religious liberty. This shaft was aimed directly at Madison who responded to Henry's hypocrisy by denying the efficacy of such documents. The Constitution, he said, does not grant the federal government so much as a shadow of authority to "intermeddle with religion." The slightest move in this direction would be a "most flagrant usurpation," he insisted. It was true, he admitted, that under the Constitution a state might undertake some "religious project," but Congress would not be likely to do so because the United States abounds with such "a variety of sects" that they constitute a "a strong security against religious persecution." Virginia's own experience with its Declaration of Rights demonstrated that the variety of sects needed to constitute a legislative majority, not a paper barrier of words, is the only real security which can be relied on to guard such rights.[3] This clever riposte was undoubtedly intended to discredit Henry in the eyes of all who recalled that he had led the legislative battle in favor of religious assessments in 1784–85 and that Madison had been his successful opponent. In 1788 Madison regarded Henry as the most dangerous of all the Anti-Federalists in Virginia who were calling for a bill of rights as an artful dodge calculated to prevent ratification of the Constitution.

AN ARCHITECT OF THE BILL OF RIGHTS

It is in this light that one ought to understand Madison's slow and reluctant conversion from an opponent to a bill of rights in 1788 to its chief author and advocate in 1789. The first of Madison's reasons for opposing a bill of rights during this period was that its addition would complicate the process of ratification of the Constitution which he, himself, regarded as seriously flawed. If the freshly framed plan were to be opened to amendments, as it must be to add a bill of rights, then no one could predict what the final result of such tampering would be. Even before the Constitution was signed on 17 September 1787 Madison reported to Jefferson that it was basically flawed. Should the plan be ratified it would not serve the "national object" of the project, nor prevent the "local mischiefs which every where excite disgust against the state governments." The delegates were universally anxious about the reception which the public would give to the fruit of their arduous and extended labors. Furthermore, Madison predicted, "certain characters will wage war against any reform whatever." Despite this situation, Madison judged that the public was ready for constitutional reforms likely to produce stable government and to secure individual rights. "If the present moment be lost it is hard to say what will be our fate."[4]

The moment the Convention sent the Constitution to Congress to start the process of ratification, trouble was stirred up, as Madison expected it to be. From New York where he was serving in Congress, he reported to George Washington that the "national" issue as well as efforts by Richard Henry Lee of Virginia and Nathan Dane of Massachusetts to add a bill of rights had sown confusion and discord which jeopardized acceptance of the reforms. These two members of Congress moved to add a bill of rights. This appendage was to be adopted by Congress and sent with the Constitution to the states for ratification. Supporters of this ploy argued that Congress had both the authority (under the Articles of Confederation, still in effect) and the duty to add these "essential guards to liberty" to a Constitution sorely deficient in this characteristic. Opponents of this dilatory stratagem agreed that Congress retained its authority to propose amendments (to the Articles of Confederation), but they opposed the move on four grounds. First, Congress was included in the process of constitutional reform at this time only as a matter of "form and respect." It was not expected to take any such drastic action as adding to the Convention's proposals. Second, a discussion of the merits of specific amendments would consume valuable time. (This was probably the main reason why the Convention did not act to accept Mason's move for a bill of rights on 14 September.) Third, the intervention of Congress would be contrary to the requirement that the Convention send its product directly to the states. Finally, this maneuver confused the important difference between amending the Articles of Confederation and ratifying the Constitution. The former required the unanimous consent of the states; whereas the latter required the consent of only nine of them. Fortunately, the infinite confusion which this problem alone would have caused was avoided. The opponents defeated this diversionary tactic with a suitable resolution. This victory left ratification of the Constitution to the state conventions exclusively as the Framers provided and postponed any action on a bill of rights.[5]

Nevertheless, the ground had been laid for opposing the Constitution because of the lack of a bill of rights. Or, to put the matter as Madison perceived it, the lack of a full bill of rights had been artfully raised by opponents seeking to mask the true grounds of their opposition to the Constitution. Three weeks later Madison reported to Jefferson, who was in Paris, that Edmund Randolph and George Mason had defected from the supporters of the Constitution. He reported the antifederalist maneuver in Congress to secure a bill of rights and said that it was intended to "embarrass" the plan of constitutional reforms. On the same day he reported to William Short, Jefferson's secretary, that "Virga. will be divided and extremely agitated" over ratification.[6]

The opponents to the Constitution were outmaneuvered and outvoted in Congress, but they were still in a position to take their case to the ratifying conventions in the states. This was the source of Madison's extreme anxiety over the prospects for ratification and his opposition to adding a bill of rights which could be used as a political lever to unhinge the work of the Convention. At this time he refused even to argue the issue in the abstract. As the recipient of a constant stream of reports from correspondents in several of the states, Virginia in particular, Madison had ample reason to fear rejection of the Constitution without anyone's adroit complication of the issue with calls for a bill of rights–or other amendments for that matter.[7]

Finally, the cries of alarm from Madison's political friends in Virginia reached a crescendo which he could not ignore. Archibald Stuart reported from Richmond that, during the current sitting of the legislature which had to authorize the ratifying convention, "Mr. [Patrick] Henry has upon all Occasions however foreign to his subject attempted to give the Constitution a side blow."[8] Once the convention was authorized, Stuart implored Madison to serve as a member. "It is generally considered necessary that you should be [a member] of the convention, not only [so] that the Constitution may be adopted but with as much unanimity as possible. For God's sake do not disappoint the Anxious expectations of your friends and let me add your Country."[9] Soon thereafter Madison agreed to serve as a delegate, despite his initial conviction that members of the Philadelphia Convention ought to leave ratification to other individuals.[10] A neighbor pointed to the fears which prompted this decision. Madison needed to be present because there would otherwise be "no guarding against artfull persons from injecting their poison into the unwary." Please, this correspondent begged, be present at the ratifying convention "as soon as conveniently possible."[11]

Jefferson inadvertently contributed to the confusion created by the call for a bill of rights. He added his name to the list of its supporters. On 20 December 1787 he told Madison that among his few objections to the proposed Constitution was the absence of a bill of rights guaranteeing freedom of the press and religion, forbidding standing armies and monopolies, an unqualified writ of habeas corpus, and jury trials.[12] In voicing this criticism, Jefferson still had no knowledge of the opportunity he was providing guileful Anti–Federalists in Virginia. When Jefferson let out other criticisms to other individuals, Madison's anxiety was heightened even further.[13]

In January, 1788, Madison publicly noted that among the charges against the Constitution was the absence of a bill of rights to protect those of persons or states. To the critics who assumed this ground of objection or some other one he responded by asking rhetorically whether a second convention could produce a perfect plan of government. There was more bravado than conviction, however, in this challenge.[14] To his dismay, it was taken up in June by the Anti–Federalists in Virginia's ratifying convention. They demanded adoption of amendments as a precondition for ratification. By the last week in June, however, Madison sensed the likely defeat of this movement with a counter–strategy which he reported to Rufus King of Massachusetts. The "moderate and respectable" supporters of the Constitution would move to preface the resolution of ratification with "a declaration of a few obvious truths" and follow it with a recommendation for a "few amendments to be pursued in the constitutional mode."[15] The

Anti–Federalists' final gasp, Madison reported to Washington, took the form of a motion for "previous amendments," but it was defeated by a vote of 88 to 80. The question of ratification was then put, and it carried 89 to 79. Amendments would be added subsequently, he promised.[16] These two votes convinced Madison that, ever since the move to send both the Constitution and a bill of rights to the states for concurrent ratification was made in Congress in September, 1788, this profession of a love of rights was no more than a stratagem to defeat ratification, at least in Virginia and Massachusetts.[17]

Apparently without knowing that he was being the unwitting ally of Anti–Federalists, Jefferson reissued his call to Madison for a bill of rights on 31 July 1788. He did not know that Virginia had ratified the Constitution with the promise of suitable amendments to come. He repeated his specification of the rights which ought to be guaranteed against violation. In particular, he thought there ought to be a declaration that the federal government would never keep the presses from printing what they please. It would "not take away the liability of printers for false facts printed." To this apparent allusion to the common law definition of a free press, he added another interesting observation. Neither would a declaration that religious faith should go "unpunished" give "impunity to criminal acts dictated by religious error."[18] Before Madison received this letter he reported to Jefferson that there was a new move underway in New York for amendments "from which mischiefs are apprehended." It was a call for a second constitutional convention. A delay of this move for "a few years will assuage the jealousies which have been artificially created by designing men and will at the same time point out the faults which really call for amendment."[19] Madison voiced his concern for this "extremely dangerous" movement to Edmund Randolph, Washington, and Jefferson once again during the next two weeks.[20]

Madison did not receive Jefferson's second call for a bill of rights until 15 October 1788. He answered it within two days. In all likelihood this quick response reflected Madison's fear that his friend would go to the public with this issue at this inauspicious time. He admitted that some of both the critics and advocates of the Constitution wanted further safeguards for "individual rights" added. He thought it likely such a declaration would be adopted. "My own opinion has always been in favor of a bill of rights; provided that it be so framed as not to imply powers not meant to be included in the enumeration. At the same time I never thought the omission a material defect, nor been anxious to supply it even by subsequent amendment, for any other reason than it is anxiously desired by others. I have favored it because I supposed it might be of use, and if properly executed could not be of disservice." There are four reasons for taking this position.[21] First, the rights in question are reserved to a certain degree by the manner in which powers are granted in the Constitution, although "Mr. [James] Wilson" carried this argument too far. Second, there is good reason to believe that the rights of "conscience" will be more greatly narrowed by a formal definition of them than they are likely to be injured by the exercise of assumed power. In New England there were objections to the prohibition of religious tests for holding office under the Constitution. It was contended that this provision opened the doors to public officeholding by "Jews Turks and Infidels." Third, the fact that the powers of the federal government are limited will stir the state governments to a degree of jealousy of them; this passion provides some security. Fourth and finally, experience demonstrates how ineffective bills of rights are, when they are most needed.

In every state there have been repeated instances in which the "parchment barriers" to violation of individual rights have been ignored by "overbearing majorities." In Virginia, despite an explicit avowal of the "rights of Conscience" in its bill of rights, a religious establishment would have been erected by the legislature, if its majority had found, as they expected, a majority of the people in favor of it. "I am persuaded that if a majority of the people were of one sect, the measure would still take place," despite the obstacle which the "law has since created." In our governments "real power lies in the majority of the Community, and the invasion of private rights is chiefly to be apprehended, not from acts of Government contrary to the sense of its constituents, but from acts in which the Government is the mere instrument of the major number of the constituents." This very important truth has not received the attention it deserves, but it has been impressed on "my mind by facts" and reflections on them different from "yours which has contemplated abuses of power arising from a very different quarter."[22]

This difference is between the effects of bills of rights in republics and monarchies, respectively. There is no question but what wrong will generally be done where there is an interest in it and the power to do it. This rule holds regardless of whether there is a powerful and interested party or a prince. The superiority of republics in this regard lies in the probability that interest is less likely to abuse power in a republic than in a monarchy, the power of which can reach to the whole of society rather than merely a part of it. The difference in regard to the effectiveness of a bill of rights in controlling the abuse of power is due to basic differences in the two types of political systems. In a monarchy the "latent force of the nation is superior to that of the sovereign." Therefore, a charter of popular rights must have a "great effect, as a standard for trying the validity of public acts." It serves, also, as a "signal for rousing and uniting the superior force of the community" against the monarch. In a popular government, however, the political and physical power of the nation are both vested in the majority of the people. Consequently the "tyrannical will of the sovereign is not [to] be controlled by the dread of an appeal to any other force within the community." Therefore, the question is what use can there be for a bill of rights in popular governments? The answer to this question is that there are two considerations which make a bill of rights worthwhile in popular governments, but to a lesser degree than in others. The first reason is that "political truths solemnly declared" gradually acquire the status of "fundamental maxims of free Governments." As such, they become incorporated as a part of "national sentiment" to the point where they may be used to counteract the "impulses of interest and passion." The second consideration favoring such precautions against the abuse of power is that they may help to define the line between the danger to liberty from both a deficiency of power and an excess of it.[23]

If it be supposed that a bill of rights is the proper instrument for drawing the line between these two extremes despite the failure of experience as a guide, then "I am inclined to think that absolute restrictions in cases that are doubtful, or where emergencies may overrule them, ought to be avoided." No matter how emphatically they are stated on paper, restraints will never be heeded when they are opposed by the decided sense of public opinion. No written prohibitions on earth will prevent a government from suspending the writ of habeas corpus, when rebellion or insurrection cause a general alarm among the people and their government. No constitutional prohibition of a standing army in peacetime would be heeded, if Britain or Spain established armies in our neighborhood. Monopolies are great nuisances, but are they not too valuable as encouragements to literary works and "ingenious discoveries" to be renounced totally?[24] Jefferson had recommended that all of these restrictions be absolute.

Jefferson did not receive this letter until 23 February 1789, and he delayed a reply to it until 15 March. Apparently he thought that a response was not an urgent matter because he understood that on the whole Madison was favorable to a bill of rights and had only undertaken to report the prevailing objections under discussion. He conceded that Madison had raised a number of points to which assent could be given on a moment's reflection, but he thought that Madison had omitted mention of one great benefit of a declaration of rights: "the legal check it puts in the hands of the judiciary...a body, which if rendered independent and kept strictly to their own department merits great confidence for their learning and integrity." To Madison's four main points he wished to add some short comments. First, it is true that in theory a constitution may be framed so as not to require a bill of rights, but in view of the nature of the new government, prudence requires some fence against the abuse of power even though the federal grant is limited and enumerated. Second, even if a full bill cannot be secured, a partial one is better than none at all. Third, a declaration will provide the "text" to be used by the state governments serving as jealous guardians against federal violation of individual rights. Finally, experience has proved the value of such declarations so that the limitations they place on governments do not last for long times and any harm done is easily reparable. The absence of a declaration of rights is not so easily corrected.[25]

By May, 1789, when Madison presented his proposed amendments to Congress, the first election had assured him that the president and a majority of Congress would support the Constitution. The danger of antifederalism had subsided, but Madison was still sufficiently wary to take notice of it in his speech introducing his proposed amendments. In the face of dilatory motions in the House of Representatives, Madison called for immediate consideration on 8 June 1789. Any further delay, he warned, would create suspicions, at least, and might even inflame public opinion among the warm supporters of a bill of rights. Deliberate delay would give them reason to believe that the House had no intention of taking up this business within the foreseeable future. Therefore, he thought it was his duty to introduce and explain this "great work" at once and to push for its serious consideration despite the pressure of other important business. If the House followed this lead, the numerous and "respectable" persons who were dissatisfied with the Constitution as it stood might be better pleased. Otherwise, they might not support it. Among these critics were individuals who were devoted to liberty and republican government, but feared that the Constitution was intended to lay the foundation for an aristocracy or a despotism. Then, too, the amendments might make the Constitution sufficiently attractive to induce the two states which had not ratified the document to do so soon. Beyond all of these prudent considerations, however, is the possibility that the powers of the federal government ought to be more carefully guarded against abuse. It would be necessary to proceed with caution, however, because "I should be unwilling to see a door opened for a re-consideration of the whole structure of the government." Amendments should be limited to guarantees of rights to which no objections have been made, for which support has been voiced, and to which both houses of Congress and three-fourths of the states are likely to give their concurrence.[26]

He acknowledged the four main arguments against a bill of rights by turning them into arguments favoring such a declaration. It had been argued with great ingenuity, for example, that there was no bill of rights in the British constitution. Therefore, none was needed in the American constitution. The two systems are not comparable, however, because the British have raised barriers against the crown, but they have left the power of Parliament "indefinite." Although able advocates may be found in favor of these rights in the latter branch of the British government, their "Magna Charta" does not contain a single provision for the security of those rights which most concern the American people. "The freedom of the press and rights of conscience, those choicest privileges of the people, are unguarded in the British constitution." In the United States the prevailing opinion is that constitutional restraints must be raised against every branch of government. The state bills of rights do so with considerable variations of form without necessarily distinguishing between the "pre-existing rights of nature" and others which result from "the social compact" such as trial by jury. Some of them even lay down dogmatic axioms regulating the structure of government. What they have in common, however, is their great object. It is to "limit and qualify the powers of government, by excepting out of the grant of power those cases in which the government ought not to act, or to act only in a particular mode. They point these exceptions sometimes against the abuse of the executive power, sometimes against the legislative, and sometimes against the community itself..."[27]

Some people may argue that paper barriers are too weak to withstand the majority in the community where the highest power exists in our governments. Formal declarations of rights are valuable, however, because they have a "tendency to impress some degree of respect for them, to establish public opinion in their favor, and to rouse the attention of the whole community" so as to control a majority which might be inclined to act otherwise without such a restraint.[28]

Opponents say, also, that it is unnecessary to add restraints on a government which possesses only limited and enumerated powers with the residue left elsewhere. This argument overlooks the grant to Congress of its discretionary power to pass laws for carrying its enumerated powers into effect. Congress is to be the sole judge of the necessity and propriety of choosing such legislative means. This potential prompted Madison to say in 1791 that by loose construction of this discretionary authority "Congress might even establish religious teachers in every parish, and pay them out of the Treasury of the United States, leaving other teachers unmolested in their functions."[29]

In response to the argument that state bills of rights were still in effect, he answered that some states did not have one and others had defective ones. They did not necessarily protect the rights which the public considered to be most important. The argument that declarations have been violated does not prove that a formal statement does not restrain the abuse of power at all. If a bill of rights is incorporated into the Constitution of the United States, then the independent courts will consider themselves to be in a special sense "the guardians of those rights" and a "bulwark against every assumption of power [over them] in the legislative or executive" branches. The courts will be naturally led to resist every encroachment upon rights stipulated in the constitution. Besides this security, it is highly probable that such a declaration would be enforced in the federal system because the state legislatures will "jealously and closely watch the operations of this government." They will be able to resist, more than any other power on earth, every assumption of power. Even the greatest opponents to a federal government admit that the state legislatures are sure guardians of the people's liberty.[30] Apparently Jefferson's hope that the courts would be special guardians of rights moved Madison to add this argument to others he believed more likely to prevail.

In order to conform with American public opinion favoring he most important rights of all, Madison proposed to insert in Article 1, Section 9, a long list of further exceptions to the power of the federal government. Between the third and fourth clauses Madison wanted these words inserted:

The civil rights of none shall be abridged on account of religious belief or worship, nor shall any national religion be established, nor shall the full rights of conscience be in any manner, or on any pretext infringed.

The people shall not be deprived or abridged of their right to speak, to write, or to publish their sentiments; and the freedom of the press, as one of the great bulwarks of liberty, shall be inviolable.

The people shall not be restrained from peaceably assembling and consulting for their common good; nor from applying to the legislature by petitions, or remonstrances for redress of their grievances.

The right of the people to keep and bear arms shall not be infringed. But no person religiously scrupulous of bearing arms, shall be compelled to render military service in person.

To these fundamental freedoms he added a list which constitutes the bulk, but not the whole, of the amendments which were adopted as numbers three through ten in the Bill of Rights.[31]

To the tenth section of Article 1 he proposed to add exceptions to the power of state governments. "I wish also, in revising the constitution we may throw into that section which interdicts the abuse of certain powers in the state legislatures, some other provisions of equal or greater importance than those already made." His recommended words were: "no [sic] state shall violate the equal right of conscience, freedom of the press, or trial by jury in criminal cases; because it is proper that every government should be disarmed of powers which trench upon those particular rights."[32]

This striking assertion is worthy of careful attention. It is an additional, unequivocal statement that the object of a bill of rights is to deny to government any power whatsoever to legislate on the subjects named in the declaration. The form of such a declaration is a specification naming the rights which are exceptions to legislative, judicial, or executive power. In 1785 Madison said in recommending characteristics of a constitution for Kentucky that legislative power tends by its nature to be "indefinite." Therefore, a constitution should name the exceptions to it in order to exempt basic rights from legal restraints. These exceptions should include ones which would "keep them from meddling with religion–from abolishing juries from taking away the Habeus corpus [sic]–from forcing a citizen to give evidence against himself, from controlling the press, from enacting retrospective laws at least in criminal cases, from abridging the right of suffrage, from seizing private property for public use without paying its full Value" and so forth.[33]

The Framers followed this same understanding at the Convention. They followed the sixth Article of Confederation by listing a number of exemptions to federal power. On 28 August they added several clauses to both sections, including the provision for suspending habeas corpus only when specified conditions require it. During the debates on these exemptions which were being increased in number and precision, Madison moved that the words "nor lay imposts or duties on imports" be placed in an article then numbered twelve "which will make the prohibition on the States absolute."[34] Jefferson objected to the qualified privilege of the writ of habeas corpus in the Constitution on the ground that it would not prevent almost constant suspension in a nation where acceptance of this condition had become habitual, as British experience demonstrated.[35] Madison responded that this provision demonstrated the need to avoid making all exceptions to governmental power absolute. Some must be conditional. Otherwise, they will not be heeded in periods of emergency, regardless of whether they are qualified or not. There would be no reason to qualify some exemptions from power, if the others were not believed to be absolute. There can be no other interpretation of Madison's remarks on this subject.

The idea that exceptions named in the Constitution might be converted into constructions supporting power occured to Edmund Randolph who, like Madison, was a Framer and a member of Washington's first cabinet in which he served as attorney general. On 29 February 1788, when Madison was still publishing his essays in The Federalist, Randolph ended a letter to Madison with this question: "Does not the exception as to a religious test [for any office under the authority of the United States] imply that Congress by the general words had power over religion?"[36]

Madison replied on 10 April after he had returned home to Orange, Virginia: "As to the religious test, I should conceive that it can imply at most nothing more than that without that exception, a power would have been given to impose an oath involving a religious test as a qualification for office. The constitution of necessary offices being given to Congress, the proper qualifications seem to be evidently involved. I think too there are several other satisfactory points of view in which the exception might be placed." Undoubtedly, one of these was the explanation he gave to Edmund Pendleton who feared that this constitutional prohibition would destroy the efficacy of oaths. Madison demurred on the ground that an oath is an implied religious test insofar as the person who swears it believes in "the supreme Being who is invoked, and the penal consequences of offending him, either in this or a future world or both..." Such a person will be under the "same restraint from perjury as if he had subscribed [overtly] to a test requiring this belief." If anyone taking an oath is "an unbeliever in these points...a previous test would have no effect. He would subscribe to it as he would take the oath without any principles that could be affected by either."[37]   In this secular republic, government cannot require anyone to profess a belief, implied or otherwise, in a supernatural being in order to perform a governmental function.

Hamilton provided further support for Madison's understanding that the Bill of Rights contains exceptions to governmental power. In explaining the utility of adding a judicial branch to the federal government, Hamilton maintained that judicial independence is essential to a "limited Constitution " It is defined, he said, as one which "contains certain exceptions to the legislative authority" so that it may not pass such acts as bills of attainder and ex post facto laws. These limitations on power cannot be "preserved" in practice except through the actions of courts of law having the duty to declare all such acts void as contrary to the Constitution.[38]   He reinforced this understanding of a limited constitution in his defense of the lack of a bill of rights. After naming several of the exceptions to federal power listed in Article 1, section 9, he pointed out that such a declaration would contain "various exceptions to powers granted..." Why, he asked, "declare that things shall not be done for which there is no power to do?" Take liberty of the press, for example. Should a declaration of rights say that the press shall not be restrained, "when no power is given by which such restraints may be imposed?" Instead of serving to deny power over the press, such a provision might well supply a "pretext...a plausible pretense for claiming that power." The formally declared exception to power might well encourage "the doctrine of constructive powers" over the subjects named in a bill of rights.[39] It is difficult to imagine a more prescient insight into the fate of the First Amendment than this one.

Additional evidence that Madison thought he was following the understanding of the Framers is to be found in the form in which he proposed his amendments. All of the exceptions to the powers of the federal government were to be inserted into the original ninth section of the first article. He proposed to insert the exceptions to state power in the tenth section of the first article. He made form and substance inseparable, but Congress did not agree, of course. Over time the result has been a tendency to obscure the distinction between absolute exemptions from power and qualified grants of it. The real problem of interpreting the exceptions has arisen, however, as it did in Madison's time, from the difference between naming rights and defining them.

He addressed this problem to a limited degree in the few remarks he made in the debates over the amendments. On 15 August 1789 the discussion concerned words proposed by the select committee appointed to deliberate on Madison's original proposals. The committee proposed that "no religion shall be established by law, nor shall the equal rights of conscience be infringed." In opposition it was urged that the words might tend to abolish religion entirely or, on the other hand, they might not secure the beliefs of many sects who felt exposed to interference under the existing language of the Constitution. Madison tried to assure both sides that the words meant Congress would have no power to "establish a religion, and enforce the legal observation of it...nor compel men to worship God in any manner contrary to their conscience." He would not vouch for the necessity of these words in the Constitution, he said, but he would support them to quiet the concerns of some of the state ratifying conventions. They feared that the clause empowering Congress to make all laws necessary and proper for carrying the Constitution into effect would be construed as authority to infringe on the rights of conscience or to establish a "national religion." The amendment was intended, therefore, to prevent these effects insofar as the nature of language will permit.[40]

This explanation notwithstanding, a fear was then expressed that the federal courts would be excluded from jurisdiction over cases brought to compel individuals to contribute to the support of religious societies in the states such as Connecticut where this practice was established by law. Indeed, the proposed amendment might even comfort persons who profess no religious beliefs at all, it was avowed. To assuage these fears, Madison suggested that the word national be inserted before the word religion in the clause under debate. The prevailing fear, he believed, was that one sect or two of them combined might become preeminant and use the power of government to compel others to conform to their demands. His addition would point the amendment to the practice it was meant to prevent.[41]

On 17 August Madison defended his proposed amendment to deny the states power to violate "the equal rights of conscience" as well as free speech and press along with trial by jury in criminal cases. He called it "the most valuable amendment in the whole list." If there were good reasons for denying power over these rights to the United States, then there were equally good ones for doing so in the case of the individual states.[42] It is notable that Madison did not propose to deny states the power to maintain religious establishments. It seems apparent from this omission and his proposal to insert the word *national* in the First Amendment that his actions were deliberate and well understood by his peers in the House.

His only other comment on the amendments while they were pending in the House concerned the Tenth Amendment. He objected to a motion to add the word *expressly* before the word *delegated*. He insisted that this limitation was too confining; powers must be admitted by implication unless the Constitution is to be cluttered with *minutiae*.[43] Despite the fears, real or imagined, of those who perceived the potential for using the elastic clause to regulate religion, Madison parried the thrust at this time.

ANTECEDENTS TO THE SEPARATION OF
RELIGION AND GOVERNMENT

These few and limited remarks about the meanings Madison attached to the religious clauses of the First Amendment can be illuminated readily from his private correspondence and his public papers and actions prior to 1789. In 1773 he asked his friend, William Bradford of Philadelphia, to report the extent of "your religious Toleration" in Pennsylvania. Madison required information about the practice of the Quaker commonwealth because he wished to answer a more basic question: Is an "Ecclesiastical Establishment absolutely necessary to support civil society in a surpream [*sic*] Government? And how far is it hurtful in a dependent state?" The literature immediately available to him for examination was so loosely argued as to "essential truths" as to induce the suspicion that they were "Enemies to serious religion..."[44]

The phrasing of this question reveals that Madison entertained the hypothesis that an established religion was harmful in colonial society such as his Virginia three years before independence. He revealed a positive dislike of the prevailing religious establishment the next year, when he told Bradford that, if the "Church of England had been the established and general Religion" in the northern colonies, as it was in Virginia, and had there been a general peace, then it was clear to him that a slavish subjection to colonial rule would have "insinuated" itself among Americans gradually. He ventured to conclude that unity of religious sentiments begets "confidence," and religious establishments tend to "great ignorance and Corruption," both of which conditions reinforce the execution of "mischievous Projects." In Virginia one finds "Pride, ignorance and Knavery among the Priesthood and Vice and Wickedness among the laity." Worse yet, the "diabolical Hell conceived principle of persecution rages among some and to their infernal infamy the Clergy can furnish their quota of Imps for such business. This vexes me the most of anything whatever." In an adjoining county there were five or six "well meaning men" in jail because they had published their religious sentiments...Madison judged the latter to be generally "very orthodox." He had protested these persecutions to the point where, he admitted, he had become totally impatient. Therefore, "pray for Liberty of Conscience."[45]

Three months later he despaired of greater religious liberty .in Virginia. Most people refused to reexamine their "principles..." They were too attached to their religious establishment to listen to the idea of "Toleration of dissentients..." Virginians were not interested in the "liberal" idea of the "rights of Conscience" which are enjoyed by a "free people..." The few members of the legislature who did entertain the conception of tolerating dissent from officially sanctioned doctrines were overborn by the clergy, Madison said. They are a "numerous and powerful body" who have great influence because of their dependent connection with the "Bishops and Crown..." They use their "art and interest" to depress their threatening adversaries who may rob them of their standing with the people and may eventually "endanger their living and security." The conclusion to be drawn from this cooperative relationship between church and state is that "Religious bondage shackles and debilitates the mind and unfits it for every noble enterprise, every expanded prospect."[46]

With this sweeping condemnation of the constrictive effects on the human mind of religious dogma supported by government, Madison was ready for action where it could be most effective. As a member of the House of Delegates in May, 1776, he prepared two amendments to the religious article of the Declaration of Rights then pending. The exact parliamentary situation is unknown, but the intention of his two drafts is reasonably clear in light of the state of mind with which he approached this work. The first draft provided for the full and free exercise of religion by all persons and, also, declared that no person nor class of persons ought, because of their religion, to be given "peculiar emoluments or privileges"; neither was anyone to be subjected to any penalties or disabilities because of religious beliefs. His second draft was less ambitious. It provided only for the equal right of all to exercise religious beliefs according to the "dictates of conscience" without punishment or restraint by civil government. His words which were officially adopted said "all men are equally entitled to the free exercise of religion," a passage to which he appealed in 1785.[47]

From his remarks made before 1776 and what transpired during the next nine years, it appears Madison intended that the free exercise of religion should replace both officially established religion and its doctrinal handmaiden, religious toleration. There is no record, however, of much that is important about Madison's first attempt to name in a bill of rights an exemption from the power of government. When he was asked a half-century later to illuminate these events more clearly, he said that he ought to be able to do so, but "my memory cannot do justice to my wishes."[48] It seems clear enough, however, that he hoped to substitute the free exercise of religion without civil pains or penalties as a dictate of personal conscience for a dogmatic religious establishment.

Both the language of the Virginia Declaration and subsequent events make it clear, however, that the revolutionary fervor prevailing in Virginia in 1776 did not extend to eliminating in principle or practice the mutually supporting relationship between churches and the government of Virginia. Madison had not underestimated the resistance of Virginians to a liberalizing of this relationship. It was one more proof that the dissolution of British rule did not automatically terminate existing social institutions and relationships. Indeed, this state of affairs led to something of a reaction within a decade so that Madison had new opportunities to develop and elaborate his definition of beliefs which ought to be exempt from governmental influence or control.

In 1784–85 three attempts to legislate support of religion aroused Madison's opposition. The first of these incidents occured in May, 1784, when the "Episcopal Clergy introduced a notable project for reestablishing their independence of the laity," he reported to Jefferson. The bill was to incorporate the entire body of the church, to give it title to all its property, to delegate to it power to make bylaws not inconsistent with the laws of the state, and to divest vestries of the church of their power to remove incumbent officers independent of the church's Convocation. Madison was dismayed to report, further, that this "extraordinary" effort of clergy to enlist the aid of the state to wrest control of affairs from their congregations was preserved from a deserving "death" by the "talents of Mr. [Patrick] Henry."[49] This measure was laid over until the fall session, however, when Madison voted for an amended version because, he said, it was necessary to incorporate for "the purpose of holding and managing the property of the Church." If the law proved to be unpopular with the lay members, it would serve as a "standing lesson to them of the danger of referring religious matters to the legislature." In addition, he thought that passage of this law, which might stir a reaction against it from the church's members, would also serve as a stratagem to dampen the "eagerness and the pretexts for a much greater evil, a General Assessment..."[50]

He was referring to the second attempt by the legislature to support Christian sects, but no others, with a special tax and appropriations. The bill required that each person paying the tax name the sect to which it was to be paid. If individuals refused to do so, the money was to be paid out to maintain a school in each county involved, provided that the use was for "pious" purposes. Despite opposition based on the charge that it violated the religious article of Virginia's Declaration of Rights and that civil government has no power to support religious establishments, the bill was supported by a heavy majority due to a coalition of Episcopalians and Presbyterians. The latter, however, opposed the exclusion of non-Christians from public tax support. Madison thought this difference might produce a split, although the Presbyterians "indirectly favor a more comprehensive establisht." The one ray of light was that Patrick Henry, the "father of the Scheme," left the session early so that the prospects for passing the bill were "very inauspicious..."[51] Madison told Jefferson that not even the substitution of the word Religious for Christian satisfied him. He predicted that, if the law were passed, it would be evaded. It deserved to be opposed because it was "obnoxious on account of its dishonorable principle and its dangerous tendency."[52]

The third attempt to legislate support of religion which Madison opposed in 1784 was made within the Congress of the Confederation. He learned that Congress had finally expunged a provision supporting religion from a bill to regulate political organization of the public lands. It was a requirement that within each township a district should be set aside for "supporting the Religion of a Majority of the inhabitants." Madison could not understand how a rule so "unjust," so clearly absent from the delegated powers of Congress, and one "smelling so strongly of an antiquated Bigotry" could have been so much as considered by that body. On the bright side, he told James Monroe, the action of Congress was better than "our own encroachments on Religious Liberty..." in Virginia... The latter might yet prove, nevertheless, the "sense of the community to be in favor of the liberty now enjoyed" as people begin to understand the probability of further interference by the legislature "once they begin to dictate in matters of religion."[53]

To oppose a pending bill for religious assessments in Virginia, Madison made notes for one or more speeches. First he noted that the courts would have to work through a "labyrinth" of dogmas in order to determine whether the parties coming before them could be defined as "Christian..." Next, he argued that religion falls outside the purview of civil authority which has the tendency to establish Christian dogmas and to enforce them with legal penalties. The problem then arises of determining the "difference between establishing [religious truth?] and tolerating error..." The true question, however, is whether religious establishments are necessary and good for either churches or government, a question he had raised in 1773. Certainly they give rise to bitter denominational conflicts as American experience alone demonstrated. Those who are in favor of establishing religion claim that it benefits civil government. They infer its necessity from the condition of a given society at a particular time of alleged distress. The truth of the matter is that the breakdown of morals which religion is supposed to prevent or cure is due to causes other than the lack of a working relationship between church and state. The two most significant causes of moral breakdown are war and bad laws. This bill would not remove either cause and only "dishonor Christianity." Finally, this proposal takes a step back from the principles of religious liberty guaranteed in Virginia's Declaration of Rights of 1776.[54]

In his famous Memorial and Remonstrance Against Religious Assessments published in 1785, Madison repeated and expanded his prudential arguments against governmental support of religion. Such a relationship rests on the supposition that persons who make and enforce the laws are competent judges of religious truth, or, if they do not make this claim, then they use religion as an instrument to support their rule. The first claim is an "arrogant pretension falsified by the contrary opinions of Rulers in all ages." The use of religion to support civil rule is a "perversion" of true religious convictions. These do not need the support of government either to establish doctrines or to secure belief in them. Often religions have flourished in the face of opposition from governments and certainly without their support. Furthermore, a religion must exist before it is established by law. Compulsory support of religion tends, also, to weaken real belief by engendering the suspicion among those who reject it that the dogmas are too fallacious to merit adherence without a governmental imprimatur. Experience demonstrates that almost invariably, religious establishments have produced "pride and indolence in the clergy; ignorance and servility in the laity; in both, superstition, bigotry and persecution." If government must establish religion by law in order for the people to be convinced, is it possible, Madison asked, that religious teachers fear the downfall of their establishments so long as they are dependent on the "voluntary rewards of their flocks?" On which side, therefore, should the greater weight be given? Is it when their testimony favors, or opposes, "their interest?"[55]

Neither can it be argued successfully that civil government requires the support of religion. Experience demonstrates that in some instances religious establishments have erected a "spiritual tyranny" on the ruins of governments. In other cases they have upheld tyrannical governments. Never, however, have religious establishments served as the guardians of the people's liberties. Therefore, a "just" government does not need them. It is best supported by protecting every citizen's equal rights in the enjoyment of religion without invading the rights of others. The failure to adhere to this rule of justice will be destruction of the moderation and harmony of beliefs which is achieved by forbearing to use laws to "intermeddle with Religion." In the past, torrents of blood have been spilled in vain attempts by governments to eliminate religious differences by requiring uniformity of opinions. Experience in some American states has demonstrated, however, that this "malignant influence" on the health and prosperity of society is inferior to providing "equal and complete liberty" of religion. In addition to dividing society into hostile groups of believers, any attempts to enforce by law acts which are "obnoxious to so great a proportion of the Citizens" should be avoided because of their tendency to erode respect for the laws generally. This effect cannot fail to follow from enactment of this "invalid and dangerous" bill.[56]

Madison rested the argument for a complete separation of church and state on the philosophical ground of natural rights, also. The equal right of every person to the free exercise of religious belief originates as the "gift of nature..." All persons are by nature equally free and independent. They enter into civil society under equal conditions. The natural rights which they retain are "unalienable..." Among them is the right to believe, if convinced, that we owe a duty to a Creator. The right to determine the proper means of discharging it is correlative and can be directed only by reason and conviction, but not by violent force. The right of every individual to determine by conviction and conscience the nature and extent of his religious beliefs is unalienable because one's "opinions" depend on the evidence which each individual alone can contemplate and choose to accept. One person's opinions do not depend on the dictates of other persons. Religious duties, therefore, are "precedent both in order of time and degree of obligation to the claims of Civil Society." Every person who becomes a member of it reserves this right. In matters of religious belief, therefore, no person's right is "abridged by the institution of Civil Society," and religion is "wholly exempt from its cognizance."[57]

With the defeat of the bill for religious assessments, the way was cleared for Madison to push for enactment of Jefferson's bill for religious liberty as part of a general revision of Virginia's laws during the legislature's session of 1785–86. On 22 January 1786 Madison reported the results of his efforts to Jefferson, who was in Paris. Some of the many bills were laid over because they were not essential, but one of "peculiar importance" which was enacted was the "Bill concerning Religious freedom." Its passage was the result of the steps taken throughout the state in 1785 against the "interposition of the Legislature in matters of Religion." In addition, the general convention of the Presbyterian Church urged that the bill for religious freedom be enacted because it was the "best safeguard short of a constitutional one, for their religious rights." The bill was approved without alteration by the House of Delegates, but the Senate objected to the preamble and proposed to substitute for it the "16th art: of the Declaration of Rights." When the House resisted this maneuver, the Senate pursued other "frivolous" objections to the philosophical preamble, and these resulted in "one or two verbal alterations" which the House accepted rather than lose the bill because of the late date of the session and the thinning ranks of its members. The resulting senatorial amendments "did not affect the substance though they somewhat defaced the composition. The enacting clauses past [sic] without a single alteration, and I flatter myself have in this Country [Virginia] extinguished forever the ambitious hope of making laws for the human mind."[58]

This report is noteworthy because it links Madison directly, and unequivocally with Jefferson, as well as Virginia's legislature in 1786, as opponents to all governmental efforts to impose any religious beliefs on their fellow human beings. The marred document was Jefferson's draft of a bill which he had framed as early as 1779. Its defacement consisted of omissions from his philosophical preamble. They included the opening declaration that the opinions and beliefs of human beings follow from the "evidence presented to their minds..." Consequently, religious beliefs can be extended by their protagonists by their influence on "reason alone." This conclusion is included within the general proposition that peoples' opinions and beliefs are "not the object of civil government, nor under its jurisdiction." These deletions are obviously not minor from a philsophical perspective and, therefore, it is not difficult to understand why Madison regarded them as disfigurations of a document which was intended by its primary sponsors to proclaim the natural right of all persons to beliefs uncoerced by civil laws. Madison used precisely the same appeal to the primacy of reason in the Memorial and Remonstrance. When the full body of Madison's convictions concerning this issue is examined, it is evident, also, that he agreed entirely with the portions of Jefferson's draft which was enacted without change. If the two friends differed at all, it was over the application of the general proposition that the opinions of people are beyond the cognizance of government, as we shall observe in regard to libels committed by a free press.

THE RELIGIOUS CLAUSES OF THE FIRST AMENDMENT

The categorical exemption of religion from both the regulatory and the supporting power of government, Madison declared in 1792, follows from the fundamental purpose for which government is instituted. That end is to protect "property of every sort," defined as one's "dominion" over "external things of the world" and in the "larger and juster" sense "every thing to which a person may attach a value and have a right; and which leaves to every one else the like advantage."[59] The latter class of rights includes "opinions and the free communication of them," especially the "peculiar value" one has in one's "religious opinions" and the profession and practice which they dictate... A "just" government is one which "impartially secures to every man, whatever is his own" property in both senses of this term... No government can be just, therefore, if it protects the rights of persons to their external goods, but not the right to the "enjoyment and communication of their opinions in which they have an equal, and in the estimation of some, a more valuable property." Even less is a government to be called just, when it violates the individual's "religious rights" by imposing penalties, restrictive "tests," or taxes imposed by a "hierarchy. Conscience is the most sacred of all property..." Other forms of it depend for their protection on "positive law," but the exercise of the right of conscience is protected as a "natural and unalienable right." The fact that government is instituted to protect one's house gives it no "title to invade a man's conscience which is more sacred than his castle..." Governments have the duty to protect the right to both castle and conscience because of the "very nature and original conditions of the social pact."[60] This right is the gift of nature, not of a government nor of any society creating a government through the exercise of its power and right as the popular sovereign. No organized society has the authority to grant, modify, abridge, or deny this natural right to one's own beliefs and their full enjoyment regardless of whether they are supported by reason or faith.

Madison called a strict separation of church and state for the additional reason that he distrusted appeals to irrational sources of authority in the American republic. There is a fragment on religion in the notes which he prepared in November, 1791, concerning the influence of various factors on the operations of government independent of its structure. This subject contains only a single sentence to indicate the thrust of his thoughts, but it is revealing: "For the cave of Jupiter in Crete where Minos, Epimenides and Pythagoras pretended to have recd. a divine sanction to their laws and see Anacharsis."[61]

This tantalizing fragment appears to have been on Madison's mind, when he composed and published a year later his homilitic, "Who are the Best Keepers of the People's Liberties?" Composing it in the form of a dramatic dialogue, Madison ascribed to an imaginary "Anti-republican" the belief that the people are "stupid, suspicious, licentious." They cannot trust themselves and, therefore, must resign themselves to "obedience," once they have established government. They should leave their liberties to the care of their "wiser rulers." To this call for elite rule, a "Republican" replies that the general lot of people throughout history has been that of "slavery" in which they have been kept in ignorance and divided in order to be ruled. The lesson to be drawn from this undoubted truth, however, is that the people ought to be "enlightened...awakened...and united" so that they may oversee governments once they are established. To this optimistic prescription the Anti–republican answers that not even "the science of the stars" can instruct the common people in the "mysteries of government." To this charge Madison's Republican answered: "Mysteries indeed! But mysteries belong to religion, not to government; to the ways of the Almighty, not to the works of man." In religion mysteries are due to the "dimness of the human sight." There need be no mysteries about institutions created by man, however, "unless for those inferior beings endowed with a ray perhaps of the twilight vouchsafed to the first order of terrestrial creation."[62]

With this ironical allusion to the Platonic cave filled with the mysterious shadows of a divine order, Madison rejected a religious sanction for the authority of government in the American republic. He had long since rejected the argument that an oath of office taken out of fear of divine retribution for its violation ever restrains those who possess and use the power of government. Madison's position in these matters was part and parcel of his rationalism, the obverse of which was his deep distrust of blind passions. The only foundations for religious duties are reason and conviction based on evidence satisfactory to each individual, he said in his *Memorial and Remonstrance..* As far as he was concerned personally, all knowledge of "nature's God" is derived from reason and not from "revelation" reported through an "oral tradition," he said in 1825. The form of proof which is most persuasive is one of "reasoning from the effect to the cause, 'from nature to nature's God'..." This is so because the finite processes of our thought are confronted with the "infinity of time and space..." Nevertheless, the human mind "prefers at once the idea of a self–existing cause to that of an infinite series of cause and effect." This preference increases the difficulty instead of avoiding it, however. It seems easier, therefore, for us to assent to the "self–existence of an invisible cause" possessing "infinite power, wisdom and goodness" than it does to accept the idea of such a first cause "destitute of these attributes." With this analysis of our comparative capacities to reason and to believe, "all philosophical reasoning on the subject must, perhaps, terminate."[63]

Reason alone is the only ultimate foundation for our political duties as well. He rejected titles imitating European orders because they would detract from the "rational" dignity of republican institutions in America.[64] He contended repeatedly that the only earthly source of governmental authority in the United States is the people acting in their sovereign capacity. As such, they had exercised their unalienable and indefeasible natural right to form a new government of their own choice. Governments are just only as they are perceived by the governed to secure this fundamental right and the others we attach value to. For this reason Americans ought to guard their constitution with the "holy zeal" reserved for "political scriptures..." They secure the American people against the "outrages" committed by despots in Europe against "the reason and rights of man."[65] The only safe grounds on which to enlist the "prejudices of the community" are those which give republican institutions that reverence which time must bestow on even the most "rational" forms of government.[66] That form is one which operates, not by pageantry, ceremony and exhalted titles, but by the "reason of its measures" as well as the "understanding and interest of society."[67] Reason, secularism, and republicanism were inseparable elements in Madison's intellectual universe which justified constitutionally limited government for Americans.

On four occasions after he proposed the Bill of Rights Madison applied his principle of strict separation to federal legislation. In 1790 he proposed to include in the first census a count of the various trades and professions as to determine their number and size. He omitted the learned professions because he would have to include persons who teach and "inculcate the duties of religion..." They could not properly be recognized by a law requiring that they be counted because the "general government is proscribed from interfering, in any manner whatever, in matters respecting religion." Therefore, this government ought not to determine "who are and who are not, ministers of the gospel."[68]

Six months later, he announced his wish to exempt conscientious objectors from militia service. He did so because it is the "pride of our present Constitution" that we respect the "rights of conscience" in the exercise of "religious sentiments." Proof of belief was to be given by the individual's making a declaration before a magistrate or by a certificate of membership in a religious society of persons professing this scruple. For this exemption such persons should "pay an equivalent in money," Madison said, but only because "justice" to members of other sects seemed to require it. The purpose of his alternative proofs of belief was to extend the exemption to all "individuals" and not merely to one religious sect or another. He believed that persons who claimed this exemption would not be likely to "put on the mask of hyprocrisy in order to avoid a duty which is honorable." Futhermore, he thought that this risk had to be taken because by "no means hitherto discovered can you make them undertake the defense of this nation" against the scruples of conscience.[69]

In 1800 he categorically reaffirmed his belief that the First Amendment absolutely and positively denies any authority whatsoever to the federal government to pass laws concerning the establishment of religion or denying its free exercise. This amendment was proposed and adopted with the understanding that these two rights, like freedom of the press, speech and political association, are *equally* and *completely* exempted from all authority whatever of the United States." The Constitution was adopted in 1788 with the widely articulated agreement that it delegated no power to the federal government to legislate on this subject. The First Amendment was proposed in 1789 and adopted two years later with the understanding that its purpose was to confirm this interpretation with the prohibitory words *no law.*[70]

As President in 1811 Madison vetoed a bill to incorporate the Protestant Episcopal Church in the Town of Alexandria, then in the District of Columbia. This bill, he declared, exceeds, first, "the rightful authority to which governments are limited by the essential distinction between civil and religious functions." It violates "in particular" the constitutional article which declares that "Congress shall make no law respecting a religious establishment." The bill does so because it establishes by law the sole rules and procedures by which the church is to be organized. As such, if enacted, it would be a religious establishment supported by the force and sanctions of law. The bill goes far beyond the mere purpose of providing "descriptive criteria" by which the "corporate identity of the society" is to be determined. The second unconstitutional flaw in the bill is the function it vests in this incorporated church for providing "support for the poor and the education of the poor children of the same." This grant of authority by law is not only "superfluous," if provisions are to be made for the poor through "pious charity", but also because it provides a "precedent for giving to religious societies as such a legal agency in carrying into effect a public and civil duty." One week later he vetoed a bill appropriating public land to a Baptist church in the Territory of Mississippi. This act, too, violated the Constitution which says that "Congress shall make no law respecting a religious establishment."[71] His use of the same words twice within one week is evidence of his understanding of the constitutional text despite his paraphrase of it. While these two messages reveal his construction of this particular application of the establishment clause, they do not dispose entirely of his conception of what he repeatedly called the separation of religion and government.

Madison broke sharply with this strict view of the separation of religion on government, however, on 9 July 1812. He issued a proclamation recommending that the third Thursday of August next be observed by the people of the United States "with religious solemnity as a day of public humiliation and prayer." Although he did so following Jefferson's precedent at the request of Congress which adopted a joint resolution, the substance and style of his text reveal a pietism which is stunning for its devotional tone. It is equally notable for the occasion which prompted it. The nation was now at war with Great Britain and a presidential election was in the offing. Madison declared that his proclamation would "enable Religious denominations and societies so disposed" to offer on a single day their "common vows and adorations of the Almighty God" on the "solemn occasion produced by the war in which He has been pleased to permit the injustice of a foreign power to involve the United States." Madison did not give any hint of his reasons for believing that religious bodies require an enabling proclamation from the government of the United States to make their prayers on a certain Thursday rather than any other day of the week, but he did specify the content of these pious appeals which might be proper for the occasion. This day should be set aside for the "devout" purpose of rendering due "homage" to the "Sovereign of the Universe and the Benefactor of

Mankind"; acknowledging our "transgressions" which "justly provoke" manifestations of "His divine displeasure"; seeking "His merciful forgiveness... and assistance in the great duties of repentance and amendment"; offering "fervent supplications" that during the war "He...take the American people under his peculiar care and protection...guide their public councils, animate their patriotism, and bestow his blessing on their arms"; and inspire all nations to love peace and justice and to observe the "unerring precept of our holy religion," the golden rule.[72]

This pious invocation of divine aid was no single aberration. He issued three more proclamations in 1813, 1814 and 1815, all equal in tone and devotional substance to his first one in calling for holy and worshipful appeals for a divine blessing on the American war effort and, finally, in thanksgiving for its successful termination in peace. When Madison issued this first invitation to prayer, he was the presidential nominee of the Republican congressional caucus which was well aware of the New England Federalists' lack of appetite for war with Great Britain. Given the firm union of church and state in that region, it would be difficult to decide whether Madison's claim that it was the deity and not his "war party" which was responsible for the war placed a greater strain on his opponents' piety or their credulity.[73]

In 1822 he tried to exculpate himself for these departures from a strict and literal interpretation of the separation of religion and government. It was not with "my approbation," he told Edward Livingston, "that the deviation from it took place in Congress, when they appointed chaplains to be paid out of the National Treasury." If the members wanted them, they should have paid for their services out of pockets of the members who were so inclined. He doubted that the precedent would ever be rescinded, however, so the most he could hope for was that it would be held to a minimum in the future. Another improper deviation from sound constitutional doctrine was the practice of his predecessors who issued executive proclamations declaring "fasts and festivals" in the form of "*injunctions*," some of which lost sight of the "equality of all religious sects" recognized by the Constitution. He followed these flawed precedents, but he satisfied his philosophical and constitutional scruples by making his proclamations mere recommendations which were "absolutely indiscriminate" with regard to all religious beliefs. Their purpose was only to designate particular days on which all persons who were disposed to exercise their beliefs might do so in common.[74] Madison did not venture, however, to recall or to explain his open call for churches to support the war.

Madison's private notes on this subject composed sometime after 1817 reveal the kind of bitingly critical opposition to a working union between government and religion which one would expect from his utterances on the subject prior to July, 1812. He still believed that there is always the danger of "silent accumulations & encroachments by Ecclesiastical Bodies" on the peoples' liberties, even when churches have the "noble merit of unshackling the conscience of persecuting laws" and establishing legal equality among religious sects. This tendency was evident in the states and in various actions of the federal government since 1789 despite the "separation of Religion and Govt in the Constitution of the United States." Moreover, those who govern the kingdom, which is not supposed to be of this world, have demonstrated an alarming passion for accumulating worldly wealth with consequent corruptions of faith so gross in Europe as to make the governments of Protestant countries disregard pleas for the sacredness of property held as a "religious trust" under the law. In the United states there were already dangerous examples of churchly wealth far beyond the foresight of the legislatures which incorporated them with the right of acquiring and holding both real and personal property. There is a real question, also, whether the appointment of chaplains in the armed forces is made with the "spiritual interest of the flocks or the temporal interests of the Shepherds most in view." The law providing congressional chaplains not only unconstitutionally established religion for both representatives and their constituents through compulsory taxation, but also secured the domination of orthodox Protestant sects over "Roman Catholics & Quakers" as well as all others who dissent from orthodoxy. This law displays the "naked deformity of the doctrine that religious truth is to be tested by numbers..." It accounts, too, for the "scanty attendance" of members at this "tiresome formality" conducted by "legal Ecclesiastics..."[75]

Executive proclamations urging prayers or other religious rituals are no less unconstitutional, even if they are only recommendations. They imply that government has a "religious agency" which is in fact denied to it under our constitutional system. Our governments have "no advisory trust from their Constituents in their religious capacities" to form synods, conventions, or councils from which to issue injunctions to the faith or consciences of the public. Furthermore, such actions not only imply, but also, "nourish the erronious [sic] idea of a *national* religion." Even Americans are too apt to embrace this idea associated with the "Jewish nation under a theocracy" and imitated by many other nations as they adopted Christianity. The idea of a union of all under one government united in worship of "the God of all is...imposing," but reason directs otherwise. In a nation consisting of a plurality of sects, some "alienated widely from others," it is doubly wrong for government to establish religion. The last and "not the least objection is the liability of the practice to a subservience to political views, to the scandal of religion, as well as the increase of party animosities. Candid or incautious politicians will not always disown such views." The truth, however, is that it is very difficult to frame religious proclamations prompted by a "political State of things" without referring to "party questions." President Washington's proclamation of thanksgiving after the "insurrection" in Pennsylvania in 1794 was "so construed by many" and explicitly admitted to be so by Alexander Hamilton, according to the documentary record. President Jefferson cautiously circumnavigated this charge by inviting a congressional resolution requesting that he call for voluntary religious observances by individuals disposed to practice them in unison.[76]

This allusion to Jefferson's procedure ended Madison's notes on this subject abruptly without any reference to his own use of it during the years of war with Great Britain. It seems almost as if Madison wished to draw a veil across his memory rather than recall the aid he gave to religious societies in composing their prayers. To do so would have been to condemn himself for acts which, he admitted in the privacy of his study, no candid or incautious president could defend while adhering to his previously strict construction of the separation of religion and government. Apparently he did wish to remind himself–or others after him–that his proclamations did exactly what he condemned. They encouraged the belief that the nation needed a religion, suggested prayers which it is the sole province of ecclesiastical authorities to compose, and undoubtedly used them to support the political views of the war party in the United States between 1812 and 1814. The procedural strategem he employed debased executive power while violating the separation of religion and government by calling for the very union of faith and sword which he had condemned as the historic threat to liberty. The whole matter demonstrates, once again, his observation that pure theory is often yielded to the political circumstances prevailing at any given moment.

In 1823 he gave some indication of the limits of governmental support of religion in a university which he probably envisioned when he moved at the Constitutional Convention to empower Congress to establish a university "in which no preferences or distinctions should be allowed on account of religion."[77] In this instance he referred to his native state of Virginia to which the First Amendment did not apply despite his wish to the contrary. In founding the University of Virginia, the Board of Visitors, of which he was a member, was authorized only to open a "public hall for religious occasions, under impartial regulations..." Had the university established "sectarian professorships," it would have given them a monopoly to propagate their beliefs. Had the university provided professorships for all "rival sects, it would have been an arena of Theological Gladiators." The obvious disadvantage of this policy was that some persons would impute to the university's Board of Visitors and administrators "irreligious tendencies, if not designs." The Board of Visitors accepted this possibility as the lesser of two evils at a risk which Madison thought was smaller in Virginia than in Edward Everett's Massachusetts. Settled opinion in Virginia favored the total exemption of religion from government, Madison said. A "legal establishment of religion without toleration" was unthinkable; and with toleration there is no security for individual rights where there is even the slightest connection between "laws and religion..." With the support of public opinion, opposing the latter, a university with "the feature peculiar to ours will succeed here if anywhere." In the following year he responded to a request from Jefferson for a list of books on the subject of religion which should be included in the library of the University of Virginia. He did so "supposing...that although Theology was not to be taught in the University, its library ought to contain pretty full information for such [person] as might voluntarily seek [it] in that branch of learning."[78]

Despite this progress toward religious liberty, there were some parts of the nation where there was still a "strong bias towards the old error that without some sort of alliance or coalition between Government and Religion neither can be duly supported." The tendency to form such an alliance is undeniable, he conceded, despite "its corrupting influence" on both parties. Consequently, the danger of a union of faith and sword can never be guarded against too carefully. In a "Government of Opinion like ours" the only effective protection against this corrupting coalition is "the soundness and stability of the general opinion on the subject."[79] Parchment barriers to the use of unauthorized power are merely nominal without the support of reason and enlightened opinion which is the real sovereign in every free government.

Obviously, Madison's prescription of separation between government and religion was not founded on any personal hostility to the private practice of religion. Early in his first term as president, he thanked the mother superior of the Ursuline convent in New Orleans for the prayers offered on his behalf by that religious community. He remarked, also, that that in a nation where all rights, "religious as well as civil," are protected by law and "guaranteed by enlightened opinion," there is security for those who train youth in the paths of "Virtue, and useful knowledge..."[80] In 1819 he was asked to comment on the moral tone of Virginians as it was affected by religion. He answered that religion had flourished ever since the Revolution, when the legislature abolished the established church and replaced it with religious liberty. Experience since that notable event had demonstrated that a stable government can function without the "prop of a religious establishment..." It was equally obvious that Christianity had not perished for the lack of legal support for its clergy. Simultaneously, the number and "morality" of the clergy as well as the religious devotion of the people have "manifestly increased by the total separation of church from State."[81]

In 1821 he thanked a correspondent for a copy of an address given at the laying of the cornerstone of St. Matthews Church in New York. This address, Madison noted, was a pleasing and persuasive example of benevolent attachment to a particular creed "untinctured by illiberality" because it recognized the "due distinction" between what is owed to God and Caesar to which the "genius and courage of Luther" led the way. This address demonstrated, also, the value of the American experience with the separation of church and state. That provides a "happy disproof of the error so long rooted in the minds of some Christians" and "persecuting usurpers" that without a "legal incorporation of religious and civil polity neither could be supported." The proper conclusion is that "mutual independence" between the two realms leads to "practical Religion, to social harmony, and to political prosperity."[82]

The conflicts arising over the proper relationship between religion and government, Madison concluded in 1832, originate in human nature. There "appears to be in the nature of man" something which impels belief in an "invisible cause of his present existence, and anticipation of future existence." All of the "propensities & susceptibilities" involving the relationship of "religion" to government arise from this original source. If one waives discussion of the "rights of Conscience" which are excluded from the surrender of other rights upon entering civil society, but are "more or less invaded by all religious Establishments," there is only one question to be answered: whether the Christian religion ought to be supported solely by private donations or by government. Experience provides the answer. The "Papal System" makes for the "worst of Govts." Among the governments of the old world, the "legal" establishment of particular religions without, or with very little, toleration of dissenting sects, makes religion a part of the political order without benefit to either church or state. Until Holland experimented with liberal toleration combined with an established creed, it was assumed, and is still believed by some persons, that an "exclusive & intolerant establishment was essential" for preserving both church and state. It has remained for the United States, however, to provide the "decisive test" of experience which counters these erroneous beliefs and practices. During the colonial period four states and part of another had no "religious Establishments..." The New England states had them for special reasons, but even they have altered their positions in the direction of "the prevailing example..." The southern states ended "legal...provision for the support of Religion" with independence. The result has been a general improvement in the quality of the clergy and an increased devotion of the faithful, although this situation has not been due entirely to the termination of the legal establishment of religion. Nevertheless, the period of fifty years which has passed since "the legal support of religion was withdrawn" demonstrates that it does not require the support of government. Moreover, it will scarcely be claimed that "Government has suffered by the exemption of Religion from its cognizance, or its pecuniary aid." Government cannot be totally blind to the existence of churches because the latter depend on charters of incorporation which legally authorize them to enjoy the rights of property. In addition, government must interfere on occasions without a "corrupt coalition or alliance" with any sect to preserve public order and to protect "each sect agst. trespasses on its legal rights by others." It may be impossible to draw a perfectly distinct line of separation which will avoid all conflicts and doubts about essential points, but any errors which are made will be corrected as reason gradually regains ascendancy over passion.[83]

Madison's objection to a union of government with the Church of Rome did not reflect anti–Catholic bias. He was pleased to believe in 1782 that the Irish Catholics were having the "shackles taken off their religious worship" by a reformist British government. In 1795 he said that they should be eligible for naturalization as Americans because there was nothing in their religion "inconsistent with the purest republicanism" as Swiss experience demonstrated. They should not be ridiculed; many of them had been "good citizens during the revolution."[84]

Madison's final words on this subject leave us to locate the line of separation with perhaps only one clear rule to follow. It is not the function of our governments to use laws to regulate our beliefs whether religious or otherwise. The latter are beyond the "cognizance" of government in the sense that it is forbidden to imply or declare that *anyone* must profess any religious beliefs or doctrines. It is the proper function of religious bodies, and not governments, to propagate such doctrines as may secure the voluntary assent of individuals. This is not to say that government must be blind to the existence of religious bodies to the extent necessary to authorize their corporate existence, to exempt all conscientious objectors from military service, or even to provide meeting rooms and a library stocked with religious tracts for the study of religion in a public university. Support of education with grants of funds or property to religious bodies, however, confuses the distinction between civil and religious functions thereby violating the separation of church and state. In addition, government has a positive duty to recognize individual conscience by securing the right of every individual to hold, enjoy, practice, and communicate his opinions and beliefs prompted by this source without either penalties or burdens for doing so. This is so because every individual enters political society with the unalienated and sole responsibility for determining the existence and extent, if any, of his or her religious duties through use of the gift of nature which makes us sentient beings. It cannot be argued with any support from Madison, therefore, that government in the United States may establish religion, or provide for public prayers as long as it gives no preference to one sect over others.

It is very important to bear in mind Madison's belief that religion benefits from a total separation from government. Theological and moral purity cannot be corrupted by governmental co–optation in the service of power. In the *Memorial and Remonstrance* he pointed to fifteen centuries of history to remind us that the legal establishment of religion had repeatedly corrupted articles of faith by placing them in the service of government. The consequences were superstition, bigotry, and persecution. Prudence demonstrates that the separation of faith and power promotes moderation and even harmony among religious sects because they have no temptation to compete with each other for assistance from government. Finally, separation makes the American republic an asylum for the persecuted and oppressed of all nations and religions so that our freedom of belief shines as a beacon on every coast.

There is no evidence to support any claim that he looked upon instruction in religious tenets to be a cultural requisite for maintaining the American republic. Neither civil rights nor civil duties are dependent upon religious faith any more than they are on any subject amenable to rational inquiry. In his polite correspondence with clerics he conceded that they may provide valuable moral instruction, but he professed no support for the idea that theological teaching is an essential support of the American system of free government. Never once did he assert that there is a necessary connection between civic excellence in a free society and the moral tuition which is claimed to follow from the profession of religious doctrines. In fact, in his memorandum called "The Vices" he pointed to the total failure of religious tuition to temper ruling majorities with a sense of justice toward those whom they may oppress with the weight of overbearing numbers. Undoubtedly recalling the rule of Oliver Cromwell and his religious zealots, Madison averred that no prudent founder wished to see religion in control of government. What is required, he explicitly asserted, is both comprehension of, and commitment to, the fundamental values of our constitutional democracy and an enlightened understanding of its operations. No laws should ever fetter the human mind in its quest for this knowledge or any other kind. This conclusion should be borne in mind, also, in the course of examining Madison's definition and defense of freedom of the press, speech, and political association.

NOTES

1.   *PJM*, 12:203 Useful studies of the framing of the Bill of Rights include Robert A. Rutland, *The Birth of the Bill of Rights* (Chapel Hill, N.C.: University of North Carolina Press, 1955; Edward Dumbauld, *The Bill of Rights* (Norman, OKla: University of Oklahoma Press, 1957; Irving Brandt, *The Bill of Rights* (Indianapolis, Ind: Bobbs Merrill and Co., Inc., 1965.)
2.   Farrand, *Records*, 2:341–42, 587–88.
3.   *PJM*, 11:130–31.
4.   Ibid., 10:163–64; italicized words encoded in the original.
5.   Ibid., 179–180.
6.   Ibid., 215, 217, 221.
7.   For some of these reports see ibid., 181, 183, 186, 190,.193, 194, 198, 227–31, 242–43, 248, 251, and so on, enough items to fill much of the second half of volume ten of his *Papers*; no good purpose could be served by citing all of them.
8.   Ibid., 202.
9.   Ibid., 234.
10.   Ibid., 244.
11.   Ibid., 344.
12.   Ibid., 336.
13.   See Malone, *Rights*, 165–76.
14.   *The Federalist*, 237, 239 (No. 38).
15.   *PJM*, 11:167; also 170.
16.   Ibid., 177–78.
17.   Ibid. 10:179, 217, 498–99, 510, 519.
18.   Ibid. 11:212–13
19.   Ibid., 226.
20.   Ibid., 238, 240.
21.   Ibid., 297; see also ibid. 1:174–75; 8:351; 11:293.
22.   Ibid. 11:297–98, italics in the original. Jefferson objected to James Wilson's defense of the lack of a bill of rights; see ibid. 10:336.
23.   Ibid., 11:298–99.
24.   *PJM*, 11:299, 300.
25.   Ibid. 12:13–14.
26.   Ibid., 196–99 passim. For an analytically and historically limited account of Madison's introduction of the Bill of Rights to the House see Brandt, *Madison*, 3:264–75.
27.   *PJM*, 12:203–4.
28.   Ibid., 204–5.
29.   Ibid., 205; 13:375–76.
30.   Ibid. 12:206–7.
31.   Ibid. 201–2.

32. Ibid. 208, italics added.
33. Ibid. 8:351.
34. Farrand, *Records*, 2:441.
35. *PJM*, 11:212–13.
36. Ibid. 10:543.
37. Ibid., 223; 11:19.
38. *The Federalist*, 505 (No. 78).
39. Ibid., 558–559 (No. 84).
40. *PJM*. 12:339.
41. *Annals of Congress* (Washington: Gales and Seaton, 1834), 1st Cong., 1st sess., 731.
42. *PJM*, 12:344.
43. Ibid., 346.
44. Ibid. 1:101.
45. Ibid., 105–6.
46. Ibid., 112–13.
47. Ibid., 174–75.
48. *LJM*, 3:607.
49. *PJM*, 8:93–94.
50. Ibid., 217, 228–29.
51. Ibid., 136–37, 157–58; 9:430–31.
52. *PJM*, 8:229.
53. Ibid., 286.
54. Ibid., 197–99. For attempts to construct one or more speeches from these notes see Brandt, *Madison*, 2:344–45; and Thomas E. Buckley, *Church and State in Revolutionary Virginia* 1776–1787 (Charlottesville, Va.: University Press of Virginia, 1977), 99–100.
55. *PJM*, 8:301.
56. Ibid., 301–3 passim.
57. Ibid., 299–300, 304.
58. Ibid., 394–401, 473–74.
59. *PJM*, 14:266, italics in the original; from "Property," 27 March 1792.
60. Ibid., 266–267,
61. Ibid., 163; see 168 n. 2 and 11:413 for notes on the source.
62. Ibid., 427, italics in the original.
63. *LJM*, 3:503–5. For an interpretation of these letters and their place in Madison's conception of church–state relations which minimizes Madison's religious scepticism see Ralph L. Ketcham, "James Madison's Religion: A New Hypothesis," in *James Madison on Religious Liberty*, ed. Robert S. Alley (Buffalo, N.Y.: Prometheus Books, 1985), 175–96.
64. *PJM* 11:155.
65. Ibid. 14:191–92.
66. *The Federalist*, 329 (No. 49).
67. *PJM*, 14:234.
68. Ibid., 13:16.
69. Ibid., 328–29, 330–31, 333 passim.
70. *LJM*, 4:551.
71. James E. Richardson, ed., *Messages and Papers of the Presidents*, 20 vols. (New York: Bureau of National Literature, 1914), 1:474–75.

72. Ibid., 498.
73. Ibid., 517, 543, 545. For the political situation then prevailing see J. C. A. Stagg, *Mr. Madison's War: Politics, Diplomacy and Warfare in the Early American Republic 1783–1830* (Princeton, NJ: Princeton University Press, 1983) 60–119; and Brandt, *Madison*, 4:452–83.
74. *LJM*, 3:274–75, italics in the original.
75. Elizabeth Fleet, ed., "Madison's Detached Memoranda," *William and Mary Quarterly*, series, 3 (1946):534–68, 554–58.
76. Ibid., 559–62.
77. Farrand, *Records*, 2:616.
78. *LJM*, 3:306–8 passim; WJM, 9:203.
79. *LJM*, 3:275.
80. James Madison, *The Papers of James Madison Presidential Series,* ed. Robert A. Rutland and others, 1 vol. to date (Charlottesville, Va.: University Press of Virginia, 1984), 1:136.
81. *LJM*, 3:124–25.
82. Ibid, 4:242–43.
83. *WJM*, 9:483–87 passim.
84. *PJM*, 4:432; 15:432–33.

Chapter 7

The Very Essence of Free and Responsible Government

Madison was no more confident about the effectiveness of constitutional exemptions of free speech, press, and association than he was about textual denials of power over religion. He made only one reluctant speech concerning the former subject, when it was pending before the House. He objected, when Representative Thomas Tucker of South Carolina moved on 15 August 1789 to add explicitly to the guarantee of free speech, press and association the right of the people to instruct their representatives. Sensing that this motion was dilatory, Madison said there was no point in proposing and arguing "abstract propositions" like this one because it might jeopardize support for the whole system of government. The people have a "right to express and communicate their sentiments and wishes" to their representatives because it is provided for by the freedom of speech and press in this amendment. Both rights are placed "beyond the reach of this government." People may do so in private or public, either individually or by petition. These are the "great and essential" rights which critics of the Constitution have demanded. They have taught the people to believe the Constitution will not protect them without these amendments. For this reason "I approve these amendments," but no others, and as a "friend to what is attainable, I would limit them to those which provide this important security."[1]

In defending this minimal position, Madison did not yield his prior convictions and doubts. On 19 August 1789 he complained bitterly to a correspondent about this "nauseous project of amendments" which had necessarily taken up so much of the House's time. He conceded that constitutional declarations favoring essential rights are "not improper," and he had always regarded them as such. They are in some degree "rational in every Govt." because power may be used to oppress and "declarations on paper, tho' not an effectual restraint, are not without some influence."[2] Within five years he had an occasion to confirm this general position, and within a decade he had an even more alarming occasion to do so. In 1794 Congress threatened the right of association. In 1798 Congress transformed the exemptions of speech and press into grants of power used to punish persons who communicated their sentiments too freely to their representatives. In time this action evoked from Madison one of his ablest defenses of these great and essential freedoms.

THE CENSORIAL POWER IS IN THE PEOPLE

The first opportunity Madison had to maintain that the First Amendment totally exempts speech, press, and association from congressional control arose in 1794. President Washington, flushed with his success in overawing the Whiskey rebels, officially denounced the numerous Democratic Societies for aiding them with sympathetic expressions of support. Obviously, Washington believed and asserted that their utterances incited disobedience to the law. When the House of Representatives chose Madison to draft its official reply to the president's message, Madison deliberately glossed over Washington's censure of the Democratic Societies because he perceived the political game which some of the Federalists were playing by trying to make the Republicans look like advocates of insurgency. To this end, a move was made in the House of Representatives to amend Madison's draft of the reply by denouncing "self-created" societies. This move challenged Madison, who refused to vote for a bad principle which he regarded as serious breach of the First Amendment and a bad precedent as well. In opposing, he made arguments which not only confirmed his belief that certain rights are wholly exempt from power, but also foreshadowed his far more comprehensive attack on the Sedition Act of 1798.

In his efforts to minimize this conflict, Madison made only one speech in the House, and he complained to Jefferson that the report of it in the newspapers was badly garbled. It appears that he was correct, but the record should be noted anyway.[3] He commenced by saying that the House would be proceeding on a novel and unsound ground if it intervened in cases "not cognizable by law..." On the contrary, the sound rule is that "an action innocent in the eye of the law, could not be the object of censure to [by] a legislative body." When the Constitution was formed, the people retained rights over which they did not grant power. The question is then raised whether this government can legislate or even notice reserved rights. Among these are the right to express "opinions [which] are not the object of legislation." Critics may denounce the "abuse of reserved rights" and ask how far it may extend. The answer is that it "may extend to the liberty of speech and of the press." In this connection it should be observed how "extremely guarded" the Constitution is with respect to subjects "not within its limits." Murder and treason, for example, cannot be "noticed" by Congress. If the measure before us were to be passed, would it not be a "vote of attainder?" It is vain to say that "indiscriminate censure is not punishment." If it is directed to classes, persons, or individuals, it will be a "severe punishment." The "law is the only rule of right"; what is consistent with it is "not punishable"; what is not contrary to it is "innocent, or at least not censurable by the legislative body." The effect of acting contrary to this principle will be "pernicious," a violation of a fundamental characteristic of "republican government..." The rule of interpretation contended for by the critics of the Democratic Societies is that they place the "censorial power" in the government over the people instead of its being "in the people over the government..."

Madison placed his confidence in their good sense and patriotism. He did not believe that there would be any "lasting evil" resulting from the publications of the Democratic Societies. The press could not shake the public's confidence in the government. "In a republic light will prevail over darkness, truth over error–he had undoubted confidence in this principle."[4]

In correspondence with Jefferson and Monroe, Madison encapsulated his arguments against this attack on "the most sacred principle of our Constitution and of Republicanism."[5] The supporters of censure maintained two principles, Madison said, and neither could be "more indefensible in reason and dangerous in practice." The first one of these is that "arbitrary denunciations may punish what the law permits, and what the legislature has no right, by law, to prohibit." The second one of these doctrines is that "Govt. may stifle all censures whatever on its misdoings; for if it be itself the Judge it will never allow any censures to be just, and if it can suppress censures flowing from one lawful source it may [gag] those flowing from any other–from the press and from individuals as well as from Societies, etc."[6]

To this lucid and cogent statement denying to the government any power whatsoever to denounce its citizens for the expression of their opinions of its conduct, Madison added that the proper remedy for erroneous opinion was functioning well. The attack by the government on the societies was not having its intended effect, he reported to Jefferson just before Christmas, 1794, because appeal to public opinion was being made by the injured societies in Baltimore, Newark, New York, and Boston. There the newspapers were arguing the issues very ably on the "republican side." And well they might, he said, because the attack on the societies was in reality one on "the essential and fundamental right of the Citizen..." It must be felt by every one who "values liberty, whatever opinion he may have of the use or abuse of it by these institutions."[7]

In responding to Madison, Jefferson said he was astonished at the boldness of the "Monocrats" and the president's willingness to be their agent in this attack on "freedom of discussion, the freedom of writing, printing and publishing." In the light of these events he was curious to know exactly what modifications of these rights their critics proposed to make. It would be equally intriguing, he thought, to know exactly what line these critics would draw between the democratic societies which were nourishing "the republican principles of our Constitution" and the "society of the Cincinnati, a self-created one," which had been seeking to establish its own hereditary rank. Some of its known members were denouncing "democrats" and slandering the friends of "popular rights." At least within his own circle, Jefferson was pleased to say, everyone understood this "abstract attempt on natural and constitutional rights in all its nakedness." Given the nature of this whole affair arising out of the anti-tax rebellion, it remained to be seen what "the court lawyers, and courtly judges and would be Ambassadors will make of it."[8]

Jefferson and Madison had to wait four years to find out exactly how some lawyers, judges, and others would draw the limits of freedom of speech and the press. They asserted that these freedoms guaranteed by the First Amendment must be defined; naming them is not enough. Anglophiles and others found the definition in the terms of the English common law. With this definition incorporated into the Sedition Act of 1798, Congress claimed the power to punish Americans not only with official censure, but also with fines and imprisonments. This act embodied the two doctrines which Madison called unreasonable and dangerous in 1794; namely, that the expression of opinions can be noticed and regulated by law, and the government may suppress its critics by punishments.

Even while the Sedition Act was merely the subject of rumors of things to be, Jefferson and Madison understood its intended immediate purpose and potential effects in the long term. This curb on free speech was meant to silence critics of the administration's foreign policy. In the longer run, the Sedition Act, if enforced with selective vigor, might enable the Federalist party to hold power in the executive branch, at least, until 4 March 1805. If it failed to do so, a succeeding party would have to reenact such a statute in order to gain vengeance against its former oppressors. It could not have escaped notice, too, that the vice-president (Jefferson) was not named in the Sedition Act as an officer privileged with this shield against public criticism. The basic strategy, however, Jefferson predicted to Madison, would be to block publication of the the circular letters between Republican representatives and their constituents. Means were needed to silence or punish the Adams administration's critics for their utterances which were unprivileged outside the halls of Congress.[9] Jefferson was observing the scene as vice-president and reporting his analyses to Madison who was then a private citizen living at his home (Montpelier). Madison responded hopefully but realistically to the first of these rumors. He was pleased to see that everything that "good sense and accurate information can supply is abundantly exhibited by the newspapers to the public." Unfortunately, this effect falls short of the ideal because truth is mixed with "indiscretion" in some of them, and this blemish limits their circulation. He remained hopeful, however, that "any arbitrary attacks on the freedom of the press will find virtue enough remaining in the public mind to make them recoil on the wicked authors." He thought, also, that the "sanguinary faction" of the Federalist party ought "not to adopt the spirit of Robespierre without recollecting the shortness of his triumphs and the perpetuity of his infamy."[10] The irony of this parallel was lost on the Federalists, who soon acted as Madison expected them to. On 10 June 1798 he predicted to Monroe that the composition of Congress and its prevailing spirit made it likely that they would seize any opportunity for "wreaking party revenge through the forms of the Constitution."[11]

The Federalists' vehicle for reaching this goal was the second section of the Sedition Act. This part of the law defined three crimes and prescribed fines, imprisonment, or both, upon conviction. The act declared it a crime to write, print, utter or publish anything "false, scandalous and malicious" about the government of the United States with the intent of defaming it, or to excite among the people any contempt, disrepute, or hatred toward members of Congress or the president. Also proscribed were combinations formed to resist, oppose, or defeat any law of the United States or act taken by the President in pursuance thereof (the moonshiners' insurgency had not been forgotten). It was made equally criminal to aid, abet, or encourage the hostile designs of any foreign government toward the United States. Any person prosecuted under this act was graciously given the right to offer the truth as evidence in his defense. Trial of both law and fact were to be by jury. The act was to continue in force until March, 1801.[12]

This law was claimed to be constitutional on three main grounds. First, the power to make all laws necessary and proper for carrying the Constitution into effect authorizes Congress to punish writings which are intended to stir up sedition against the United States. Next, the idea of a free press does not mean that every person has a "license" to publish whatever he pleases without liability for punishment, if this privilege is abused. It is only permission to publish without prior restraint. Therefore, a law punishing licentious publications cannot be an abridgement of the freedom of the press protected by the First Amendment. This definition was adopted by nearly all the states after the Revolution. Prior to that time it was the definition in England "from whence our laws are derived." Therefore, the act creates no new crime and gives no new power to the courts. The second section of the third article of the Constitution extends the judicial power of the United States to all offenses arising under it. Libels against the government are included in this class of offenses. As such they are punishable in accordance with the common law. Finally, if it were intended by the Framers of the First Amendment that Congress be absolutely prohibited from legislating at all on the subject of the press, the Constitution would contain the same language as that used to place religion beyond its reach. Concerning religion, the Constitution says that Congress shall make "no law," but it does not say it is expressly forbidden to do so in the case of the press. All that is forbidden is that Congress shall not abridge freedom of the press and speech. The inescapable conclusion, then, is that Congress may lawfully punish those persons who pervert this right and turn it into an engine of sedition against the government.[13]

It is difficult to imagine a more clever and casuistical argument to fulfill the predictions of those persons like Madison who anticipated that the enumeration of rights intended to be absolute denials of power would be transformed into grants of it by constitutional interpretation. The arguments favoring the act contravened the position Madison took in 1794 and added a new weapon to the government's arsenal. Once again, the British system provided Adams and his fellow Federalists with a model to be imitated. The right to publish is a mere license, a privilege, a permission revocable by government through punishment after utterance. The Revolution had not broken the chain of continuity; the common law was implicitly incorporated into the Constitution, they claimed. Equally striking was Congress' division of the rights enumerated in the First Amendment into two classes: those which are beyond its legistative reach and those which are not. The religious rights compose the first category and the freedoms of expression and association the other, according to the sophists who invented this argument.

In rebuttal to supporters of the act, Madison elaborated his thesis stated in 1794 that the power to censure official behavior rests with the people. It is not vested in government to stifle popular criticism. In the American republic this functional relationship is established by limiting grants of power to the federal government and positively forbidding it either to notice or control expressions of opinions and beliefs. For this constitutional reason and others, the English common law of seditious libel cannot be constructively incorporated into our Constitution in order to define freedom of speech, press, and association. It follows that modification of the common law, allowing the truth of an utterance to be offered in its defense, cannot be constitutionally valid. Madison's rejoinder was organized into three main parts: one aimed at denying that the English common law was incorporated into the Constitution; another one justifying absolute freedom of the press, and the third one stating the essential relationship between absolute freedom of utterance and the maintenance of representative government by means of free elections. This response was prepared in the fall of 1799 as a report of a select committee of the House of Delegates of Virginia and officially adopted at the end of the first week of January, 1800.

THE REPORT OF 1800

Madison opened the exposition of his thesis that the Sedition Act was unconstitutional, not merely unwise, by denying that the English common law was ever constructively incorporated into the First Amendment in order to define the freedom of the press. It was necessary to do so, he said, because supporters of the statute had made the sweeping claim that the common law of crimes was implicitly incorporated into the Constitution along with the explicitly enumerated powers. This contention reached well beyond the Bill of Rights in effect, of course. According to a contemporary legal scholar, however, the amendment did nothing more than give "constitutional recognition to common law rights."[14] It is necessary, therefore, to review in some detail Madison's arguments concerning his understanding of both the intentions of the framers of the original text of the Constitution and of the Bill of Rights with reference to the common law.

His general and fixed position before, during, and after the adoption of the Constitution was that no foreign law can be used constructively to define authoritatively the legal obligations created by the federal government or to fix the scope of powers of any of its branches. More particularly, he insisted that, if foreign laws or technical terms were adopted by Congress or incorporated into the text of the Constitution, it must be done by express act and not by implicit construction. This requirement followed from the dissolution of British authority in 1776 and its replacement, first, by independent states, then a loose confederation of them, and, finally, a federal union of republican governments. The first of these events left the states free to create new governments and to authorize them to continue or modify their varied laws individually. The Confederation did not change this situation, so that a necessary object of modifying the political system in 1787 was to authorize the federal legislature to adopt its own laws for the union without regard to either foreign or state laws, although it was left free to use or to enforce such laws by explicit actions within the limits of delegated authority.

He first identified this problem in 1784 when he expressed to Edmund Randolph a vexed concern for the lack of an authoritatively established and uniform law to settle certain kinds of controversies. In this instance, the governor of South Carolina had called on the governor of Virginia to extradite an alleged criminal. The question whether the crime was federal in nature was complicated, Madison remarked, by the lack of a clearly established law. If that of South Carolina differed from "the British law," Madison noted, there would be dispute over the meaning of the terms "Treason etc." The issue would be whether the definition taken from that source was in effect, or whether it would be one to which the "several States may annex the same titles and penalties." The text of the Articles provided no guidance, but the truth was that, had those who compiled it "severally declared their meanings," they would be as "diverse as the comments which will be made upon it." Our "experience" demonstrates a need, Madison concluded, for a "Droit Public [sic]" which presupposes a much greater "mutual confidence and animity" among the American states than the law which has grown out of the "intercourse of jealous & hostile Nations."[15] In short, no foreign law nor diverse state laws were suitable unless they were expressly adapted to fit our unique circumstances. Authority to create an American public law for the union was sorely needed.

Madison next participated in a discussion of this problem at the Constitutional Convention on 7 August 1787. At issue was the wording of the report of the Committee of Detail which authorized Congress to "declare the law and punishment of piracies and felonies..." Madison moved to strike the word *punishment*, and his motion carried. Then he and Randolph moved to substitute *define* for *declare*. James Wilson responded at once, saying that felony was a term "sufficiently defined by Common Law." Madison's immediate rejoinder was that "felony at common law is vague. It is also defective." It was improved by a "Stat: of Anne" which broadened the common law definition. *"Besides no foreign law should be a standard farther than is expressly adopted."* If, on the other hand, the laws of the states were to prevail, then there would be no "uniformity or stability" in the law of the United States. "The proper remedy for all these difficulties was to vest the power proposed by the term 'define' in the National legislature." The Framers adopted this motion forthwith without demurrer and the final language was adopted.[16]

The Framers followed this same line of reasoning in fixing a constitutional definition of treason on 20 August. Madison said the definition provided in the Report of the Committee of Detail was "too narrow. It did not appear to go as far as the Stat. of Edward III. He did not see why more latitude might not be left to the legislature" since experience might enlighten its discretion, although the latter might be used to either good or bad effect.[17] There ensued a debate over this definition which appears to have consumed almost the entire day, if Madison's record of motions, speeches and votes is reliable. Madison spoke briefly four times in order to perfect a constitutional definition of treason which expressly took into consideration the federal nature of the government which had been decided upon a month earlier.[18] If any member of the Convention thought that this definition should or could be left to be determined by the English common or statute law, he did not say so according to the only existing record.

George Washington questioned Madison about the status of the common law relative to the Constitution on 10 October 1787. Washington was confused by George Mason's claim that the Constitution was flawed because it did not secure the common law.[19] Madison could think of no valid reason for this charge. "The common law is nothing more than the unwritten law, and is left by all the constitutions equally liable to legislative alteration." He was not sure that any particular notice of it was taken in the state constitutions except possibly for a general declaration continuing it along with other branches of the law in force until legally changed in the future. The Constitution of Virginia which Mason drew up "is absolutely silent on the subject," although an ordinance passed during the same session (1776), "declared that the Common law as heretofore and all statutes of prior date to the 4 James of 1 to be still the law of the land, merely to obviate pretexts that the separation from G. Britain threw us into a State of nature, and abolished all civil rights and Obligations." Since the Revolution, every state, and certainly Virginia, has quite properly made great inroads in many instances on this *"monarchical code"* through statutory revisions. If the federal convention had in "general terms declared the Common law to be in force, they would have broken in upon the legal code of every State in the most material points: they would have done more, they would have brought over from G.B. a thousand heterogeneous and antirepublican doctrines, and even the *ecclesiastical Hierarchy* itself, for that is a part of the Common law." If they had attempted to distinguish the elements of the common law to be adopted from those which were not, they would have had to form "a digest of laws, instead of a Constitution." No objection to this omission was raised at the Convention, but if it had been, the reasons would have been explained in such a way that a repetition of Mason's confused charge in a subsequent public debate would scarcely have been attempted. The Convention could not be faulted for "ommissions which were never suggested" to its members nor for "reasons which either were not previously thought of, or must have been wilfully [sic] concealed," if Mason's charge were true.[20]

Madison next gave a public explanation in *The Federalist* in January, 1788. The congressional power to define piracies and felonies committed on the high seas marked an improvement over the Articles of Confederation. They contained no provisions for punishing offenses against the law of nations. Therefore, a legislative definition was "evidently requisite." Felony is a term loosely defined "even in the common law of England" and it varies in British statutes. "But neither the common law nor the statute law of that, or of any other nation, ought to be a standard for the proceedings of this, unless previously made known by legislative adoption." The same deficiency is found in state laws. It would be "impracticable...dishonorable and illegitimate" to follow foreign laws.[21]

The issue was raised again on 20 June 1788 at Virginia's ratifying convention. George Mason made a long speech in which he charged, among other things, that the federal courts would use the common law to displace the state courts in effect and even to destroy their governments ultimately. He drew this inference from the use in the judicial article of the phrase *law and equity*. When Madison challenged him to reveal who had told him that this result would follow, Mason admitted that it was neither Madison nor any other member of the Virginia delegation to the Convention of 1787. Mason conceded, also, that Congress was authorized to change any common law proceedings in the federal courts, but he feared that it would not do so.[22] Madison responded with the remarks he had made previously in *The Federalist* to the effect that the Constitution authorized Congress to adapt such laws as it might see fit to secure uniformity in federal laws. For this reason it was conceded on all sides that it was "necessary and expedient" for the judicial power to "correspond with the legislative." All the terms of foreign origin are either defined in the constitutional text or authorized to be defined statutorily by Congress.[23]

In June, 1789, one of the amendments Madison proposed was to change the second section of the judicial article with an explicit reference to the common law. No "fact triable by jury, according the the course of the common law" shall be "re- examinable" by any rules other than those "consistent with the principles of the common law."[24] In essence this proposal became the Seventh Amendment. It would appear that Congress agreed with Madison that, if common law rules or definitions were to be made authoritatively binding by the Constitution, it must be by specific, *express, and previous* adoption in the Constitution rather than by subsequent implication; or Congress must be authorized to adopt or adapt rules of the common law by statute.

Madison drew on this record of construction in his Report of 1800 to deny the astonishing claim of the House of Representtives that the federal courts were authorized to punish libels against the federal government *without* the authority of the Sedition Act. A majority of the House asserted that the English common law was implicitly incorporated into the second section of the judicial article of the Constitution. That section extends the judicial power of the United States to all "offenses" against the Constitution and the government it created. A libel against the government is such an offense under the English common law and, therefore, against the government of the United States, also. Moreover, the House maintained, this offense was punishable by the federal courts at their discretion in accordance with the common law. The Sedition Act simply declared this doctrine. It did not grant any new power to the courts. In fact, this law diminished their power in two respects. It limited the punishments which they might give to stated maximums instead of leaving this matter to judicial discretion. In addition, the statute permitted the truth to be offered as a defense, whereas the common law did not grant this privilege. Finally, the House alleged, the act did not violate the First Amendment because these two mitigating provisions enlarged the common law definition of freedom of the press instead of abridging it.[25]

Examined superficially, this defense might appear consistent with Madison's statement in the forty-second *Federalist*: the Framers rejected foreign laws as a standard defining federal laws unless previously adopted by Congress. Examined carefully, however, the claim that the federal courts' constitutionally declared jurisdiction is defined by the common law will be perceived as being utterly inconsistent with Madison's explanation of the Framers' intention. The object of the restriction against constructive incorporation of foreign legal terms was to authorize Congress to use them, as the Framers had done in the constitutional text, to define offenses against the United States. Congress was left free, except in the case of treason, to adopt or adapt foreign legal rules without altering their names, but to do so within the limits of power granted to the federal government. Supporters of the Sedition Act claimed, however, that the language the Framers used in the judicial article constructively incorporated the common law into part of the Constitution regardless of any authorizing statutes enacted by Congress. Even as confused as George Mason was concerning this issue, he understood that Congress was authorized to regulate the proceedings of the federal courts whether in accordance with the common law or not. Therefore, the contention of the congressional majority supporting the Sedition Act made a claim far beyond the pretense that freedom of the press in the First Amendment is defined by the common law. As Madison's political ally, John Taylor, put the matter, the strategy of some persons was to create a government which could "at pleasure dip their hands into the inexhaustable treasures of the Common Law, and thence extract as much power as they please."[26]

In order to counter this broad strategy, Madison attacked the validity of the Sedition Act by refuting the claim on which it rested. Can it be possible, he asked rhetorically, that, despite the language of the Tenth Amendment, "the common law [is] introduced by the Constitution of the United States?" This question goes beyond the admission that some of the technical language of the common law is used in the Constitution to name some of the powers delegated and to authorize Congress to adopt portions of that legal code for carrying the Constitution into effect. The "only portion" of the document relied on is the second section of the judicial article. From this language it is inferred that the common law has been adopted by the Constitution. Never, Madison asserted, was so broad a construction so clearly improper. In fact, it is only necessary to refer to the two textual descriptions of cases to which the judicial power of the United States extends in law and equity in order to demonstrate that neither of them "implies that the common law is the law of the United States."[27]

To disprove this proposition, Madison drew on his knowledge of the framing, including his contribution to this part of the text, and reason.

The purpose of the second section of the judicial article was to describe the categories of cases to which the federal judicial power extends. At the Constitutional Convention this matter was debated, and he objected to a motion to extend jurisdiction. It ought to be limited, he said, to cases of a "Judiciary nature. The right of expounding the Constitution in cases not of this nature ought not to be given to this department." When it was agreed without objection to extend jurisdiction to all cases in law and equity arising under "this Constitution" and so forth, he noted: "it being generally supposed that the jurisdiction given was constructively limited to cases of a Judiciary nature." Shortly thereafter, he and Edmund Randolph secured a favorable vote for their phrase *the Judicial power* for language referring to "jurisdiction."[28] In his Report of 1800 he concluded that the words *law* and *equity* applied to civil, not criminal, cases. Even if the judicial article were strained to embrace the common law, a multiplicity of problems would arise in determining its relationship to written law both in Britain and America at various times at least since settlement of the colonies. Finally, had it been the Framers' intention to adopt the common law for the United States, it is impossible to explain why such a decision was "not expressed in the enumeration" of the government's powers.[29]

Reason demonstrates the far–reaching implications of incorporation into the Constitution. Congress could not alter the common law, not even by the Sedition Act, which modified the English law. If it is claimed, on the other hand, that the common law defines the authority of Congress qualified by its power to alter the common law, then the Constitution imposes no limits on this branch. But most important, the effect of constructive incorporation is to give the courts a discretion "little short of legislative power," including determination of what portions of the common law shall be enforced. Furthermore, this power could be used to overrule state constitutions and laws and to "new model the whole political fabric of this country" by judicial construction. The only proper conclusion, therefore, is that the common law "never was, nor by fair construction ever can be, deemed a law for the American people as one community."[30]

Before Madison's report was adopted by the Virginia legislature, he admitted to Jefferson that the "part about the Common Law–will certainly be combated [*sic*]." On the contrary, it was not a major issue in either house and the report was readily adopted in a rather short time.[31] Twenty–four years later, Madison reviewed this subject again and noted that the common law has been called our "birthright," but it has been done without regard to "precise meaning." It is no more our birthright, he asserted, than the statute law of England nor its "Constitution."[32]

In the next part of his argument in the Report of 1800, he contended that actual practice had done much to define the meaning of freedom of the press. American experience, in particular, was due preeminent weight in defining this constitutional right, he insisted. In every state the right to comment freely on public officials and their actions had never been confined to the strict letter of the common law. It was accepted that the abuses of free expression had been greatly outweighed by the advantages. A free press had been essential for the victory of reason over error and the triumph of humanity over oppression which resulted in American independence and the constitutional improvements made since then. Otherwise, Americans might still be living under imperial rule or the infirmities of the Confederation.

The common law definition is inapplicable, also, because of basic differences between the two systems of government. In Britain the danger to individual rights is supposed to come from the executive branch. It is the latter which licenses publication without previous restraints subject to punishment for utterances which are illegal according to the common law. In theory, the members of the legislative branch are supposed to be the guardians of the people's rights against royal encroachment. Hence, Parliament is legally sovereign and the written guarantees of rights such as Magna Carta and other famous acts are restraints on the royal prerogative only and not on Parliament. Exemption from previous executive restraint of publication is all that really can be assured. In the United States, however, where the people are overeign, all branches of the government are limited by constitutions which are superior to laws. The security of a free press lies in its exemption from legislative no less than executive violations. Given this difference, it is a mockery to say, as the American Constitution does, that no laws shall be assed preventing publications, but then to claim that they may be made to punish them after the fact. It is evident, therefore, that the common law does not define an American term despite the use of the same legal language in both America and Great Britain.[33]

Enlightening though it may be, this argument is not decisive, Madison maintained, in his second general line of argument. More is involved than the distinction between statutory and constitutional restraints. The events leading up to the adoption of the Bill of Rights reveal the intentions of those who framed the First Amendment. When ratification of the Constitution was under discussion, the absence of a "positive exemption" of these press was criticized on the ground that Congress might use the necessary and proper clause to enact restraints. Defenders of this omission said that there would be no such encroachments on rights by a Congress confined to its delegated powers and those necessarily incident to them. The upshot of this debate was, nevertheless, a demand from all of the states for a guarantee of freedom of the press more than any other right. The resulting First Amendment was an "express declaration" that Congress should make no law abridging freedom of the press. It is not open to doubt thereafter that "no power whatever over the press" was granted in the original Constitution and the amendment was intended to be a "positive and absolute" confirmation of this interpretation. No one thought that the First Amendment was a fresh and additional grant of power to Congress. This conclusion is supported by the well-known desires of those who demanded amendments, by the language of Congress in transmitting them to the states for ratification, and by reason, itself. The latter is tortured by saying that the First Amendment constructively grants power in order to interpretations of this cryptic passage. Persons who wish to believe that he meant the remedy to be civil suits for libel in the state courts may do so, but Madison did not commit himself to this doctrine unless he did so anonymously as the author of a public document composed, adopted, and distributed by the General Assembly of Virginia on 23 January 1799.[43] This public paper was an exculpation of the resolutions which the legislature had adopted one month earlier on 24 December 1798. Among many other arguments, it contained a passage justifying prosecution of libels against federal officers, but not the federal government, in state courts. It is not only improbable that Madison was the author of this paper. There is no proof that he was.[44]

There are several reasons for rejecting the supposition of some scholars that Madison was the author of this "Address" and, therefore, favored civil actions for libel in the state courts in January, 1799, but not in December of that year, when he composed the Report of 1800.[45] First, he never mentioned it to his closest political friends at this time to any one else thereafter. Writing on 29 December 1798, from his home, Montpelier, to Jefferson who was in Philadelphia to attend a session of Congress, Madison said he had no news of the proceedings of the General Assembly in Richmond. There is no mention of the Address in subsequent letters, although Madison characteristically shared news of events of this sort with Jefferson at the earliest opportunity.

Had Madison been the author, he would have needed an agent to introduce it to the General Assembly and move it through the two houses as Taylor did with the draft of Madison's resolutions adopted on 24 December 1798. Furthermore, it seems most unlikely that he would have agreed, after much urging as he did in March, 1799, to seek election to the House of Delegates in order to take a seat in December for the avowed purpose of vindicating the Resolutions of 1798. The Report of 1800, which was the result of this strategy, took a great deal of time and labor, he reported to Jefferson on 29 December 1799. Furthermore, Madison sent Jefferson a copy of this report on this date despite the fact that it was then "in the press and stands the order of the day for Thursday next."[46]

This candor in reporting events which transpired in the General Assembly while Madison was a member was characteristic of his behavior where Jefferson was concerned. In this instance, it is what might be expected because of the great importance they attached to securing support for their bold resolutions of 1798 and 1799 (in the case of Jefferson's draft of resolutions to be adopted by the legislature of Kentucky). It was an enterprise in which Jefferson was the instigator and Madison a collaborator who cautioned against his friend's rash doctrines. Whether for all of these reasons, none of them, or others, neither Adrienne Koch nor Irving Brandt took any notice of the Address of 1799 which has been attributed improperly to Madison.[47]

convince the public that no power over the press was originally given to Congress.[34]

Given Madison's conclusion that the federal government was totally without authority over the press, it was not necessary in strict logic for him to comment further on the Sedition Act. He did so, however, on grounds so sweeping that no proof of a libel against a public officeholder could be maintained in any court in the United States. The act made it criminal for any person to utter or publish statements about the president and members of Congress, if they were false, malicious, and intended to defame them. The statute gave the privilege of allowing authors to prove the truth of their charges. This provision was defended, Madison noted, on the ground that it ameliorated the strict rigors of the common law of libels which would have been left in force by the operation of the indefinite discretion claimed for the federal courts. It takes very little argument, however, to demonstrate that this modification cannot diminish the "baleful tendency" of the privilege of offering the truth as a defense contained in political writings, Madison asserted. The first reason is that where facts alone are in dispute there is great "trouble and vexation" for an author to prove truth in meeting a prosecution by the government with the full and formal proof necessary in a court of law. It is equally obvious that opinions, inferences, and conjectures in political writings are inseparable from the facts. It is the former which may more often be the object of prosecutions than the latter. Even if opinions, inferences, and conjectures of the sort made criminal by this statute are separated from facts, they are not subject to the kinds of proof which relate to facts in a court of law. Finally, it is equally obvious that proof of the intent to defame cannot fail to have a "pernicious" effect. Aside from the difficulty of using the words of a publication to prove the author's intent, it is impossible to punish individuals for the "malice" of intent to bring governmental officers into contempt and disrepute without destroying a fundamental requirement for the enjoyment of free government under the Constitution. It is the right of freely discussing "public characters and measures..."[35]

With this observation, Madison turned the discussion away from the legal arcana and fictions invented by lawyers, judges and their academic adjuncts who regard themselves as the special guardians of the higher law. The "actual meaning" of the Constitution, Madison insisted, must be determined by the characteristics of the system of government which the Constitution established without regard for the former British connection. When the American people dissolved their tie of allegiance to Britain, adopted constitutions, and amended the instrument of 1787, they did so on the ground that all just and lawful governmental authority rests on the deliberate consent of the governed. The British constitution and laws, whether written or not, were certainly not binding by prescription, especially insofar as they were inconsistent with the republican governments which the Americans adopted. Upon separation from Britain, Americans became free to shape their laws in ways consistent with their new form of government. Viewed from this perspective, the Sedition Act violated the spirit of the laws in the sense in which Montesquieu had formulated a logically necessary correspondence between types of constitutions and the laws which maintain them. At the Constitutional Convention, Madison said that he would "always exclude inconsistent principles in framing a system of government."[36]   After the new government was established, he insisted that it would never be right to support an "interpretation that destroys the very characteristic of the government."[37] The Sedition Act posed a question of political philosophy, not one of mere law. Indeed, it posed in more severe and threatening form the issue involved in the government's attempt to censure its critics in 1794. That effort was invalid because, if we examine the "nature of republican government, we shall find that the censorial power is in the people over the government, and not in the government over the people."[38]

The Constitution of the American Republic presupposes that the president and Congress are responsible to their constituents for the faithful discharge of their official duties. The only proper judges of their failure to do so are the voters who put them in office with the expectation of being able to turn them out and return them to private life at stated intervals, if necessary.

The Constitution rests on the further necessary supposition that failure to perform their duties properly exposes these functionaries to public criticism which may express contempt and even hatred for their behavior and even result in their being held in disrepute. All persons holding office under the Constitution expose themselves to a free and unrestrained examination of their official conduct and the equally free communication of the public's judgments among its members. The question whether official conduct merits criticisms as harsh as those proscribed by the Sedition Act is irrelevant. It is the "duty as well as the right, of intelligent and faithful citizens" to discuss and disseminate their opinions in such matters freely in order to give effect to them in the manner presupposed by the Constitution. It is unavoidable that those who give effect to the constitutional mode of censuring official behavior must feel, and vent to some degree, "contempt or hatred against the transgressing party." The contrary tendency of this act is to jeopardize the operation of this purgative by making the exercise of this great remedial right subject to the criminal penalties of this act.[39]

This restraint on the free expression and communication of unfavorable judgments of official conduct ought to alarm every friend of liberty. If the intent to incite unfavorable judgments of those who conduct the affairs of government is a punishable offense, then the effect of this threat is to prohibit all expressions of opinions having this tendency and effect. The additional equivalent effect of lodging this censorial power in the government is to protect incumbents against robustly adverse public criticism. What is worse, the existence of this penal statute punishing exposure of public officers to ridicule, contempt and even hatred which tarnishes their fame demonstrates that proof of the intent to do so is proportional to the need for criticism. It is, also, evidence of the vigilance with which criticism will be prosecuted and punished. There can be no doubt that this statute shields a culpable adminstration from the just and natural effects of responsibility, which is the essential element in the faithful discharge of public duties.

The whole matter must be judged, therefore, in light of the principle that the very essence of "free and responsible government" consists in the right of freely electing its members. The real value of this right depends on the voters' having a knowledge of the comparative merits and demerits of all candidates for office, and to acquire it they must be free to communicate their judgments of candidates' conduct and qualifications. As long as an act of this sort is in effect, it will shield incumbents from the critical glare of adverse opinions voiced about their conduct. In this circumstance, the people are no longer "free" because they are compelled to make their choices between competitors for office whose comparative claims to election the voters are not free to determine, examine or discuss publicly. The advantage given to incumbents impairs the people's right to free elections, and with the effective loss of this right comes loss of the blessings of free government. For this reason, it was entirely just for the General Assembly of Virginia to declare in its resolutions of 24 December 1798 that the right of freely examining the records of those persons holding office is the only effectual guardian of every other right which the Sedition Act was calculated to destroy.[40] The vigorous enforcement of such an act, if it were made perpetual, would result in either the destruction of our system of free government or a "convulsion" equally fatal to it.[41]

Another consideration arising out of the adoption of the Firs[t] Amendment weighed in Madison's conviction that this addition to th[e] original constitutional text was not a qualified grant of power to th[e] federal government. The amendment was intended to clarify a[nd] reaffirm the limited scope of federal authority instead of leaving it [to] some "vague and violent construction" in the future. It is consistent w[ith] the circumstances surrounding its framing and adoption to say that [the] amendment was intended to "exempt the press altogether from t[he] authority." Several more general factors account for this policy, a[nd] These include the magnitude of the powers over some subj[ect] necessarily given to the federal government, the long terms of som[e of] its officers, the great distances between the capital city from man[y of] the representatives' constituencies, and the "peculiar difficult[y of] circulating an adequate knowledge of [that government's actions] a[mong] them through any other channel." These factors, arising in part fro[m] dispersion of the population over a large area, account for the delib[erate] policy of "binding the hands of the federal government from touchin[g the] channel which alone can give efficacy to its responsibility." [The] Framers' decision was to leave those who administer the affairs [of] federal government "a remedy for their injured reputations unde[r the] same laws, and in the same tribunals which protect their lives...lib[erties] and...properties."[42]

This last sentence is noteworthy for its ambiguity whic[h was] probably deliberate. Madison did not identify either the specific r[emedy] or the proper arena for vindicating the injured reputations of pre[sident] or members of Congress. He merely eliminated criminal [libel] prosecuted in the federal courts. Into this vacuum of studied am[biguity] his contemporaries were free (as ours are) to rush with their pr[oposals]

A CONSISTENT CIVIL LIBERTARIAN

Once it is established that Madison was not the author of the Address of 1799, it can be demonstrated from all the evidence presented in this book that his views about freedom of speech, press, and political association before 1800 were consistent with the libertarian theory which he developed in the Report of that year.[48] As I pointed out in the previous chapter, Madison said in 1785 that freedom of the press, religion, and certain other individual rights ought to be made *exempt* from legislative power in a state constitution. In the same year he argued for absolute freedom of religion and the expression of religious beliefs, including the right to have none, from government power. He called the enactment of Jefferson's statute for Religious Freedom a victory for the freedom of the human mind from legal restraints. In *The Federalist* number ten he stated that liberty is essential to political life even though its full enjoyment divides society into bitterly contending parties, sects and interests who are unequally affected by the actions of government. In the fiftieth paper he reminded readers that the conflict of political parties cannot be avoided unless we are prepared to extinguish liberty. In the sixty-third essay he conceded that the American people were vulnerable to the artful manipulation of public opinion because of their dispersion over an extended territory.

In 1789 he called his proposals to guarantee liberty of conscience, speech, and press against violation by the state governments the most valuable of all his proposed amendments. The language of his proposed restrictions on the federal government was somewhat more emphatically limiting. He wanted it said in section nine of Article 1 that the right to speak, write or publish one's "sentiments" shall not be "deprived or abridged," so that "the freedom of the press" might be maintained "inviolable" as one of the great bulwarks of liberty.[49] In ordinary language as defined in the dictionary Madison meant that the named rights shall neither be violated nor encroached upon, nor shall they be curtailed or reduced in scope because the freedom to communicate beliefs is a sacred and indestructable bulwark of liberty which ought never to be violated or profaned. If Madison had intended to follow the common law definition of a free press, he needed only to paraphrase it or to incorporate it explicitly as he did in his proposal which became the Seventh Amendment (instead of an alteration in the second section of the Judicial article as he recommended). He did not refer to the common law, however, and neither did Congress, in using the phrase *freedom of the press*. Given his well-established views on the general problem of incorporating the common law into the Constitution, there is no reason to believe that he intended to do so in this matter. Those who contend that Congres entertained this intention rely on the supposition that there was an unspoken uniformity of belief supporting the common law definition and a continuity of adoption by implication rather than by express authorization. If so, how does one account for instances of the latter practice as well as others in which the Framers provided new definitions of crimes?[50]

Apparently Madison was satisfied with the final language of the First Amendment because it said that Congress shall pass "no law" *abridging* free speech and press. It was left free, therefore, to *support* a free press should the members chose to do so in an appropriate way. Consequently, in 1790 Madison urged the House of Representatives to purchase all the newspapers published in Philadelphia (then the capital). This action would provide members with more information than was available otherwise, and it would give "encouragement to the press which was thought advantageous to the public." A few months later he was alarmed by a proposal in Congress to tax newspapers. He considered it to be of "great importance" that the proposal be changed so as to remove the obstacle which would be raised against "information to the people." In all governments "public censorship [of government] is necessary" to prevent "abuses." In a government such as ours, however, "where the members are so far removed from the eye of their Constituents, an easy and prompt circulation of public proceedings is peculiarly essential."[51] In his essay, "Public Opinion," published in December, 1791, it should be recalled, he warned against the ease with which public opinion, the sovereign in every free government, can be counterfeited in a nation of extended territory. The proper corrective, he said, was the combination of a free press and representatives circulating without hindrance between the capital city and their constituencies. It was the enjoyment of this essential combination of rights which was jeopardized by the Sedition Act.

Within three months after calling for a free press and representation to enable true public opinion to control the tendency of government to expand its power, he published his essay defending the right of individuals to hold and freely communicate opinions, if a government is to be judged just. In 1794 he risked an unwanted political break with Washington, when he defended the right of the Democratic Societies to criticize the federal government's enforcement of the excise tax with armed force of dimensions sufficient to discourage resistance to enforcement of the laws. Freedom of utterance is a reserved right, he insisted. He did so, let it be recalled, on the ground that opinion is beyond legislation in a republic where the people are properly the censors of the government and not the reverse.

This record is consistent with his interpretation of the First Amendment in 1800. Judicial proceedings to vindicate the injured reputations of public officeholders strike at the very heart of the right to enjoy the fruits of a free and responsible government. It stretches credulity to say that Madison suddenly discovered within the span of a year or less that any proceedings, whether civil or criminal, in any court, state or federal, for seditious libel unconstitutionally inhibit the free and unrestrained criticism of persons who hold public offices. To say that his silence in the face of earlier opportunities to reject state proceedings is evidence of inconsistency is to draw an unwarrantable inference from silence.[52] The evidence is truly compelling that Madison consistently held, even in opposing adoption of amendments in 1787–88, that certain individual rights ought to be *exempt absolutely* from control by governments, both state and federal.

Madison did not leave this conclusion to subsequent scholarly conjecture. He publicly declared that the right of free expression of opinions is absolute because it is a natural, not a social or conventional, right. In 1785 he declared in his *Memorial and Remonstrance* that the right of conscience is the gift of nature every person reserves for his or her exercise in accordance with reason, when entering into the social compact. In 1789, while introducing the Bill of Rights to the House of Representatives, he pointed out that persons who had drafted such documents in the past had not always distinguished "pre-existing" natural rights from those rights which result from the creation of the social compact. This observation was certainly true of the British constitution which did not secure the two rights which Americans regarded as the choicest of all, freedom of press and of conscience.[53] Madison regarded these two rights to be the endowment of nature, not of the English common law. The purpose of the First Amendment was to affirm the former, not the latter.

The common law, as Madison understood it, provided the definition of freedom of the press in Great Britain and the status of the religious hierarchy as well. Given the absence of any accepted limits on parliamentary power, there was even less security for these rights which Americans cherished. It was for this reason that Madison called attention in the Report of 1800 to the statement made by Virginia's legislature in ratifying the First Amendment. Liberty of conscience and of speech were equally and completely exempt from regulation by the authority of the United States. If it were claimed, however, that the common law defines one of these rights, then it must be conceded that it governs the other one as well.[54]

Madison could not have argued otherwise, since he was already on record publicly with his declaration that the measure of a just government is the degree to which it protects conscience even more than castle. A just government protects individuals in the enjoyment and communication of their opinions in which they have an equal, if not a more, valuable property than in any other.[55] Nothing about the British constitution and laws met this standard in Madison's judgment. Consequently, Americans were free to innovate laws and institutions consistent with their own circumstances and wishes. They were not bound prescriptively to their colonial past.

Finally, Madison explictly upheld the right of the American people to commit seditious libel in its ultimate form. He proposed a prefix to the Constitution declaring the right of the people to alter or change their government when it is found to be "adverse or inadequate" to the purposes which it is intended to serve. This right cannot be exercised effectively if Americans are liable to punishment for the publication of their criticisms as Thomas Paine was for publishing *The Rights of Man* in Great Britain. If Madison were to have taken any other position, he would have had to deny what he called the principle of right by which the American people became a self-governing nation, free to choose those political institutions which seemed to them to be conducive to the enjoyment of life, liberty, and that degree of happiness they might obtain. He continued to maintain this position in both public and private papers for more than thirty years after the turbulent events of 1798 to 1800.[56]

In 1825 he reaffirmed the interpretation of freedom of the press expounded in the Report of 1800. In responding to Jefferson's suggestion that the report be required reading at the University of Virginia, Madison pointed out that such a rule might involve the new institution in partisan conflict. The interpretation expounded in the report corresponded with "the predominant sense of the nation," in Madison's judgment, but it was of "local origin" and it referred implicitly to a division between parties which had not ended yet. Therefore, he suggested resolutions to be adopted by the Board of Visitors to include the "Resolutions of the General Assembly of Virginia of 1799, on the subject of the Alien and Sedition Laws, which appear to accord with the predominant sense of the people of the United States." This resolution was adopted by the board with Madison present as a member on 4 March 1825. Despite the date he gave this report, he referred beyond doubt to the document commonly known as the Report of 1800, adopted during the legislative session which commenced in January, 1799. In 1834 he referred again to "the Resolutions of Virginia in 1798, as expounded and vindicated in the Report of 1799..." They were deliberately supported by popularly elected representatives who expressed the views of the public and not his private beliefs only.[57]

Unobserved in scholarly reports of this exchange is the important fact that the two friends never agreed about the power to punish libels against governments or their officials. Jefferson never yielded the belief expressed to Madison on 31 July 1788 that a Bill of Rights ought not to protect publishers from liability for printing "false facts," provided, he added some years later, that they are tried in state courts.[58] In a letter to Nicholas P. Trist prompted by references to Jefferson's views on this subject, Madison delicately revealed their differences. The press, Madison affirmed, is a "necessary guardian of free government." Jefferson was justified in criticizing newspapers for occasionally playing fast and loose with the truth. Nevertheless, the effect of their "falsehoods and slanders must always be controlled in a certain degree by contradictions in rival or hostile papers where the press is free." There are times when "gross and injurious untruths" may predominate. The persons who do not enjoy the satisfaction of seeing fallacious and specious comments challenged or contradicted will be "generally under the delusions so strongly painted by Mr. Jefferson," despite his devotion to liberty of the press. "It has been said that any country might be governed at the will of one who had the exclusive privilege of furnishing its popular songs. The result would be far more certain from a monopoly of the politics of the press." Of course, there is an ideal remedy, but it could never be put into practice without revolutionary changes: let each party print its views of politics on the two opposite sides of a sheet of newsprint.[59]

WAR, FREE PRESS, ACCOUNTABILITY AND GOVERNMENTAL AUTONOMY

President John Adams' preparations for war in 1798, including the Sedition Act, and Madison's claims that the latter violated the constitutional right to freedom of the press, confirmed his thesis that accountability under our written constitution is likely to be overridden by the tendency of government toward autonomy because of its power to make war. This truth becomes apparent once we recall that the Sedition Act was enacted and enforced to silence or punish the critics of the Adams administration's apparent determination to entangle this nation in a war with France. On 2 April 1798 Madison wrote in great alarm to Vice President Jefferson about President Adams' "violent passions and heretical politics" which prompted him to seek war, as Madison believed. Adams' public pronouncements about his authority to do so were particularly alarming. The Constitution, Madison pointed out, "supposes, what the History of all governments demonstrates, that the Executive is the branch of power most interested in war, and most prone to it." Accordingly, the Constitution has "with studied care, vested the question of war with the Legislature." The doctrines recently advanced by President Adams, however, strike at the "root" of all these provisions and leave the question of peace for the country to be decided by the discretion of that department of the government the "Constitution distrusts as most ready, without cause, to renounce" peace in favor of war. This reversal of functions is inevitable, if our new constitutional doctrine is that it is "the opinion of the President, not the facts and proofs themselves," which is "to sway the judgment of Congress in declaring war." Furthermore, if the president is as free as Adams claimed to be to "create a foreign mission, appoint the Minister, and negotiate a war Treaty without the possibility of a check, even from the Senate, until measures present alternatives overriding the freedom of its judgment"; or, if a treaty, once made, obligates Congress to declare war "contrary to its judgment" and to "grant the requisite supplies" until such a treaty is repealed, then the American people are "cheated out of the best ingredients in their Government, the safeguards of peace, which is the greatest of their blessings." Congress ought to adjourn at so members could consult with their "constituents on the subject of war," and make opposition to the president's order arming vessels "more striking to the public eye." Direct consultation with constituents would be desirable because it would be impossible to "call forth the sense of the people generally before the season [session?] will be over, especially as the towns, etc., where there can be most despatch in such an operation, are on the wrong side" of this issue of war and peace. Also, it is to be feared that a "partial expression of the public voice may be misconstrued or miscalled [as] evidence in favor of the War party." If the members of Congress cannot sound out public opinion in all of its diversity, the measures being taken by the president will end in war "contrary to the wish of the Body which alone can declare it."[60]

In mid–April Madison commented with equal dismay on the President's command of public opinion which can be excited to favor war. He was convinced that Adams was using diplomatic correspondence very selectively to enforce measures for war and to divert "public attention from the other more important part" which shows that the president's speech and conduct were the real obstacles to an accommodation with France. The fact that these documents were communicated to Congress would be praiseworthy, Madison thought, if other circumstances did not persuade him that Adams' purpose was "more to inflame than to inform the public mind."[61]

Within another week Madison was able to report to Jefferson the use which Adams had made of limited diplomatic correspondence with France was "kindling a flame among the people" against "extending taxes, armies and prerogative..." Because newspapers were airing the administration's words and behavior toward France, people were learning "solemn lessons, which I hope will have their proper effect, when the infatuation of the moment is over." Such instruction to be used in the long term is highly desirable because the "management of foreign relations appears to be the most susceptible [to] abuse of all [the] trusts committed to a Government because they can be concealed or disclosed, or disclosed in such parts and at such times as will best suit particular views." This power is peculiarly subject to abuse, also, because "the body of the people are less capable of judging, and are more under the influence of prejudices, on that branch of their affairs, than of any other." Perhaps, Madison concluded, "it is a universal truth that the loss of liberty at home is to be charged to provisions against danger, real or pretended, from abroad." He found this truth particularly galling because he was convinced that Adams' strategic objective was to implement the "maxims of the British constitution" by making the United States "into the makeweight of the European balances of power."[62]

These were the circumstances, let it be recalled once again, which moved the Adams administration to enact and enforce the Sedition Act against both the publishers of newspapers and members of Congress who dared to denounce the President. It is equally important to recall that Madison's Virginia Resolutions of December, 1798, and his justification of them in the Report of January 1800 were directed at President Adams' attempts to gain a free hand to conduct war, if necessary in his judgment, without opposition from either the press or persons within the government itself.

The Alien and Sedition Laws, Madison pointed out to Edward Everett in 1830, were "usurpations and abuses, measures of Government violating the will of constituents..." They were fundamentally different, therefore, from the oppression of a minority by a majority governing through the "forms of the Constitution." The hated acts of 1798 violated "the fundamental principles of Republican Government..."[63] They did so, Madison believed, because a president used his superior control of information about the conduct of foreign policy to manipulate and inflame the public against a potential enemy and secured legislation contrary to the literal text of the First Amendment to punish critics who challenged either the accuracy of offical news releases or the policy of making war itself. It is difficult to imagine a more clear-cut example of the tendency of governments toward self-directed actions, especially waging wars, to satisfy the motives for ruling at the cost of shattered constitutional barriers and genuine accountability to the general public. The fact that President Adams drew back from war does not change the power of Madison's analysis of the effects of even the threat of war on freedom of expression.

The vigorous enforcement of these laws and others by the federal courts suggested to Madison an additional problem. He asked: are there constitutional remedies open to the American people to be used to counteract "usurpations in which the Supreme Court of the United States concurs?" The answer is affirmative, of course. Some of them have already been found effectual, "particularly in the case of the alien and sedition laws..." Such measures as "remonstrances and instructions, recurring elections and impeachments; amendments to the Constitution" will all be effective as long as the federal government is responsible to its constituents.[64] The fact that these dangerous laws were enacted and then enforced vigorously by the federal courts certainly disappointed what little expectation Madison ever entertained that they would be independent guardians of the Bill of Rights. The experience fully confirmed his guarded commitment to paper declarations of rights. They are of scant value once a government is determined to pursue a largely self-directed course of action in order to pursue its interest through gradual, well-timed, and constructive claims of power.

The most Madison ever expected was that the declarations in the Bill of Rights would become fundamental precepts of free government embodied in national sentiment. So established, appeals might be made to them as necessary in order to counteract the interest and passions of those who rule. Unfortunately, Madison said years after the framing, the attempts which were made, when the federal government was first put into operation, to "defeat those safe, if not necessary, and those politic, if not obligatory amendments introduced in conformity with the known desires of the body of the people...were not a little ominous." Soon after they were adopted, support was voiced for new "political tenets," and proper rules of constitutional interpretation were abandoned. These new doctrines were "capable of transforming [the Constitution] into something very different from its legitimate character" as an expression of the will of the nation. "I wish I could say that constructive innovations had altogether ceased."[65]

NOTES

1. *PJM*, 12:340–42.
2. Ibid., 346–47.
3. Ibid., 15:397–98.
4. Ibid., 391–92.
5. Ibid., 397.
6. Ibid., 406–7.
7. Ibid., 419–420.

8. Ibid., 426–27, 487.
9. Malone, *Ordeal*, 386–94.
10. *LJM*, 2:139–40.
11. Ibid., 146; note also, 142.
12. United States *Statutes at Large*, 1:596–97.
13 Leonard Levy, ed., *Freedom of the Press From Zenger to Jefferson* (Indianapolis, Ind: The Bobbs–Merrill Co., Inc. 1966), 172–76 contains extracts from the report of the select committee appointed to consider repeal of the Sedition Act in 1799. See also *Annals of Congress,* 5th Cong., 3rd Sess., 2987–90, 3003–14.
14. Leonard Levy, *Emergence of a Free Press* (New York and London: Oxford University Press, 1985), 319.
15. *PJM*, 8:3–4.
16. Farrand, *Records*, 2:315–16 italics added.
17. Ibid., 345.
18. Ibid., 346–49.
19. *PJM*, 10:189–90.
20. Ibid., 196–97, italics in the original. Madison referred to the select committe appointed by the legislature in 1776 with Jefferson in the chair to revise Virginia's colonial laws so as to make them consistent with republican government. See Dumas Malone, *Jefferson the Virginian* (Boston: Little Brown, & Co., 1948), 261–85.
21. *The Federalist*, 272 (No. 42).
22. Elliot, *Debates*, 3:474–79 passim.
23. *PJM*. 11:158–159.
24. Ibid., 202. In 1811 and 1828, respectively, he repeated this explanation to the English philosopher, Jeremy Bentham, and the American jurist, Thomas A. Grimke; *WJM*, 8:400 and *LJM* 3:311–12.
25. Levy, *Freedom of the Press*, 175.
26. Simms, *Life of John Taylor*, 87.
27. *LJM*, 4:535.
28. Farrand, *Records*, 2:430–31.
29. *LJM*, 4:536–37 passim.
30. Ibid., 539.
31. Ibid. 2:153, 154.
32. *WJM*, 9:200, see also 198–202 and 299–300.
33. *LJM*, 4: 542–44 passim.
34. Ibid., 545–46.
35. Ibid., 548–49 passim.
36. Farrand, *Records*, 1:475–76.
37. *PJM*, 13:374.
38. Ibid. 15:391.
39. *LJM*, 4:547–48.
40. Ibid., 549–50
41. Ibid., 548.
42. Ibid., 546–47.
43. Walter Berns, *The First Amendment and the Future of American Democracy* (New York: Basic Books, Inc., 1976), 118; and by Levy, *Emergence*, 306–07, 320. The document in question was entitled "Address of the General Assembly to the People of the Commonwealth

convince the public that no power over the press was originally given to Congress.[34]

Given Madison's conclusion that the federal government was totally without authority over the press, it was not necessary in strict logic for him to comment further on the Sedition Act. He did so, however, on grounds so sweeping that no proof of a libel against a public officeholder could be maintained in any court in the United States. The act made it criminal for any person to utter or publish statements about the president and members of Congress, if they were false, malicious, and intended to defame them. The statute gave the privilege of allowing authors to prove the truth of their charges. This provision was defended, Madison noted, on the ground that it ameliorated the strict rigors of the common law of libels which would have been left in force by the operation of the indefinite discretion claimed for the federal courts. It takes very little argument, however, to demonstrate that this modification cannot diminish the "baleful tendency" of the privilege of offering the truth as a defense contained in political writings, Madison asserted. The first reason is that where facts alone are in dispute there is great "trouble and vexation" for an author to prove truth in meeting a prosecution by the government with the full and formal proof necessary in a court of law. It is equally obvious that opinions, inferences, and conjectures in political writings are inseparable from the facts. It is the former which may more often be the object of prosecutions than the latter. Even if opinions, inferences, and conjectures of the sort made criminal by this statute are separated from facts, they are not subject to the kinds of proof which relate to facts in a court of law. Finally, it is equally obvious that proof of the intent to defame cannot fail to have a "pernicious" effect. Aside from the difficulty of using the words of a publication to prove the author's intent, it is impossible to punish individuals for the "malice" of intent to bring governmental officers into contempt and disrepute without destroying a fundamental requirement for the enjoyment of free government under the Constitution. It is the right of freely discussing "public characters and measures..."[35]

With this observation, Madison turned the discussion away from the legal arcana and fictions invented by lawyers, judges and their academic adjuncts who regard themselves as the special guardians of the higher law. The "actual meaning" of the Constitution, Madison insisted, must be determined by the characteristics of the system of government which the Constitution established without regard for the former British connection. When the American people dissolved their tie of allegiance to Britain, adopted constitutions, and amended the instrument of 1787, they did so on the ground that all just and lawful governmental authority rests on the deliberate consent of the governed. The British constitution and laws, whether written or not, were certainly not binding by prescription, especially insofar as they were inconsistent with the republican governments which the Americans adopted. Upon separation from Britain, Americans became free to shape their laws in ways consistent with their new form of government. Viewed from this perspective, the Sedition Act violated the spirit of the laws in the sense in which Montesquieu had formulated a logically necessary correspondence between types of constitutions and the laws which maintain them. At the Constitutional Convention, Madison said that he would "always exclude inconsistent principles in framing a system of government."[36] After the new government was established, he insisted that it would never be right to support an "interpretation that destroys the very characteristic of the government."[37] The Sedition Act posed a question of political philosophy, not one of mere law. Indeed, it posed in more severe and threatening form the issue involved in the government's attempt to censure its critics in 1794. That effort was invalid because, if we examine the "nature of republican government, we shall find that the censorial power is in the people over the government, and not in the government over the people."[38]

The Constitution of the American Republic presupposes that the president and Congress are responsible to their constituents for the faithful discharge of their official duties. The only proper judges of their failure to do so are the voters who put them in office with the expectation of being able to turn them out and return them to private life at stated intervals, if necessary.

The Constitution rests on the further necessary supposition that failure to perform their duties properly exposes these functionaries to public criticism which may express contempt and even hatred for their behavior and even result in their being held in disrepute. All persons holding office under the Constitution expose themselves to a free and unrestrained examination of their official conduct and the equally free communication of the public's judgments among its members. The question whether official conduct merits criticisms as harsh as those proscribed by the Sedition Act is irrelevant. It is the "duty as well as the right, of intelligent and faithful citizens" to discuss and disseminate their opinions in such matters freely in order to give effect to them in the manner presupposed by the Constitution. It is unavoidable that those who give effect to the constitutional mode of censuring official behavior must feel, and vent to some degree, "contempt or hatred against the transgressing party." The contrary tendency of this act is to jeopardize the operation of this purgative by making the exercise of this great remedial right subject to the criminal penalties of this act.[39]

This restraint on the free expression and communication of unfavorable judgments of official conduct ought to alarm every friend of liberty. If the intent to incite unfavorable judgments of those who conduct the affairs of government is a punishable offense, then the effect of this threat is to prohibit all expressions of opinions having this tendency and effect. The additional equivalent effect of lodging this censorial power in the government is to protect incumbents against robustly adverse public criticism. What is worse, the existence of this penal statute punishing exposure of public officers to ridicule, contempt and even hatred which tarnishes their fame demonstrates that proof of the intent to do so is proportional to the need for criticism. It is, also, evidence of the vigilance with which criticism will be prosecuted and punished. There can be no doubt that this statute shields a culpable adminstration from the just and natural effects of responsibility, which is the essential element in the faithful discharge of public duties.

The whole matter must be judged, therefore, in light of the principle that the very essence of "free and responsible government" consists in the right of freely electing its members. The real value of this right depends on the voters' having a knowledge of the comparative merits and demerits of all candidates for office, and to acquire it they must be free to communicate their judgments of candidates' conduct and qualifications. As long as an act of this sort is in effect, it will shield incumbents from the critical glare of adverse opinions voiced about their conduct. In this circumstance, the people are no longer "free" because they are compelled to make their choices between competitors for office whose comparative claims to election the voters are not free to determine, examine or discuss publicly. The advantage given to incumbents impairs the people's right to free elections, and with the effective loss of this right comes loss of the blessings of free government. For this reason, it was entirely just for the General Assembly of Virginia to declare in its resolutions of 24 December 1798 that the right of freely examining the records of those persons holding office is the only effectual guardian of every other right which the Sedition Act was calculated to destroy.[40] The vigorous enforcement of such an act, if it were made perpetual, would result in either the destruction of our system of free government or a "convulsion" equally fatal to it.[41]

Another consideration arising out of the adoption of the First Amendment weighed in Madison's conviction that this addition to the original constitutional text was not a qualified grant of power to the federal government. The amendment was intended to clarify and reaffirm the limited scope of federal authority instead of leaving it to some "vague and violent construction" in the future. It is consistent with the circumstances surrounding its framing and adoption to say that the amendment was intended to "exempt the press altogether from that authority." Several more general factors account for this policy, also. These include the magnitude of the powers over some subjects necessarily given to the federal government, the long terms of some of its officers, the great distances between the capital city from many of the representatives' constituencies, and the "peculiar difficulty of circulating an adequate knowledge of [that government's actions] among them through any other channel." These factors, arising in part from the dispersion of the population over a large area, account for the deliberate policy of "binding the hands of the federal government from touching the channel which alone can give efficacy to its responsibility." The Framers' decision was to leave those who administer the affairs of the federal government "a remedy for their injured reputations under the same laws, and in the same tribunals which protect their lives...liberties, and...properties."[42]

This last sentence is noteworthy for its ambiguity which was probably deliberate. Madison did not identify either the specific remedy or the proper arena for vindicating the injured reputations of presidents or members of Congress. He merely eliminated criminal libels prosecuted in the federal courts. Into this vacuum of studied ambiguity his contemporaries were free (as ours are) to rush with their preferred interpretations of this cryptic passage. Persons who wish to believe that he meant the remedy to be civil suits for libel in the state courts may do so, but Madison did not commit himself to this doctrine unless he did so anonymously as the author of a public document composed, adopted, and distributed by the General Assembly of Virginia on 23 January 1799.[43] This public paper was an exculpation of the resolutions which the legislature had adopted one month earlier on 24 December 1798. Among many other arguments, it contained a passage justifying prosecution of libels against federal officers, but not the federal government, in state courts. It is not only improbable that Madison was the author of this paper. There is no proof that he was.[44]

There are several reasons for rejecting the supposition of some scholars that Madison was the author of this "Address" and, therefore, favored civil actions for libel in the state courts in January, 1799, but not in December of that year, when he composed the Report of 1800.[45] First, he never mentioned it to his closest political friends at this time to any one else thereafter. Writing on 29 December 1798, from his home, Montpelier, to Jefferson who was in Philadelphia to attend a session of Congress, Madison said he had no news of the proceedings of the General Assembly in Richmond. There is no mention of the Address in subsequent letters, although Madison characteristically shared news of events of this sort with Jefferson at the earliest opportunity.

Had Madison been the author, he would have needed an agent to introduce it to the General Assembly and move it through the two houses as Taylor did with the draft of Madison's resolutions adopted on 24 December 1798. Furthermore, it seems most unlikely that he would have agreed, after much urging as he did in March, 1799, to seek election to the House of Delegates in order to take a seat in December for the avowed purpose of vindicating the Resolutions of 1798. The Report of 1800, which was the result of this strategy, took a great deal of time and labor, he reported to Jefferson on 29 December 1799. Furthermore, Madison sent Jefferson a copy of this report on this date despite the fact that it was then "in the press and stands the order of the day for Thursday next."[46]

This candor in reporting events which transpired in the General Assembly while Madison was a member was characteristic of his behavior where Jefferson was concerned. In this instance, it is what might be expected because of the great importance they attached to securing support for their bold resolutions of 1798 and 1799 (in the case of Jefferson's draft of resolutions to be adopted by the legislature of Kentucky). It was an enterprise in which Jefferson was the instigator and Madison a collaborator who cautioned against his friend's rash doctrines. Whether for all of these reasons, none of them, or others, neither Adrienne Koch nor Irving Brandt took any notice of the Address of 1799 which has been attributed improperly to Madison.[47]

A CONSISTENT CIVIL LIBERTARIAN

Once it is established that Madison was not the author of the Address of 1799, it can be demonstrated from all the evidence presented in this book that his views about freedom of speech, press, and political association before 1800 were consistent with the libertarian theory which he developed in the Report of that year.[48] As I pointed out in the previous chapter, Madison said in 1785 that freedom of the press, religion, and certain other individual rights ought to be made *exempt* from legislative power in a state constitution. In the same year he argued for absolute freedom of religion and the expression of religious beliefs, including the right to have none, from government power. He called the enactment of Jefferson's statute for Religious Freedom a victory for the freedom of the human mind from legal restraints. In *The Federalist* number ten he stated that liberty is essential to political life even though its full enjoyment divides society into bitterly contending parties, sects and interests who are unequally affected by the actions of government. In the fiftieth paper he reminded readers that the conflict of political parties cannot be avoided unless we are prepared to extinguish liberty. In the sixty-third essay he conceded that the American people were vulnerable to the artful manipulation of public opinion because of their dispersion over an extended territory.

In 1789 he called his proposals to guarantee liberty of conscience, speech, and press against violation by the state governments the most valuable of all his proposed amendments. The language of his proposed restrictions on the federal government was somewhat more emphatically limiting. He wanted it said in section nine of Article 1 that the right to speak, write or publish one's "sentiments" shall not be "deprived or abridged," so that "the freedom of the press" might be maintained "inviolable" as one of the great bulwarks of liberty.[49] In ordinary language as defined in the dictionary Madison meant that the named rights shall neither be violated nor encroached upon, nor shall they be curtailed or reduced in scope because the freedom to communicate beliefs is a sacred and indestructable bulwark of liberty which ought never to be violated or profaned. If Madison had intended to follow the common law definition of a free press, he needed only to paraphrase it or to incorporate it explicitly as he did in his proposal which became the Seventh Amendment (instead of an alteration in the second section of the Judicial article as he recommended). He did not refer to the common law, however, and neither did Congress, in using the phrase *freedom of the press.* Given his well-established views on the general problem of incorporating the common law into the Constitution, there is no reason to believe that he intended to do so in this matter. Those who contend that Congres entertained this intention rely on the supposition that there was an unspoken uniformity of belief supporting the common law definition and a continuity of adoption by implication rather than by express authorization. If so, how does one account for instances of the latter practice as well as others in which the Framers provided new definitions of crimes?[50]

Apparently Madison was satisfied with the final language of the First Amendment because it said that Congress shall pass "no law" *abridging* free speech and press. It was left free, therefore, to *support* a free press should the members chose to do so in an appropriate way. Consequently, in 1790 Madison urged the House of Representatives to purchase all the newspapers published in Philadelphia (then the capital). This action would provide members with more information than was available otherwise, and it would give "encouragement to the press which was thought advantageous to the public." A few months later he was alarmed by a proposal in Congress to tax newspapers. He considered it to be of "great importance" that the proposal be changed so as to remove the obstacle which would be raised against "information to the people." In all governments "public censorship [of government] is necessary" to prevent "abuses." In a government such as ours, however, "where the members are so far removed from the eye of their Constituents, an easy and prompt circulation of public proceedings is peculiarly essential."[51] In his essay, "Public Opinion," published in December, 1791, it should be recalled, he warned against the ease with which public opinion, the sovereign in every free government, can be counterfeited in a nation of extended territory. The proper corrective, he said, was the combination of a free press and representatives circulating without hindrance between the capital city and their constituencies. It was the enjoyment of this essential combination of rights which was jeopardized by the Sedition Act.

Within three months after calling for a free press and representation to enable true public opinion to control the tendency of government to expand its power, he published his essay defending the right of individuals to hold and freely communicate opinions, if a government is to be judged just. In 1794 he risked an unwanted political break with Washington, when he defended the right of the Democratic Societies to criticize the federal government's enforcement of the excise tax with armed force of dimensions sufficient to discourage resistance to enforcement of the laws. Freedom of utterance is a reserved right, he insisted. He did so, let it be recalled, on the ground that opinion is beyond legislation in a republic where the people are properly the censors of the government and not the reverse.

This record is consistent with his interpretation of the First Amendment in 1800. Judicial proceedings to vindicate the injured reputations of public officeholders strike at the very heart of the right to enjoy the fruits of a free and responsible government. It stretches credulity to say that Madison suddenly discovered within the span of a year or less that any proceedings, whether civil or criminal, in any court, state or federal, for seditious libel unconstitutionally inhibit the free and unrestrained criticism of persons who hold public offices. To say that his silence in the face of earlier opportunities to reject state proceedings is evidence of inconsistency is to draw an unwarrantable inference from silence.[52] The evidence is truly compelling that Madison consistently held, even in opposing adoption of amendments in 1787–88, that certain individual rights ought to be *exempt absolutely* from control by governments, both state and federal.

Madison did not leave this conclusion to subsequent scholarly conjecture. He publicly declared that the right of free expression of opinions is absolute because it is a natural, not a social or conventional, right. In 1785 he declared in his *Memorial and Remonstrance* that the right of conscience is the gift of nature every person reserves for his or her exercise in accordance with reason, when entering into the social compact. In 1789, while introducing the Bill of Rights to the House of Representatives, he pointed out that persons who had drafted such documents in the past had not always distinguished "pre–existing" natural rights from those rights which result from the creation of the social compact. This observation was certainly true of the British constitution which did not secure the two rights which Americans regarded as the choicest of all, freedom of press and of conscience.[53] Madison regarded these two rights to be the endowment of nature, not of the English common law. The purpose of the First Amendment was to affirm the former, not the latter.

The common law, as Madison understood it, provided the definition of freedom of the press in Great Britain and the status of the religious hierarchy as well. Given the absence of any accepted limits on parliamentary power, there was even less security for these rights which Americans cherished. It was for this reason that Madison called attention in the Report of 1800 to the statement made by Virginia's legislature in ratifying the First Amendment. Liberty of conscience and of speech were equally and completely exempt from regulation by the authority of the United States. If it were claimed, however, that the common law defines one of these rights, then it must be conceded that it governs the other one as well.[54]

Madison could not have argued otherwise, since he was already on record publicly with his declaration that the measure of a just government is the degree to which it protects conscience even more than castle. A just government protects individuals in the enjoyment and communication of their opinions in which they have an equal, if not a more, valuable property than in any other.[55] Nothing about the British constitution and laws met this standard in Madison's judgment. Consequently, Americans were free to innovate laws and institutions consistent with their own circumstances and wishes. They were not bound prescriptively to their colonial past.

Finally, Madison explictly upheld the right of the American people to commit seditious libel in its ultimate form. He proposed a prefix to the Constitution declaring the right of the people to alter or change their government when it is found to be "adverse or inadequate" to the purposes which it is intended to serve. This right cannot be exercised effectively if Americans are liable to punishment for the publication of their criticisms as Thomas Paine was for publishing *The Rights of Man* in Great Britain. If Madison were to have taken any other position, he would have had to deny what he called the principle of right by which the American people became a self–governing nation, free to choose those political institutions which seemed to them to be conducive to the enjoyment of life, liberty, and that degree of happiness they might obtain. He continued to maintain this position in both public and private papers for more than thirty years after the turbulent events of 1798 to 1800.[56]

In 1825 he reaffirmed the interpretation of freedom of the press expounded in the Report of 1800. In responding to Jefferson's suggestion that the report be required reading at the University of Virginia, Madison pointed out that such a rule might involve the new institution in partisan conflict. The interpretation expounded in the report corresponded with "the predominant sense of the nation," in Madison's judgment, but it was of "local origin" and it referred implicitly to a division between parties which had not ended yet. Therefore, he suggested resolutions to be adopted by the Board of Visitors to include the "Resolutions of the General Assembly of Virginia of 1799, on the subject of the Alien and Sedition Laws, which appear to accord with the predominant sense of the people of the United States." This resolution was adopted by the board with Madison present as a member on 4 March 1825. Despite the date he gave this report, he referred beyond doubt to the document commonly known as the Report of 1800, adopted during the legislative session which commenced in January, 1799. In 1834 he referred again to "the Resolutions of Virginia in 1798, as expounded and vindicated in the Report of 1799..." They were deliberately supported by popularly elected representatives who expressed the views of the public and not his private beliefs only.[57]

Unobserved in scholarly reports of this exchange is the important fact that the two friends never agreed about the power to punish libels against governments or their officials. Jefferson never yielded the belief expressed to Madison on 31 July 1788 that a Bill of Rights ought not to protect publishers from liability for printing "false facts," provided, he added some years later, that they are tried in state courts.[58] In a letter to Nicholas P. Trist prompted by references to Jefferson's views on this subject, Madison delicately revealed their differences. The press, Madison affirmed, is a "necessary guardian of free government." Jefferson was justified in criticizing newspapers for occasionally playing fast and loose with the truth. Nevertheless, the effect of their "falsehoods and slanders must always be controlled in a certain degree by contradictions in rival or hostile papers where the press is free." There are times when "gross and injurious untruths" may predominate. The persons who do not enjoy the satisfaction of seeing fallacious and specious comments challenged or contradicted will be "generally under the delusions so strongly painted by Mr. Jefferson," despite his devotion to liberty of the press. "It has been said that any country might be governed at the will of one who had the exclusive privilege of furnishing its popular songs. The result would be far more certain from a monopoly of the politics of the press." Of course, there is an ideal remedy, but it could never be put into practice without revolutionary changes: let each party print its views of politics on the two opposite sides of a sheet of newsprint.[59]

WAR, FREE PRESS, ACCOUNTABILITY AND GOVERNMENTAL AUTONOMY

President John Adams' preparations for war in 1798, including the Sedition Act, and Madison's claims that the latter violated the constitutional right to freedom of the press, confirmed his thesis that accountability under our written constitution is likely to be overridden by the tendency of government toward autonomy because of its power to make war. This truth becomes apparent once we recall that the Sedition Act was enacted and enforced to silence or punish the critics of the Adams administration's apparent determination to entangle this nation in a war with France. On 2 April 1798 Madison wrote in great alarm to Vice President Jefferson about President Adams' "violent passions and heretical politics" which prompted him to seek war, as Madison believed. Adams' public pronouncements about his authority to do so were particularly alarming. The Constitution, Madison pointed out, "supposes, what the History of all governments demonstrates, that the Executive is the branch of power most interested in war, and most prone to it." Accordingly, the Constitution has "with studied care, vested the question of war with the Legislature." The doctrines recently advanced by President Adams, however, strike at the "root" of all these provisions and leave the question of peace for the country to be decided by the discretion of that department of the government the "Constitution distrusts as most ready, without cause, to renounce" peace in favor of war. This reversal of functions is inevitable, if our new constitutional doctrine is that it is "the opinion of the President, not the facts and proofs themselves," which is "to sway the judgment of Congress in declaring war." Furthermore, if the president is as free as Adams claimed to be to "create a foreign mission, appoint the Minister, and negotiate a war Treaty without the possibility of a check, even from the Senate, until measures present alternatives overriding the freedom of its judgment"; or, if a treaty, once made, obligates Congress to declare war "contrary to its judgment" and to "grant the requisite supplies" until such a treaty is repealed, then the American people are "cheated out of the best ingredients in their Government, the safeguards of peace, which is the greatest of their blessings." Congress ought to adjourn at so members could consult with their "constituents on the subject of war," and make opposition to the president's order arming vessels "more striking to the public eye." Direct consultation with constituents would be desirable because it would be impossible to "call forth the sense of the people generally before the season [session?] will be over, especially as the towns, etc., where there can be most despatch in such an operation, are on the wrong side" of this issue of war and peace. Also, it is to be feared that a "partial expression of the public voice may be misconstrued or miscalled [as] evidence in favor of the War party." If the members of Congress cannot sound out public opinion in all of its diversity, the measures being taken by the president will end in war "contrary to the wish of the Body which alone can declare it."[60]

In mid–April Madison commented with equal dismay on the President's command of public opinion which can be excited to favor war. He was convinced that Adams was using diplomatic correspondence very selectively to enforce measures for war and to divert "public attention from the other more important part" which shows that the president's speech and conduct were the real obstacles to an accommodation with France. The fact that these documents were communicated to Congress would be praiseworthy, Madison thought, if other circumstances did not persuade him that Adams' purpose was "more to inflame than to inform the public mind."[61]

Within another week Madison was able to report to Jefferson the use which Adams had made of limited diplomatic correspondence with France was "kindling a flame among the people" against "extending taxes, armies and prerogative..." Because newspapers were airing the administration's words and behavior toward France, people were learning "solemn lessons, which I hope will have their proper effect, when the infatuation of the moment is over." Such instruction to be used in the long term is highly desirable because the "management of foreign relations appears to be the most susceptible [to] abuse of all [the] trusts committed to a Government because they can be concealed or disclosed, or disclosed in such parts and at such times as will best suit particular views." This power is peculiarly subject to abuse, also, because "the body of the people are less capable of judging, and are more under the influence of prejudices, on that branch of their affairs, than of any other." Perhaps, Madison concluded, "it is a universal truth that the loss of liberty at home is to be charged to provisions against danger, real or pretended, from abroad." He found this truth particularly galling because he was convinced that Adams' strategic objective was to implement the "maxims of the British constitution" by making the United States "into the makeweight of the European balances of power."[62]

These were the circumstances, let it be recalled once again, which moved the Adams administration to enact and enforce the Sedition Act against both the publishers of newspapers and members of Congress who dared to denounce the President. It is equally important to recall that Madison's Virginia Resolutions of December, 1798, and his justification of them in the Report of January 1800 were directed at President Adams' attempts to gain a free hand to conduct war, if necessary in his judgment, without opposition from either the press or persons within the government itself.

The Alien and Sedition Laws, Madison pointed out to Edward Everett in 1830, were "usurpations and abuses, measures of Government violating the will of constituents..." They were fundamentally different, therefore, from the oppression of a minority by a majority governing through the "forms of the Constitution." The hated acts of 1798 violated "the fundamental principles of Republican Government..."[63] They did so, Madison believed, because a president used his superior control of information about the conduct of foreign policy to manipulate and inflame the public against a potential enemy and secured legislation contrary to the literal text of the First Amendment to punish critics who challenged either the accuracy of offical news releases or the policy of making war itself. It is difficult to imagine a more clear–cut example of the tendency of governments toward self–directed actions, especially waging wars, to satisfy the motives for ruling at the cost of shattered constitutional barriers and genuine accountability to the general public. The fact that President Adams drew back from war does not change the power of Madison's analysis of the effects of even the threat of war on freedom of expression.

The vigorous enforcement of these laws and others by the federal courts suggested to Madison an additional problem. He asked: are there constitutional remedies open to the American people to be used to counteract "usurpations in which the Supreme Court of the United States concurs?" The answer is affirmative, of course. Some of them have already been found effectual, "particularly in the case of the alien and sedition laws..." Such measures as "remonstrances and instructions, recurring elections and impeachments; amendments to the Constitution" will all be effective as long as the federal government is responsible to its constituents.[64] The fact that these dangerous laws were enacted and then enforced vigorously by the federal courts certainly disappointed what little expectation Madison ever entertained that they would be independent guardians of the Bill of Rights. The experience fully confirmed his guarded commitment to paper declarations of rights. They are of scant value once a government is determined to pursue a largely self–directed course of action in order to pursue its interest through gradual, well–timed, and constructive claims of power.

The most Madison ever expected was that the declarations in the Bill of Rights would become fundamental precepts of free government embodied in national sentiment. So established, appeals might be made to them as necessary in order to counteract the interest and passions of those who rule. Unfortunately, Madison said years after the framing, the attempts which were made, when the federal government was first put into operation, to "defeat those safe, if not necessary, and those politic, if not obligatory amendments introduced in conformity with the known desires of the body of the people...were not a little ominous." Soon after they were adopted, support was voiced for new "political tenets," and proper rules of constitutional interpretation were abandoned. These new doctrines were "capable of transforming [the Constitution] into something very different from its legitimate character" as an expression of the will of the nation. "I wish I could say that constructive innovations had altogether ceased."[65]

NOTES

1. *PJM*, 12:340–42.
2. Ibid., 346–47.
3. Ibid., 15:397–98.
4. Ibid., 391–92.
5. Ibid., 397.
6. Ibid., 406–7.
7. Ibid., 419–420.

8. Ibid., 426–27, 487.
9. Malone, *Ordeal*, 386–94.
10. *LJM*, 2:139–40.
11. Ibid., 146; note also, 142.
12. United States *Statutes at Large*, 1:596–97.
13 Leonard Levy, ed., *Freedom of the Press From Zenger to Jefferson* (Indianapolis, Ind: The Bobbs–Merrill Co., Inc. 1966), 172–76 contains extracts from the report of the select committee appointed to consider repeal of the Sedition Act in 1799. See also *Annals of Congress,* 5th Cong., 3rd Sess., 2987–90, 3003–14.
14. Leonard Levy, *Emergence of a Free Press* (New York and London: Oxford University Press, 1985), 319.
15. *PJM*, 8:3–4.
16. Farrand, *Records*, 2:315–16 italics added.
17. Ibid., 345.
18. Ibid., 346–49.
19. *PJM*, 10:189–90.
20. Ibid., 196–97, italics in the original. Madison referred to the select committe appointed by the legislature in 1776 with Jefferson in the chair to revise Virginia's colonial laws so as to make them consistent with republican government. See Dumas Malone, *Jefferson the Virginian* (Boston: Little Brown, & Co., 1948), 261–85.
21. *The Federalist*, 272 (No. 42).
22. Elliot, *Debates*, 3:474–79 passim.
23. *PJM*. 11:158–159.
24. Ibid., 202. In 1811 and 1828, respectively, he repeated this explanation to the English philosopher, Jeremy Bentham, and the American jurist, Thomas A. Grimke; *WJM*, 8:400 and *LJM* 3:311–12.
25. Levy, *Freedom of the Press*, 175.
26. Simms, *Life of John Taylor*, 87.
27. *LJM*, 4:535.
28. Farrand, *Records*, 2:430–31.
29. *LJM*, 4:536–37 passim.
30. Ibid., 539.
31. Ibid. 2:153, 154.
32. *WJM*, 9:200, see also 198–202 and 299–300.
33. *LJM*, 4: 542–44 passim.
34. Ibid., 545–46.
35. Ibid., 548–49 passim.
36. Farrand, *Records*, 1:475–76.
37. *PJM*, 13:374.
38. Ibid. 15:391.
39. *LJM*, 4:547–48.
40. Ibid., 549–50
41. Ibid., 548.
42. Ibid., 546–47.
43. Walter Berns, *The First Amendment and the Future of American Democracy* (New York: Basic Books, Inc., 1976), 118; and by Levy, *Emergence*, 306–07, 320. The document in question was entitled "Address of the General Assembly to the People of the Commonwealth

of Virginia," included as Madison's work in both *LJM*, 4:509–14 and *WJM*, 6:332–40. Madison's authorship of this paper was accepted by Malone, also, in *Ordeal*, p. 408, but without providing any evidence that Madison and Jefferson had ever mentioned the subject of Madison's supposed authorship. Jefferson did allude, however, to a paper published by Edmund Pendleton and reprinted in Republican newspapers in Philadelphia and elsewhere; *WJM*, 7: 375–76. See further Cunningham, *The Jeffersonian Republicans*, 130–38 for Jefferson's role in establishing the party's position regarding this matter.

44. Neither of the two handwritten copies of the *Address* of January, 1799, in the Madison Papers, DLC: Wilson Carey Nicholas Papers (copies in the Alderman Library, University of Virginia) is written in Madison's hand.

45. Levy reached this conclusion without explicitly noting the ambiguous passage which I examine in the paragraph previous to this one; Levy, *Emergence*, 320–25.

46. *LJM*. 2:151.

47. Koch, *Jefferson and Madison*, 189–211; Brandt, *Madison*, 3:132–36.

48. The name of this theory is Levy's, but my conclusion is contrary to his; see Levy, *Emergence*, 321.

49. *PJM*, 12: 201.

50. The criticism of Madison for "faulty" draftsmanship of the First Ammendment is misleading because of the evidence omitted by Levy, *Emergence*, 323–24.

51. *PJM*, 13:315, 420; supported by Madison's essay, "Public Opinion," published the previous March as noted in chapter 4.

52. Levy did so in *Emergence*, 321.

53. See chapter 7, above.

54. *LJM*, 4:551–52.

55. *PJM*. 14:266.

56. *LJM*, 4:204; 392–93, 417.

57. Ibid. 3:481–483; 4:348. All existing documents relating to this episode are found in Arthur Bestor, David C. Mearns, and Jonathan Daniels, *Three Presidents and Their Books* (Urbana, Ill: University of Illinois Press, 1963), 39–44. For the conclusion that Madison referred to the Report of 1800 in his exchange with Jefferson see Leonard Levy, *Jefferson and Civil Liberties: The Darker Side*, (Cambridge, MA: Harvard University Press, 1963), 153. In addition, there is no evidence that Madison departed from his publicly stated position while he served in Jefferson's administration. See Brandt, *Madison*, 4:51, 355; Dumas Malone, *Ordeal* 463–66; and *Jefferson the President First Term 1801–1805* (Boston: Little Brown & Co., 1970), 225–32; and *Jefferson the President Second Term 1805–1809* (Boston: Little Brown & Co., 1974), 371–91.

58. *LJM.*, 4:515.

59. Ibid. 3: 629–30.

60. Ibid., 2:131–133

61. Ibid., p. 139.

62. Ibid., pp. 142; see also, 117, 119, 121. The resolution transmitting to members of Congress the famous resolutions of 21 December 1798 expressed the belief that the Alien and Sedition Laws were enacted to support an "aggressive foreign policy" which was deplored. There is no handwritten document in Madison's papers indicating that he was the author of this second resolution, although it was published in *LJM*, 4:508 and *WJM*, 6:331–32.
63. Ibid., 4:73.
64. Ibid., 19.
65. Ibid., 3:245.

Chapter 8

The Framers' Muse

After leaving the presidency in 1817, Madison looked back with cautious satisfaction on the republican institutions he had shared in shaping. He assessed their probable durability with his characteristic mixture of hope and philosophical skepticism. He was particularly gratified with the fruits of independence which left us free to perform our natural duty to increase the happiness of a constantly growing population. Our revolution was a model to be emulated by all persons desiring to overthrow Europe's traditional orders of monarchy, aristocracy, church and standing army. It was especially a prototype for Latin Americans who were eager to throw off Spanish imperial rule. A generation of experience in framing our Constitution of 1787 and of maintaining its republican institutions gave him reason to believe that there is a progressive science of government. This system was certainly not perfect and, therefore, the experiment was not without its strains. Government by constitutional majority was adapted to our peculiar circumstances, and it could provide about as much security for the rights of individuals and minorities as can prudently be expected from institutions of human design and operation. Madison could not give unequivocal assurances, however, in his ninth decade that this extended republic would endure.

AN EXAMPLE TO THE WORLD

In 1818, released from the burdens of the presidency, Madison composed an extended and illuminating essay on the natural order which he sent to the Agricultural Society of Albemarle County, Virginia. He asserted that the natural right of Americans to their independence was self-evident because "the earth was intended for those who would make it most conducive to the sustenance and increase of the human race" in a civilized and comfortable condition.[1] Nature has given to man alone the capacity for increasing the supply of food instead of hoarding what is provided spontaneously by nature. This capacity accounts for human preeminence over the irrational creatures and, also, distinguishes "enlightened and refined nations" from "rude and wretched tribes..." They prefer a savage existence to one of "plenty and comfort," despite examples of the latter resulting from an interaction between civilization and agriculture. Nature supplies some stimulus to the multiplication of food through the operation of its generative faculty which creates a constantly increasing number of mouths to feed. Man provides an additional stimulant, however, through the "advantages incident to the acquisition of property in the civilized state." It is apparent, however, from "the symmetry of nature" and its "principles and laws," known through both common sense and "philosophic researches," that not all of nature's productive capacity and creatures can rightly be appropriated to "the exclusive support and increase of the human part of creation."

It is difficult to believe that man was intended to "remodel nature" by destroying every species of life not essential to human existence simply to fill up the whole of the "habitable earth" to the level of density known only in its most thickly populated parts. Neither can we properly suppose that the "system of nature" permits no variations in the numbers and proportions of creatures living on earth. These truths are known to us by the fact that we are "essentially distinguished " from all other living things by "the intellectual and moral powers with which (we are) endowed ...reason and will." These powers enable us to act on matter so as to alter its form from the condition in which it appears spontaneously in nature. It is a "reasonable conclusion," because mankind has been made "in his capacity as an intelligent and voluntary agent, an integral part of the terrestrial system," that the other parts of the natural order are to be shaped by human agency for human benefits. Human efforts must be confined, however, within limits which are intelligible to us as rational creatures.

Even if Americans were to suppose, however, that the "symmetry of nature" decrees a fixed total population on earth, they have motives for obtaining their fullest share commensurate with their resources for improving human life. Where, Madison asked, is climate more favorable, soil more fertile relative to the labor required to make it productive, and "above all where will be found institutions equally securing the blessings of personal independence and of social enjoyments?" The enviable condition of America is often ascribed to its great natural resources. Much credit is due to this source of our well being, but we should not overlook "the fertile activity of a free people, and the benign influence of responsible Government." This combination of freedom, political responsibility, and natural abundance ensures Americans that "the resources of our country may not only contribute to the greater happiness of a given number, but to the augmentation of the number enjoying a greater happiness..."[2]

Madison's conviction that we have a natural duty to use nature's bounty for the general benefit of mankind prompted him to say privately in 1830 that the Cherokee Indians' claim to their lands was valid. They were in fact "incorporating" their labor with the land, thereby improving the soil on which they lived and using it to its full capacity in order to increase the "number and enjoyments of the human race." They were making use of their human capacity which justifies the appropriation of idle or underutilized lands by cultivators. Incredibly, the very people who had taught the Cherokees the arts of cultivation were then seeking to take their lands from them by arguing that the tribe had failed to meet this test of ownership sanctioned by the natural order.[3]

Americans ought not to forget that they justified their revolution on this ground supporting the Cherokee's claim.

Despite his initial disappointment with the efforts of other nations, especially France, to copy the essentials of our revolution in government, he remained hopeful during his later years. During the first four years of the French Revolution he was initially certain that the French were engaged in a deliberate and rational emulation of the American model of political reconstruction. He even overlooked some "adventitious" riots because he was certain that the French would succeed in the great work, thereby "chasing darkness and despotism from the old world..." Thereafter, Madison moved from enthusiasm, despite the imperfections of the Constitution of 1791, to deep dismay over the Reign of Terror which, he feared, encouraged "disaffection to Republican Government in America..."[4]

Long after this disappointment, he hoped that Britain was ripe for republican government, but he doubted that it would be adopted. Reform probably would be deterred there because of the "horror" instilled by the excesses of the French Revolution.[5] Six years later events in Spain and Portugal rekindled his hope that the American model of revolution would inspire reforms there. He was afraid, however, that the people of these two nations needed more of the "light and heat" of our example before they could overcome their miserable circumstances. They would have to overcome their leaders' treachery and, above all, their "Priests and their prejudices." The peoples' cause was so just that we ought not to abandon hope for their improvement. Madison never had a high regard for Spain. In 1786 he had been disgusted with Americans who then wanted an alliance with Spain. The "genius of [its] government, religion and manners unfit them, of all the nations of Christendom, for a coalition with this country."[6] It pleased Madison, therefore, in 1824 to note that the United States, consisting of ten million people and soon to be twenty, enjoyed freedom, tranquility and "the rich fruits of successful revolution." It inspired hope among some Europeans, he noted with satisfaction, but "envenomed alarm" among others who favor "despotism." Our example was the antidote to the latter, and surely it "must regenerate the old world, if its regeneration is possible."[7]

Spain's American colonies were the natural objects of Madison's solicitude in the early 1820's. In 1822 he wanted President Monroe to show our sympathy with, and hope for the success of, their moves for independence. It was desirable that the United States stand as a model for the republican cause. Therefore, this country should adhere to its principles and secure Spain's former colonies in defense of their national rights and "reforms" of which we had given such a "formidable example..." The newly emerging nations of Spanish America were all engaged in the same great experiment of self-government Americans undertook in 1776. Furthermore, if the United States did not encourage their success, the members of the Holy Alliance might regain "command of their resources" and confederate generally against the right of all nations to self-government.[8]

In this spirit he told the Marquis de Lafayette that "the most glorious cause which can animate mankind" is improving and ameliorating the human condition.   To this end "representative and responsible governments" contribute greatly by coinciding with the rights and sentiments of all nations, and thereby eradicating arbitrary governments from the civilized world.   The forms of representative governments will surely improve, Madison predicted, as new types are attempted.   For this reason, the American "experiment...cannot fail to add new lights to the science of constitutions."[9]

THE INTENTIONS OF THE FRAMERS

Despite this optimism, Madison was almost obsessed during the last ten years of his life with maintaining a pure interpretation of the Constitution, especially its federal feature.   In his efforts to expound the authentic meaning of the Constitution, it is surprising, perhaps, to learn that he categorically rejected the debates of the Constitutional Convention as a proper source of interpretations of the finished text.   In 1821 he admitted that he possessed materials for a "pretty ample view of what passed" at the Convention, and he did not intend for them to remain under a veil of secrecy forever.   They would remain shrouded, however, until after his death.   Then "the Constitution should be well settled by practice" and knowledge of the "controversial part" of the Convention's proceedings can no longer be put to "improper account." As a "guide in expounding and applying the Constitution, the debates and incidental decisions of the Convention can have no authoritative character."   It is desirable to have the record published, however, in order to satisfy historical curiosity and to illuminate the science of government.   The "legitimate meaning" of the Constitution must be derived only from "the text itself; or if a key is to be sought elsewhere, [it is found] in the sense attached to it by the people in their respective state conventions, where it received all the authority it possesses."[10]

Madison subsequently explained why he held this belief.   Views expressed by the members reflected both the chronic crisis inherent in all confederations and the acute one existing in the minds of Framers alarmed by the Shays affair.   As a consequence of the latter, many delegates ignored the distinction between temporary and permanent flaws in popular governments so as to exaggerate the latter.   In addition, proposals were advanced and opinions expressed as negotiating grounds more remote from each side initially than the "real opinions of each other were from the point at which they finally met."   This behavior was to be expected in a body in which so much depended on compromises. His own views, Madison explained, had always started in favor of the "principles of self-government," and his purpose was to rescue it from the dangers which then seemed to threaten it.   These included his fear that events in America had reached a crisis in which our republican experiment would fail, blasting the "hopes which the republican cause had inspired..."   Given this countervailing climate of opinion, there was a disposition on the part of the supporters of republican government to give the system "vigor" to satisfy opponents who harbored a "secret dislike to popular Government..."   These individuals hoped that the

American experiment would be disgraced in order to pave the way for a form of government "more congenial with monarchical or aristocratical predilections." For this latter reason, Madison admitted, he was willing to give a system resting on the theory of self–government as much "energy" as it needed to be stable and effective. It is possible, he conceded, that in pursuit of this objective he may have given in "some instances this consideration" more weight than he might have after further reflection during the Convention or in the actual operation of the government once it was established. Also, opinions were occasionally voiced about some particular "modification or... power [having] a conditional reference to others" which, when considered in relation to them, would "vary the character of the whole."[11]

Insensitive, uninformed, or biased readings of the debates, he said on another occasion, easily follow from a failure to define precisely the terms which describe our unprecedented political system. The only curb on fruitless and endless discussions of its nature is a careful definition of words. Existing ones express known ideas, whereas a unique political system requires either new words to describe it or old ones redefined. Madison had made the same point in *The Federalist* thirty–six years earlier, but in vain.[12] Failure to observe this caution in defining the term *national* as it was used in the Virginia Plan at the Convention leads to "constructive ingenuity." The words used in these resolutions were " never meant to be inserted in their loose form in the text of the Constitution." All of the delegates understood that they were to be "reduced by proper limitations and specifications" to a final and operative form–as they were in fact. The word *national* was used to mean that the government was to "operate within the extent of its powers directly and coercively on individuals, and to receive the higher sanction of the people of the states." This term was used because there was "no technical or appropriate" existing word to apply accurately to the "new and unique system..." There were no more than "two or three members" of the Convention who were theoretically rather than practically in favor of a unitary government.[13]

He defined *national* more fully for another correspondent, saying that the word was to be distinguished from *federal*, *not* to describe the "*extent* of power but the *mode of its operation*," despite erroneous interpretations to the contrary advanced by such antifederalist delegates as Robert Yates and Luther Martin.[14] In fact, the "abstract leanings" of individual delegates toward consolidated and limited government depended on the resolution of two intertwined issues: "the structure of the Govt. and the *quantum* of power entrusted to it, were more or less inseparable in the minds of all," so that decisions about one of these issues depended on determinations of the other one. Only after the compromise on representation was reached did some delegates make their theoretical inclinations about the proper division of power known.[15]

The resulting system could not properly be called national because of the ultimate source of its power, its operations on individuals, and its structure. Too much emphasis cannot be placed on this last point. From Madison's perspective the government could not be national because of its flawed structure. It is useful to recall the distinction he made in the sixty-second *Federalist* between a people incorporating themselves into one nation as distinguished from those linking themselves in a league of independent states. In the former case, they would distribute power proportionally among all parts as Americans had done in the House. In the latter case, they would distribute power equally among the states as the Framers had done with the Senate. The failure to make and comprehend Madison's distinction between the scope and structure of power leads readily to the popular, but unwarranted, belief that there were two Madisons, the first one an ardent nationalist before the Convention of 1787 and the second one an antinationalist by 1791-92.[16]

Madison first contended in 1791 that the only authentic interpretations of the Constitution were to be found in the proceedings of the state ratifying conventions. During a debate in the House, he read from debates in the conventions of North Carolina, Pennsylvania, and Virginia in order to prove that the principal advocates of the Constitution did not intend to confer unlimited power on Congress. He said he could not vouch for the accuracy or even the authenticity of the publications on which he relied because the arguments made may have been mistaken or poorly recorded. Nevertheless, they were useful, when used in conjunction with the explanations attached to their notices of ratification and the amendments desired by many of them. They were all of the same complexion in opposing unlimited national power. The same inference could be drawn from the amendments proposed to the states by Congress in 1789 and ratified by the states. These renunciations of power demonstrated the "sense in which the Constitution was understood and adopted."[17]

On the basis of his own later statements, it appears that this source of original intentions was of little value to Madison and his contemporaries in the absence of their publication in complete form. According to two statements made to Jonathan Elliott in 1827, it appears that the "debates" from Pennsylvania which Madison possessed consisted of the speeches of only two members of its ratifying convention. The proceedings of North Carolina were those of its first convention which rejected the Constitution, not those of the second one which he never possessed. At some time he did acquire the published proceedings of the convention held in Massachusetts, but he never acquired those of any state other than Virginia. It may be said in Madison's favor in regard to the records of Virginia's convention that he declined Elliott's offer to let him edit the record of his speeches made there despite his claim that the printed record contained defective, erroneous, obscure and sometimes unintelligible reports of what he really said. It would be neither "safe" nor "fair," to rewrite them after a lapse of forty years into "what might be believed they ought to be."[18] He repeated his general position in 1830. Although "respect may be thought due to the intention of the Convention as presumptive evidence of the general understanding of the time," the "only authoritative intentions" are those of the people of the states expressed through their ratifying conventions.[19]

One notable omission from Madison's restricted list of sources of authentic interpretations of the Constitution is *The Federalist*. In 1824 he said that it would be wise to keep human nature in mind while reading the "contemporary writings which vindicated and recommended the Constitution..." So cautioned, one would realize that the "authors might sometimes be influenced by the zeal of advocates."[20] In 1825 Jefferson wanted Madison to approve the work as required reading at the University of Virginia. In 1788 however, Jefferson had flattered the authors by saying that it was the best commentary ever written on the principles of government, but it was evident that in some essays the author argued only what might be "best said in defence of opinions in which he did not concur."[21] Evidently the Sage of Monticello remembered only the flattering part of this judgment in 1825. Madison had not forgotten the rest of it, however, so he apparently thought it was best to remind his aged friend gently that, although these essays constituted the "most authentic exposition of the text of the Federal Constitution" as it was understood by the Framers and Ratifiers, it had never served as an infallible guide to interpretation of the text because the "great rival parties have [not] acquiesced in all its comments."[22] Madison evidently thought that the distinction between advocacy and authentic interpretation was crucial.

Even more revealing was Madison's admission in 1829 that he did not have a copy of *The Federalist* at hand for consultation on a point of constitutional meaning. Nicholas P. Trist wanted to know what the word contract meant in the Constitution. Madison answered: "The Federalist touches on the origin of the prohibition; but my copy not being at home, I cannot refer to the passage. The debates at the state conventions would seem to promise much information, but I am not sure that such will be the case." The "best resource" will be the "contemporary state of things" as revealed in numerous publications in "pamphlet form and in newspapers."[23] If Madison heaped any other faint praise on *The Federalist* as an exposition of "the" intentions of "the" Framers, it remains well hidden.

The one early document which in Madison's opinion authentically interprets a part of the Constitution–The First Amendment–was the Virginia Report of 1800 as we noted in the previous chapter.

Madison's great difficulties in establishing authentic sources of constitutional interpretation were paralleled by his search for rules guiding it. Normally, he dealt only with specific issues of public policy and only rarely did he try to lay down general, but unambiguous, rules of enduring value. For example, he enjoined all concerned not to "exercise doubtful powers..."[24] He urged, also, that the distinction between the "utility" and the "constitutionality" of measures be maintained in favor of the latter.[25] Yet, a purely "literal" textual reading may be a "hard rule of construction" because it may be injurious to the public interest as well as a "hard imputation on the Framers and Ratifiers of the Constitution."[26] Among the "obvious and just guides applicable to the Constn. of the U. S. may be mentioned: 1. the evils & defects for curing which the Constitution was called for & introduced. 2. The comments prevailing at the times it was adopted. 3. The early, deliberate &

continued practice under the Constitution as preferable to constructions adopted on the spur of occasions, and subject to the vicissitudes of party or personal considerations."[27]

In 1831 he elaborated the last of these general perspectives. From the premise that the Constitution is derived from an authority superior to both legislators and judges, it follows that it is to be "expounded and obeyed, not controlled or varied" by either branch. A precedent is a "rule of decision" having "authoritative force" for all branches of the government because certain and known rules serve a social good; also, repeated public expositions of statutes and the Constitution permit the inference that they originated in those who ultimately authorized the performance of these functions. The value of "fixed and known" legal rules is that it avoids instability in constitutional interpretations. All officers of the government take an oath to uphold the Constitution so it binds them all with equal force. It has has never been supposed that a judge is free to disregard all precedents in order to give effect to his "own abstract and individual opinions...." Not even "the wisest and most conscientious judge" has failed to acquiesce in decisions in which he has been overruled by the "matured opinions of the majority of his colleagues" in establishing authoritative expositions. There is a common understanding that a "course of practice" serves as a rule for interpreting the Constitution.[28]

There may be "extraordinary and peculiar" circumstances which allow for exceptions to the binding force of precedents. Nevertheless, the established rule will "force itself on the practical judgment of the most ardent theorist." He will find it impossible to *act officially* on his "solitary opinions" about the meaning of the Constitution, when others have been determined by practice over a reasonable period of time, especially if there is no prospect of a change of meaning by "the public or its agents." If this rule of restraint were inoperative, then there would be no limitation on the exercise of this power. Furthermore, the danger of erroneous interpretations increases with the "increasing oblivion of explanatory circumstances, and with the continued changes in the import of words and phrases." Therefore, the "true and safe construction" of the constitutional text is the one having the "uniform sanction of successive legislative bodies; through a period of years and under the varied ascendency of parties..."[29] Madison wrote this letter to make it clear that his rule applies to Presidents no less than it does to legislators and judges.

He continued to insist, also, as he had forty years earlier, that the Constitution should not be construed by reference to either learned foreign commentators or other political systems. In 1825 he cautioned Jefferson against using two well-known British treatises to interpret the Constitution. The famous works of Algernon Sidney and John Locke were "admirably calculated to impress on young minds the right of nations to establish their own governments and to inspire a love of free ones..." However, they provide "no aid in guarding our Republican charters against constructive violations."[30] In 1829 he insisted that the "compound" American system is without "a model." Therefore, it is to be "explained by itself, not by similitudes or analogies." Its key terms must never be used without the qualifications appropriate to its unique characteristics. For example, the British government is "*sui generis*" so that the terms "Monarchy used by those who look to the executive head only and Commonwealth by those looking at the representative member chiefly are inapplicable in a strict sense" to the American system.[31] In 1835 he insisted again that we ignore or even abandon all obscure, ingenious and technical commentaries on politics in expounding the Constitution. Appeals should be confined to the "law and the testimony of the fundamental charter...which constitutes it" because ours is a "system hitherto without a model..." The Constitution must be construed according to the "actual" division and distribution of powers which it provides.[32]

His efforts to establish authentic and usable sources and rules of constitutional interpretation are particularly instructive. They demonstrate conclusively that he had litle success despite his overwhelming firsthand knowledge of events which transpired at the Convention and in the first several Congresses; his secondhand knowledge of debates in some of the state ratifying conventions; and his keen awareness of the climate of belief prevailing in centers of informed opinion during his lifetime. Moreover, despite his exhortations to rely on the constitutional text alone for its meaning, it is not self–explanatory, and only rarely does it provide explicit standards to guide decisions and actions (such as those allocating representation and forbidding religious tests for holding office). Otherwise, its key terms are as protean now as Madison well knew them to be in his time. Furthermore, his experience in trying to establish the authentic sources of the Framers' intentions ought to instill a due humility in all who have followed him in these efforts. Finally, his argument that long–standing practice supported by successive majorities of alternating parties ought to be regarded as authoritative is a sound rule. Of course, it is subject to exceptions, as he noted, especially in novel circumstances. In all, Madison's observations are a counsel of prudence calling for full discussion and mutual accomodation among the the branches of the government, if the constitutional system is to be stable.

GOVERNMENT BY CONSTITUTIONAL MAJORITY

One other subject captured Madison's attention during his last years. He became increasingly uncertain that the more perfect and durable union which he had sought to forge in 1787 would endure. The changing circumstances of a nation pregnant with the explosive forces of growth and the nature of political man account in large measure for his uncertainty that the constitution would endure. In 1833 he noted centrifugal forces consisting of the rapid growth within individual states of population, wealth and power; the growing belief that there was an incompatibility of interests among the sections resulting in the oppression of a minor by the major part; and the encouragement which this situation gave to "the natural aspirations of talented ambition for new theatres multiplying the chances of elevation in the lottery of political life." The "counter tendencies" included the "complicated form of our political system," the "links and ligaments" of interstate commerce, the prospects for assimilating the agricultural and manufacturing sections of the country, and finally, "the obvious consequences of disunion." Nevertheless, the decreasing influence of the fear created by external danger, *the most powerful control of disuniting propensities in the parts of a political community*," required the aid of "moral causes" to maintain the "equilibrium supposed by the Theory of our compound Government." Among the causes of this sort, appeals to patriotism must be preeminent, provided that they are not co-opted by a political party to advance its own interest.[33]

In about 1834, Madison composed, but did not publish, his final defense of the Constitution. This essay recalled his explanation and justification of representative government first expounded in the tenth and fourteenth *Federalist* essays. His target was people who claimed the right of a state to nullify federal statutes. They asserted, in effect, that majority rule is the most oppressive form of government. This doctrine must be challenged, he insisted, because it "strikes at the very heart of republicanism" by denying the possibility of rule by moderate majorities. Nullifiers said that majority rule is dangerous only where there is a difference of interests or classes which compose the political community. They added the erroneous doctrine that this difference and the danger which it generates are proportional to the territorial extent of the political system. In the extended United States, the discord of interests is so great, they contended, that majority rule cannot be trusted to avoid oppressing minorities. This contention repeats the discredited theory that a republic is naturally limited to a territory small enough to permit its citizens to assemble in one place in order to exercise the powers of government in person. Once again, this erroneous theory has been supported with reference to the history of both ancient and modern republics.[34]

On the contrary, Madison insisted. The introduction of representative governments, first in Europe and then in the United States, demonstrated that popular governments could be established over extended territories. American experience suggested that representative government is the "cure" for many of the evils previously associated with small republics which were direct democracies. It remained for the people of the United States, however, to add a new security against the old dangers by combining a "federal with a republican organization..." Experience and study have demonstrated not only the error of the old theory requiring republics to be small, but also, a new and "important truth: namely, that both the representative and federal structures provide responsible governments to an extent which ought to satisfy the reasonable hopes of the friends of free government." As "Montesquieu" observed long ago, a federal system allows its members to disapprove of the "pernicious measures" of any one of its members without infecting the others. Quite aside from the question of the effectiveness of federal governments, however, or "the interpretation of our own," every supporter of republican government ought to object to the charge that rule by a majority is "the most tyrannical and intolerable of all..."[35]

The friends of this "new heresy" ought to look to the multiplicity and variety of discordant interests existing within their own states, if they are so eager to discredit the form of majority rule established by the Constitution, Madison pointed out. Once they have observed both existing and prospective social reality, these enemies to majority rule must join either the open advocates of aristocracy, oligarchy, or monarchy with their dependence on a standing military force, or they must seek and find a "Utopia exhibiting a perfect homogeneousness of interests, opinions and feelings nowhere yet found in civilized communities. Into how many such parts must [a state] be split before the semblance of such a condition could be found in any of them?[36]

Certain theoretical objections to the form of majority rule established in the United States may be raised. The majority formed by the Constitution may be a minority when it is compared with a "popular majority." This situation prevails in some states and in the United States. It will continue to do so in the former where property is combined with population in apportioning and electing representatives. Constitutional and popular majorities differ even more in the case of the United States as a whole because of the great differences in their respective populations. This arrangement clearly departs from the "rule of equality" because it creates a "political and constitutional majority in contradistinction to a numerical majority of the people..." It is true, also, that such a constitutional majority may oppress a numerical minority. It may do so, furthermore, to such an extent and by such means as to drive the latter to use "ultra or anti–constitutional" measures of relief. Nevertheless, a constitutional minority must acquiesce in rule by a constitutional majority. The moment the former disobeys the latter, the Constitution is subverted. Therefore, the only remedy open to those persons who consider themselves to be insufferably oppressed is either to amend the Constitution or to undertake its "subversion..." While the Constitution is in force, the power created by it, regardless of whether it is a "popular minority or majority," must be obeyed as the "legitimate" authority because this rule provides the only alternative to the "dissolution of all government." The favorable consideration which ought to counter this destructive consequence is the fact that, when a constitutional minority is in power, a numerical majority with "justice on its side, and its influence on public opinion, will be a salutary control on the abuse of power..." These countervailing influences can operate effectively, however, only if military power is not used on the side of the ruling minority.[37]

It is prudent to recall that "no government of human device and human administration can be perfect." Therefore, the best government is the one which is the "least imperfect." Judged by this standard, republican government is the best because its vital principle is that the majority rules. If its will cannot be trusted where there are diverse and conflicting interests, then it can be trusted nowhere.[38]

Unquestionably, Madison conceded in one of his last letters, federal organization leads to rival claims of power derived from a compact which created a government, armed it with "moral power," and endowed it with the physical means of executing its authority. Such disputes can be settled only by the terms of the compact itself. It is fortunate for Americans that the powers of government can be distributed by the people over whom they are to be exercised so as to be most suitable to their circumstances, most likely to guard their freedom, and to secure their safety and happiness.[39] Any political system which fails to provide an effective institution for deciding all controversies between the part and the whole is a government in "name only." Final appeal in all systems must be to the "authority of the whole." It was this understanding which underlay the specific provisions of the Constitution forbidding certain exercises of state legislative power. This conception of the relationship of the whole to its parts was incorporated deliberately in the supremacy clause. He had justified it, Madison recalled, in the thirty–ninth *Federalist*, which defended judicial review of state action, and by the section of the Judiciary Act of 1789 which established the appellate jurisdiction of the federal over the state courts. It can be prophesied, therefore, that despite the "clouds" which obscure this truth at present, it is the view which must be taken "permanently" of this power and with "surprise hereafter that any other should ever have been contended for."[40]

In March, 1836, with only a few months to live, Madison said that in the course of a long life, much of it in public service, he had witnessed the alternate popularity and unpopularity of the three branches of the federal government. This situation undoubtedly reaffirmed the belief he had expressed in 1787 that the separation of powers is an equivocal guide at best to both constitutional creation and interpretation. The three powers "touch so closely or rather run the one so much into the other, as to...leave the lines of division obscure." Therefore, "settled practice, enlightened by concurring cases...obviously conforming to the public good" must be relied upon for guidance. He had observed, too, the tendencies of the federal and state governments to encroach on each other's powers. Still, he was unable to predict with any certainty the "final operation of the causes" of this ebb and flow of the political tides. He found it even more difficult to calculate the "mingled and checkered influences" on the system in the future because of the nature and number of variables involved. These included expanding territorial limits; the number of new states admitted; the "great and growing power of some of them"; the "absence of external danger"; the combinations of some states in parts of the union and the collisions between them in other parts; and, finally, the refusal of some unsuccessful parties to abide by judicial determination of their controversies. To all of these uncertainties he had to add the effects of a "dense population" and the number and nature of the relations of the classes composing it. "I am far, however, from desponding of the great political experiment in the hands of the American people. Much as already been gained...Much may be expected..."[41]

Apparently Madison still believed in 1836 as he did in 1787 that any American rational enough "not to assume an infallibility in rejudging the fallible opinions of others" would vote to ratify the Constitution. Such a person would have understood why the Framers were forced to deviate from the "artificial structure and regular symmetry which an abstract view of the subject might lead an ingenious theorist" to give a constitution planned in "his closet or his imagination." Comparing the Constitution with its predecessor, no "man would refuse to give brass for silver or gold, because the latter had some alloy in it."[42]

From all that Madison said to justify, explain, and support the American constitutional system over nearly a half-century despite its obvious flaws, it is evident that he considered its active support by the American people to be in the public interest. It is correct, also, to conclude that he judged all measures to support this system and to secure the happiness of the American people to be equally in the public interest. The fact that the latter can be realized only through the pursuit of self-interest by those who rule and conflict among the interests which produce wealth in a free and heterogeneous society in no way condemns all to a neglect of the common good. Madison did not define the public interest as no more than a Newtonian vector of political forces, because he recognized that diversity of opinions and interests is natural in a free society and is partially the inescapable result of governmental actions. He believed that the full enjoyment of a free, constitutionally limited, and responsible government is the highest political value to be cherished, enjoyed, and defended by mankind. He saw no inconsistency, no contradiction, between realizing this value and aggrandizing social wealth through the fertile activity of a free and industrious people bent on securing a constantly increasing standard of living for an ever-growing population. Therefore, in Madison's thought one does not find any evidence of the putative tension between the pursuit of private and public interests which is so characteristic of much hortatory political theory and tendentious social analysis.

Final judgments of Madison's efforts to shape the Constitution, the new government, and the Bill of Rights during its early years will necessarily differ, if his understanding of the roots of human diversity is correct. Nevertheless, there might be widespread agreement that a fitting epitaph is found, ironically, in the words of Edmund Burke whom Madison looked upon as an avowed enemy of the founding principles of the American Republic.

> To make a government requires no great prudence. Settle the seat of power, teach obedience, and the work is done. To give freedom is still more easy. It is not necessary to guide. It requires only to let go the rein. But to form a free government, that is, to temper those opposite elements of liberty and restraint in one consistent work, requires much thought, deep reflection, a sagacious, powerful and combining mind.[43]

NOTES

1. *LJM*, 3:55.
2. Ibid., 63–76 passim.
3. Ibid. 4:114.
4. *PJM*, 11:304–5, 307, 332; 12:23, 420; 13:4, 86; 14:78, 108, 157, 251–52, 266, 420, 472.
5. *LJM*. 3:40.
6. Ibid., 336; *PJM*, 9:82.
7. *LJM*. 3: 433–34.
8. Ibid., 267.
9. Ibid., 238.
10. Ibid., 228.
11. Ibid., 243–45 passim.
12. *The Federalist*, 229–230 (no. 37) .
13. *LJM* 3:367, 520–21; 4:280–89, especially 286–287, 310–315.
14. Ibid. 3:546.
15. Ibid. 4:162; see also 209.
16. See for example Charles F. Hobson, "The Negative on State Laws: James Madison, the Constitution, and the Crisis of Republican Government," *William and Mary Quarterly*, 3d Series, (April 1979), 36:215–35.
17. *PJM*, 13:380–81.
18. *LJM*, 3:544, 598.
19. Ibid. 4:74, 128–29, 211. For earlier statements of this claim see 3:442; 4:17.
20. Ibid. 3:436.
21. *PJM*, 11:353.
22. *LJM*, 3:481.
23. Ibid. 4:17.
24. Ibid. 3:436.
25. Ibid. 56, 483.
26. *WJM*, 9:91–93.
27. *LJM*, 4:74.
28. Ibid., 183–87 passim.
29. Ibid.
30. Ibid. 3:481. He referred to Algernon Sidney, *Discourses on Government*, 2 vols. (Edinburgh, Scotland: G. Hamilton and Jay Balfour, 1750).
31. *LJM*, 4:18.
32. Ibid., 420.
33. Ibid., 298 emphasis added; see also, 358.
34. Ibid., 326.
35. Ibid., 327.
36. Ibid., 328–32 passim.
37. Ibid., 333.
38. Ibid., 334.
39. Ibid., 391, 395, "Sovereignty," 1835.

40. Ibid., 425, "On Nullification," 1835–36. Also see Burns, *Madison Philosopher*, 119–154. For some of Madison's early comments on judicial review see *PJM*, 12:238, 244; *LJM*, 1:479, 554; 3:56. In the remarks contained therein he distinguished between the limited scope of review of executive and legislative actions at the federal level and the unlimited power to review state acts.

41. *LJM*, 4:417, 429–430.

42. *The Federalist*, 226, 231, 239 (Nos. 37, 38).

43. Edmund Burke, *Reflections in the Revolution in France*, edited by Thomas H. D. Mahoney, The Library of Liberal Arts (Indianapolis, Ind.: The Bobbs–Merrill Co. Inc., 1955), 288–89.

Selected Bibliography

ORIGINAL SOURCES

Public

Annals of Congress. Washington: Gales and Seaton, 1834.

The Public Statutes at Large of The United States of America, 17 vols. Boston: 1843–73.

Elliott, Jonathan. ed., *Debates in the Several State Conventions on the Adoption of the Federal Constitution,* 2d ed. Philadelphia: N.p., 1866.

Evans Micro Print #36642, *Journal of the House of Delegates*. Virginia, Dec. 3, 1798–Jan. 26, 1799.

Private

Aristotle, *The Politics of Aristotle*, Edited and translated by Ernest Barker. Oxford: Oxford University Press, 1946.

Fleet, Elizabeth, ed., "Madison's Detached Memoranda," *William and Mary Quarterly*, third series, 3:(1946) 534–568; 554–558.

Adams, John. *The Works of John Adams*, Edited by Charles Francis Adams, 10 vols. Boston: Little, Brown and Co., 1850–56.

Burke, Edmund. *Reflections on the Revolution in France*, Edited by Thomas H.D. Mahoney, The Library of the Liberal Arts. Indianapolis, Ind.: The Bobbs–Merrill Co. Inc., 1955.

Farrand, Max, ed., *The Records of the Federal Convention of 1787.* 4 vols. New Haven, Conn.: Yale University Press, 1966; first published in 1911.

Hamilton, Alexander, John Jay, and James Madison, *The Federalist*, Introduction by Edward Mead Earle, The Modern Library. New York: Random House, N.d.

Hume, David, *Essays and Treatises on Several Subjects*, 4 vols. London: T. Cadell; Edinburgh: A. Kinlaid and A. Donaldson, 1770.

Jefferson, Thomas. *The Works of Thomas Jefferson*, Edited by Paul Leicester Ford, 12 vols. New York: G.P. Putnam's Sons, 1904–1905.

Jefferson, Thomas. *The Papers of Thomas Jefferson*, Edited by Julian Boyd, 21 vols. to date (Princeton, N.J.: Princeton University Press, 1950–).

Jefferson, Thomas. *Notes on the State of Virginia*, Introduction by Thomas Perkins Abernathy. New York: Harper Torchbooks, 1964.

Kant, Immanuel. *Perpetual Peace*, Preface by Nicholas Murry Butler. Westwood, Calif.: U.S. Library Association, 1932; English edition published in London in 1796.

Locke, John. *An Essay Concerning the True Original, Extent, and, End of Civil Government*, Edited and with an introduction by J. W. Gough. Oxford: Basil Blackwell and Mott, 1946.

Madison, James. *The Papers of James Madison*, Edited by William T. Hutchinson, William M. E. Rachal, Robert A. Rutland, and others, 15 vols. to date. Chicago: University of Chicago Press; Charlottesville, Va.: University Press of Virginia, 1962 to date.

Madison, James. *The Papers of James Madison Presidential Series*, Edited by Robert A. Rutland and others, 1 vol. to date. Charlottesville, Va.: University Press of Virginia, 1984.

Madison, James. *The Papers of James Madison, Secretary of State Series*, Edited by Robert J. Brugger and others, 1 vol. to date Charlottesville, Va: University Press of Virginia, 1984–.

Madison, James. *The Writings of James Madison*, Edited by Gaillard Hunt, 9 vols. New York: G.P. Putnam's Sons, 1900–1910.

Madison, James. *Letters and Other Writings of James Madison*, 4 vols. New York: Worthington, 1884.

Madison Papers, DLC: Wilson Carey Nicholas Papers. Alderman Library, University of Virginia.

Montesquieu, Charles Louis de Secondat, Baron de. *The Spirit of the Laws*, Translated by Thomas Nugent with an introduction by Franz Neumann, 2 vols. New York: Hafner Press, 1949.

Richardson, James D., ed., *Messages and Papers of the Presidents*, 20 vols. New York: Bureau of National Literature, 1914.

Secondary Works

Alley, Robert S. ed. *James Madison on Religious Liberty* (Buffalo, NY: Prometheus Books, 1985).

Appleby, Joyce. *Capitalism and A New Social Order: The Republican Vision of the 1790s*. New York and London: New York University Press, 1984.

Bailyn, Bernard. *The Ideological Origins of the American Revolution.* Cambridge, Mass.: Harvard University Press, The Belknap Press, 1967.

Banning, Lance. *The Jeffersonian Persuasion.* Ithaca, NY: Cornell University Press, 1978.

Berns, Walter. *The First Amendment and the Future of American Democracy.* New York: Basic Books, Inc., 1976.

Bestor, Arthur, David C. Mearns, and Jonathan Daniels. *Three Presidents and Their Books.* Urbanna, Ill.: University of Illinois Press, 1963.

Brandt, Irving. *James Madison: Father of the Constitution, 1782–1800.* 6 vols; Indianapolis, Ind.: The Bobbs–Merrill Co. Inc., 1941–1961.

_____, *The Bill of Rights*. Indianapolis, Ind.: The Bobbs Merrill Co. Inc., 1965.

Buckley, Thomas E. *Church and State in Revolutionary Virginia 1776–1787*. Charlottesville, Va.: University Press of Virginia, 1977.

Burns, Edward M. *James Madison; Philosopher of the Constitution.* New York: Octagon Books, 1968; first published in 1938.

Burns, James M. *Deadlock of Democracy.* Englewood Cliffs, N.J.: Prentice–Hall, 1967.

Chambers, William M. *Political Parties in a New Nation.* New York and Oxford: Oxford University Press, 1963.

Charles, Joseph. *The Origins of the American Party System.* New York: Harper and Row, 1956.

Corwin, Edward S. *The President: Office and Powers*, 3d ed. New York: New York University Press, 1957.

Cunningham, Jr., Nobel E. *The Jeffersonian Republicans: The Formation of Party Organization.* Chapel Hill, N.C.: University of North Carolina Press, 1957.

Dumbauld, Edward. *The Bill of Rights*, Norman, Okla.: University of Oklahoma Press, 1957.

Eidelberg, Paul. *The Philosophy of the American Constitution*. New York: The Free Press, 1968.

Epstein, David F. *The Political Theory of the Federalist*. Chicago: University of Chicago Press, 1984.

Ferguson, E. James. *The Power of the Purse: A History of American Public Finance, 1776–1790*. Chapel Hill, N.C.: University of North Carolina Press, 1961.

Forbes, Duncan *Hume's Philosophical Politics*. Cambridge: Cambridge University Press, 1975.

Hofstadter, Richard. *The Idea of a Party System: The Rise of Legitimate Opposition in the United States, 1780–1840*. Berkeley: University of California Press, 1972.

Holcombe, Arthur N. *Our More Perfect Union*. Cambridge, MA: Harvard University Press, 1950.

Kenyon, Cecilia. *The Antifederalists*. Indianapolis, Ind.: The Bobbs–Merrill Co. Inc., 1966.

Ketcham, Ralph. *James Madison: A Biography*. New York: Macmillan Co., 1971.

Koch, Adrienne. *Jefferson and Madison: The Great Collaboration*. London and New York: Oxford University Press, 1950.

Kohn, Richard. *Eagle and Sword: The Federalists and the Creation of the Military Establishment in America, 1783–1802*. New York: The Free Press, 1975.

Levy, Leonard. *Emergence of a Free Press*. New York and London: Oxford University Press, 1985.

_____, ed., *Freedom of the Press from Zenger to Jefferson*. Indianapolis, Ind.: The Bobbs–Merrill Co. Inc. 1966.

Main, Jackson T. *The Antifederalist: Critics of the Constitution*. Chapel Hill, N.C.: University of North Carolina Press, 1961.

Malone, Dumas. *Jefferson the Virginian*. Boston: Little, Brown & Co., 1948.

_____, *Jefferson and the Rights of Man*. Boston: Little, Brown & Co., 1951.

_____, *Jefferson and the Ordeal of Liberty*. Boston: Little, Brown & Co., 1962.

_____, *Jefferson the President: First Term, 1801–1805*. Boston: Little, Brown & Co., 1970)

_____, *Jefferson the President Second Term 1805–1809*. Boston: Little, Brown & Co., 1974.

_____, *Jefferson and His Time: The Sage of Monticello*. Boston: Little, Brown & Co., 1977.

Mason, Alpheus T. *The States Rights Debate*. New York: Prentice–Hall, 1972.

May, Henry *The Enlightenment in America*. New York: Oxford University Press, 1976.

McDonald, Forrest. *Alexander Hamilton: A Biography*. New York: W. W. Norton and Co., 1979.

_____, *E. Pluribus Unum: The Formation of the American Republic*. Boston: Houghton Mifflin Co., 1965; Penguin Books, 1967.

_____, *We the People*. Chicago: The University of Chicago Press, 1958.

_____, *Novus Ordo Seclorum*. Lawrence, Kans.: University Press of Kansas, 1985.

Miller, William L. *The First Liberty: Religion and the American Republic*. New York: Alfred A. Knopf, 1986.

Mitchell, Broadus. *Alexander Hamilton: The National Adventure, 1788–1804*. New York: Macmillan Co., 1962.

Pocock, J. G. A. *The Machiavellian Moment: Florentine Political Thought and the Atlantic Republican Tradition*. Princeton, N. J.: Princeton University Press, 1975.

Pole, J. R. *Political Representation in England and the Origins of the American Republic*. New York: Macmillan Co., 1966.

Ranney, Austin. *Curing the Mischiefs of Faction*. Berkeley: University of California Press, 1975.

Reichley, A. James. *Religion in American Life*. Washington, D.C.: The Brookings Institution, 1985.

Riemer, Neal. *James Madison: Creating the Constitution.* Washington, D.C.: Congressional Quarterly, Inc., 1986.

Rossiter, Clinton. *Alexander Hamilton and the Constitution.* New York: Harcourt, Brace and World, Inc., 1964.

Rousseau, Jean Jacques. *The Social Contract,* trans. G. D. H. Cole. London: J.M. Dent and Sons, 1973.

Rutland, Robert A. *James Madison: The Founding Father.* New York: Macmillan Co., 1987.

_____,*The Birth of the Bill of Rights.* Chapel Hill, N.C.: University of North Carolina Press, 1955.

Schultz, Harold S. *James Madison.* New York: Twayne Publishers, 1970.

Simms, Henry H. *Life of John Taylor.* Richmond, Va.: The William Byrd Press, 1932.

Smith, Adam. *The Wealth of Nations.* The Modern Library. New York: Random House, 1937.

Smith, David G. *The Convention and the Constitution: The Political Ideas of the Founding Fathers.* New York: St. Martin's Press, 1965.

Stagg, J.C. A., *Mr. Madison's War: Politics, Diplomacy and Warfare in the Early American Republic, 1783–1830.* Princeton, N. J.: Princeton University Press, 1983.

Stourzh, Gerald. *Alexander Hamilton and the Idea of Republican Government.* Palo Alto, Calif.: Stanford University Press, 1917.

de Vattel, Emmerich. *The Law of Nations, or the Principles of the law of Nature Applied to the Conduct and Affairs of Nations and Their Sovereigns.* Neuchatel, 1758.

Vile, M. J. C. *Constitutionalism and the Separation of Powers.* Oxford: The Clarendon Press, 1967.

Weiss, Anne. *God and Government: The Separation of Church and State.* Boston: Houghton Mifflin Co., 1982.

White, Leonard D. *The Federalists.* New York: The Free Press, 1948.

White, Morton. *Philosophy, The Federalist, and the Constitution.* New York and London: Oxford University Press, 1987.

Wills, Garry. *Explaining America: The Federalist*. New York: Penquin Books, 1981.

Wilmerding, Lucius. *The Electoral College*. New Brunswick, N.J.: Rutgers University Press, 1958.

Wood, Gordon S. *Representation in the American Revolution*. Charlottesville, Va: The University Press of Virginia, 1969.

_____, *The Creation of the American Republic*. New York: W. W. Norton and Co., 1972.

Zvesper, John. *Political Philosophy and Rhetoric: A Study of the Origins of American Party Politics*. Cambridge: Cambridge University Press, 1977.

Articles Cited

Adair, Douglas "The Tenth Federalist Revisitied,: *William and Mary Quarterly*, 3rd Series, 8 (1951): 48–67 .

_____, "That Politics May be Reduced to a Science: David Hume, James Madison, and the Tenth Federalist," *The Huntington Library Quarterly* 20 (August 1957):343–359.

Carey, George W. "Separation of Powers and the Madisonian Model: A Reply to the Critics," *The American Political Science Review* 72(March 1978):151–64 .

Corwin, E. S. "The Progress of Consitutional Theory Between the Declaration of Independence and the Meeting of the Philadelphia Convention," *American Historical Review* 30 (1925):511–36.

Hobson, Charles F. "The Negative on State Laws: James Madison, the Constitution, and the Crisis of Republic Government," *William and Mary Quarterly*, 3rd Series, 36 (April 1979): 215–35.

Ketcham, Ralph. "James Madison and Judicial Review," *Syracuse Law Review*, 8 (1957):158–65.

Morgan, Robert J. "Madison's Theory of Representation in the Tenth Federalist," *The Journal of Politics* 36 (November 1974):852–85.

_____, "Madison's Analysis of the Sources of Political Authority," *The American Political Science Review* 75 (September, 1981):613–25.

Mullett, Charles F. "Classical Influences on the American Revolution," *Classical Journal* 35 (November, 1939):92–104.

Index

About the Author

ROBERT J. MORGAN is Professor of Government, University of
Virginia. He is the author of *A Whig Embattled, Governing Soil
Conservation,* and numerous articles published in the *American Political
Science Review, Journal of Politics,* and *Law and Contemporary Problems.*